JULIUS VON BISMARCK

Edited by Dehlia Hannah and Susanne Pfleger

JULIUS VON BISMARCK

TALKING
TO
THUNDER

Städtische Galerie Wolfsburg

HATJE
CANTZ

7 Foreword
Susanne Pfleger

9 Introduction
Dehlia Hannah

11 Man in the Holocene
Max Frisch

18 Taita Is Talking
Wiwa Shaman in Conversation with Julius von Bismarck

21 TALKING TO THUNDER

51 Struck by Lightning (in His Car)
Nadim Samman

56 APOCALYPSOID

73 The State of Nature
Dehlia Hannah

82 IRMA TO COME IN EARNEST

111 The Irrelevant Lamb
Jürgen Trittin in Conversation with Julius von Bismarck

116 ONE MUST THINK AWAY THE AIR

124 THE EXPRESSIONS OF TETHYS

136 FIRE WITH FIRE

146 Reflections on the Pyrocene
Stephen Pyne in Conversation with Dehlia Hannah

165 The Psychoanalysis of Fire
Gaston Bachelard

169 List of Illustrations
171 Artist's Biography
175 Authors' Biographies

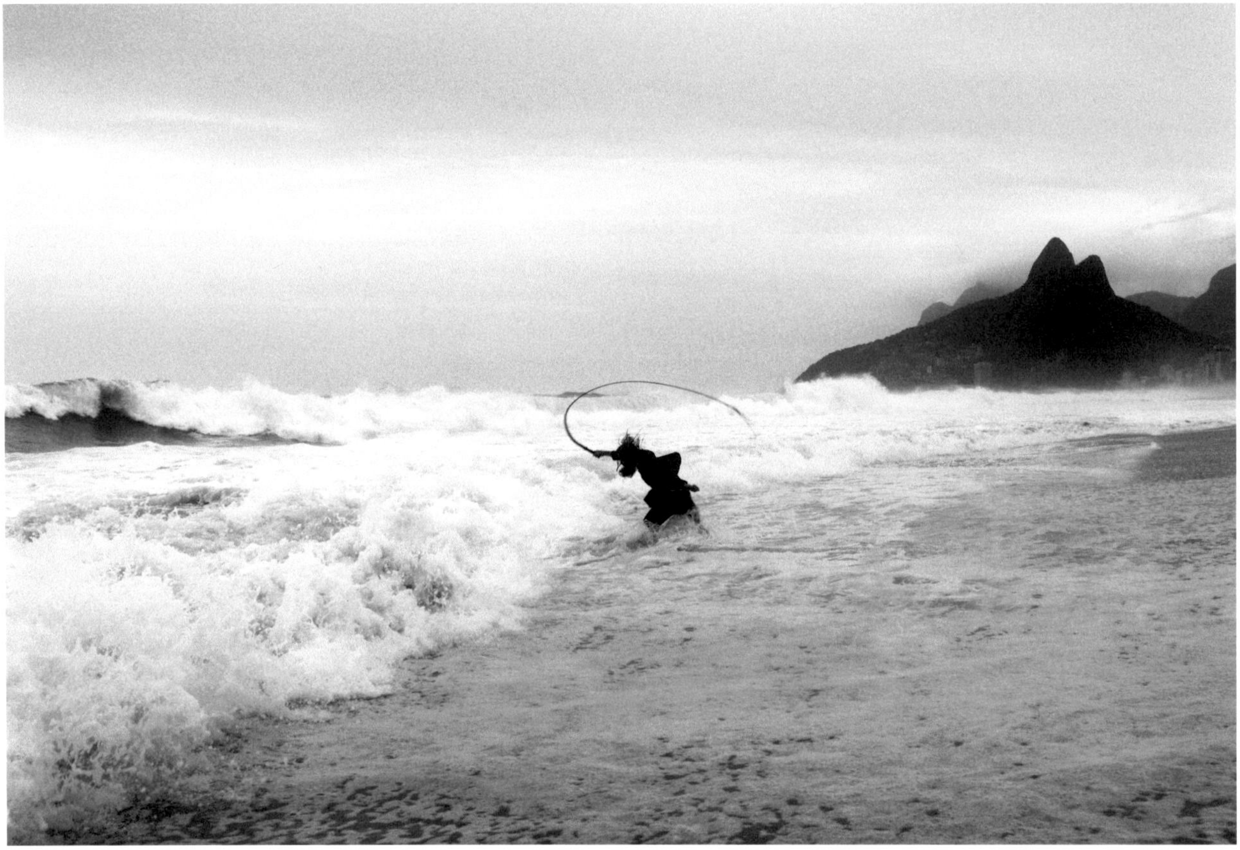

Punishment #7 2011

Foreword

Anyone to whom nature begins to unveil its open mystery feels an irresistible yearning for nature's most noble interpreter, for art.
—Johann Wolfgang von Goethe [1]

My first encounter with Julius von Bismarck occurred eight years ago. I did not meet him personally at the time, but instead saw the artist performing in one of his video works: a young man flogging the sea with a several-meter-long bullwhip made of plaited strips of leather. The urgency and unconditionality of this action made a long-lasting impression on me.

The work is part of the *Punishment* series created between 2011 and 2012. For it, Bismarck traveled to the mountains of Switzerland as well as to South America and the United States in order to whip specific locations in the landscape—a simultaneously enraged and meditative action that the artist captured in photographs and films. The idea for this series is based on a story from 480 BC, when the Persian king Xerxes had two pontoon bridges built to enable his army to cross the Hellespont. However, the bridges, which were held by ropes of papyrus and flax, were destroyed in a storm. Xerxes ordered the two constructors to be beheaded, but, still not satisfied, he also had the sea itself, representative for Poseidon, the god of the sea, whipped with three hundred lashes as punishment. It is a futile notion to think that one can control or influence nature. Bismarck takes this up in *Punishment* and, with a whip, battles to exhaustion against the natural elements, in settings that call to mind the landscape depictions of Romanticism.

I am very happy that is was possible at the time to acquire one of the video works for the collection of the Städtische Galerie Wolfsburg, especially since the *Punishment* series involves several aspects that run through Bismarck's multilayered oeuvre. They include, on the one hand, an approach that emphasizes action, and, on the other, above all, the conflict between human beings and nature. Nature is thus not brought to mind as a landscape or aestheticized in the form of materials but is instead dealt with in an experimental way. For Bismarck, there is no good or evil nature; it is neither hostile to us, nor is it a place of longing.

A central topic in his artistic research is thus the forces that impact nature. With experimental openness, he makes use of all mediums so as to develop experimental arrangements that address complex correlations from our relationship to nature, to landscape and culture. He consequently creates quasi a *theatrum naturae et artis* in the sense of the philosopher and scholar Gottfried Wilhelm Leibniz. Everything is of equal interest for his oeuvre—whether a product of nature, art, or technology. Bismarck develops frameworks that shift the normalized view of things and link the systems of art and science, which are generally regarded as separate. "I draw my inspiration from science and work artistically," he says. His interdisciplinary approach is a creative interrogation of the world and nature, which human beings are increasingly transforming. By contrast with scientific disquisitions, in artistic works this fact can be perceived and experienced differently as a result of their aesthetic transformation. What arises are ruptures that communicate insights to viewers in the truest sense of the word.

When Bismarck pursues Hurricane Irma to shoot footage on site, this is not a sensationalist action or a case of catastrophe voyeurism; with the video work that results, the artist instead addresses the force of nature itself—and he shows it in unsettlingly beautiful pictures. Hurricane Irma, which was the most powerful hurricane on record, left behind a trail of destruction. In the video work, however, the raging hurricane seems less terrible due to the fifty-fold slowing down of real time. The gusts of wind caress the tops of palms and play with the leaves of trees. The camera's proximity to the scenario is astonishingly close. There is no distance, no overall view; the camera is often in the middle of what is taking place and seems to be an active participant—an observer that creates a haunting presence as a result of its being there.

The images have a great forcefulness and a contemplative character. One nearly forgets what ferocious force gave rise to the pictorial content. The sound of the video work further intensifies this

1 Johann Wolfgang von Goethe, *Maxims and Reflections* (New York and London, 1999), p. 23.

effect. In contrast to the pictures of Hurricane Irma that were shown everywhere in the media, which worked with the horror and presented sensational motifs of a natural catastrophe, Julius von Bismarck chose the opposite strategy: he shows highly aesthetic images. Nature per se has nothing catastrophic about it, or, as Max Frisch put it: "only human beings can recognize catastrophes, provided they survive them; Nature recognizes no catastrophes."[2] Bismarck's video work addresses the existential challenge to a society that is little prepared for it, as well as its vulnerability as a result of natural catastrophes in an artistically impressive way.

Julius von Bismarck enjoys wandering between worlds. He is a scientist and artist at the same time: "My perspective on art is an experimental perspective. For me, each work is an experiment. The curiosity that I have and the curiosity that a scientist has are very similar, but the means with which we work are different." His unconventional approach and the open and precarious research require not only boldness, but also an extremely personal commitment. He thus does not shy away from either hardships or dangers in order, for instance, to investigate the elemental force of lightning. In his photographs and videos, a natural phenomenon becomes a sculptural object, and nature becomes a projection surface for ideas and emotions. Bismarck's experimental arrangements do not deal solely with art and science, but also with individual thinking, freedom, integrity, and independence as dimensions of life.

His works again and again take aim at our perception. Art becomes effective as a change in thinking. How, for instance, do we perceive spaces? The installation of bent wire that was presented at the exhibition in Wolfsburg in 2017 develops an enthralling structure in space with a reduced language of forms. It seems heavy and floating, restless and balanced at the same time. The seemingly unstable steel wires that are irregularly positioned against one another give rise to nervous vibrations in the space. It is no longer a real space but rather a conceptual one. The basis for the floating wire works is data collected by means of photogrammetry on the coast of Ireland during Hurricane Ophelia (2017), a wave that was scanned from the steep coast downward. In an interview, Bismarck describes his experience with a small boat in rough seas during a trip in the South of France. He was at the mercy of the waves and felt the power of the force of nature very directly—a physical reality that he describes as beautiful and terrifying at the same time. With the installation *Die Luft muss man sich wegdenken* (One Must Think Away the Air), he brought the ocean into the exhibition space and created a contemporary landscape picture.

The exhibition and this publication were created in connection with the awarding of the Wolfsburg art prize "Junge Stadt sieht Junge Kunst" to Julius von Bismarck in November 2017. The prize is intended as a supporting and perhaps also challenging initiative at a point when no definitive assessment has been made about work of the artist being honored. It ideally encourages the artist to look back and ahead. This publication bears witness to the inexhaustible fantasy of Julius von Bismarck, to whom I express my heartfelt gratitude for the enriching collaboration. My thanks also go to all the individuals involved who made this project possible with their support and ideas and contributed to its success. Gratitude is due to the team of Bismarck's studio as well as to the entire team of the Städtische Galerie Wolfsburg. It would also not have been possible to realize this project without the active involvement of alexander levy, Berlin, and Sies + Höke, Düsseldorf. I am thankful to Dehlia Hannah and Nadim Samman for their texts, and to Dehlia Hannah for laying the conceptual groundwork for the book and editing its content with great dedication. I am grateful to Jürgen Trittin for agreeing to participate in an interview with Julius von Bismarck, thus adding an enriching aspect to this book. The design lay in the hands of Karsten Heller, and I thank Corinna Wolfien for her capable assistance in realizing the publication. The association "jugend in der galerie" provided generous support for the project.

Susanne Pfleger
Director Städtische Galerie Wolfsburg

2 Max Frisch, *Man in the Holocene*, trans. Geoffrey Skelton (McLean, IL, 2007), p. 79.

Introduction

Dehlia Hannah

At a moment in which environmental disasters threaten the well-being of a growing number of communities and species, it becomes almost obscene to observe the forces of nature in the act of destruction. To look is an obligation and a taboo, for where one trains one's attention with intensity, the pleasure of fascination follows. Julius von Bismarck risks the wrath of nature, and a culture that guards her ideal with jealous pride, to perform immodest acts of observation. On behalf of us who shield our eyes from smoke and fire, our property from hurricane-force winds, our bodies from the strike of lightning, Bismarck stills water droplets and fragments of stone, shaping them into slow-motion disasters calibrated to the rate of human comprehension. In the series of works presented in *Talking to Thunder*, questions of causality and ethical reckoning are uncomfortably suspended in the interest of contemplation and bodily exposure to the raging elements of earth, wind, water, and fire.

There are no longer such things as natural disasters; they belong to an environmental age of innocence. Those hazards that we have not caused directly, we have brought within our sphere of control through prediction: earthquakes, tsunamis, severe weather. We bear responsibility for putting ourselves in harm's way—for building cities on the slopes of volcanoes and vulnerable coastlines; for continuing to burn fossil fuels. This book explores what it means to hold that responsibility and examines what insights follow when we allow ourselves to be mesmerized by perturbations in the unnatural order of our comfort zones. Accompanied by essays and interviews, it presents a collection of recent projects including the title work *Talking to Thunder* (2016–17), a series of close encounters with lightning, pursued in Venezuela, Colombia, and Norway; *Irma to Come in Earnest* (2017), a video portrait of the category-five hurricane and its aftermath, shot in Florida; and *Die Luft muss man sich wegdenken* (One Must Think Away the Air; 2017), a sculptural manifestation of the wind-whipped sea off the Irish coast during Hurricane Ophelia; and *Die Mimik der Tethys* (The Expressions of Tethys; 2019), a dynamic installation reproducing the movements of a high-sea buoy; and filmic and photographic work in progress that addresses wildfires burning above the Arctic Circle in Sweden, in Germany, and across California in 2018. At the heart of this geographical and elemental dialogue, *Apocalypsoid* (2017) stages the meticulously planned explosion and reassembly of granite boulder, whose planetary allusions cannot be overlooked.

As lightning streaked across the sky, Bismarck huddled with me and another author in this volume, Nadim Samman, beneath the eves of a stone church in

Berzona—an Alpine hamlet in the Swiss canton of Ticino where the artist's family has a home. Over the drum of raindrops and reverberating thunder, he recalled to us his enduring fascination with stormy weather; an obsession shared with one of the town's most celebrated residents, the author Max Frisch. Frisch's slim volume *Man in the Holocene* stages a weeklong meditation by an elderly man, cut off from the rest of the valley by relentless rainstorms. An extract, reprinted in these pages, offers a portrait of a person striving to keep a mental grip on his place in the world through scientific lists and taxonomies. Bismarck's affinity with this semifictional struggle with the elements was cemented by his own formative encounter, he continued . . . Nearing the end of a road trip along the Italian coast, he stopped on a mountain backroad to spend the night in his car. Sometime after drifting off, he was awoken by a shattering blast of light and sound. Imagining that his car had been hit by an exploding missile, he was terrified to step outside. When he finally did, rain and thunder confirmed that his vehicle had, rather, been struck by lightning. In a state of shock, Bismarck drove white-knuckled through the night, back to Berzona. This moment would resonate through his artwork and his person for years to come. As a wave of thunder rolled through the network of valleys below us, I was struck by a deeper insight into both his work and our collective encounter with environmental extremes.

Man in the Holocene

Max Frisch

It began on Thursday last week when it was still possible to sit outside, muggy as usual before a thunderstorm, the mosquitoes piercing through socks, no heat lightning; it was merely uncomfortable. No birds over the area. The guests, a younger married couple on their way to Italy, abruptly decided to leave, even though they could have slept in the house. It was in fact not a cloud mass, just a yellowish haze as if before a sandstorm in the Arabian desert; no wind. The faces also looked yellowish. The guests were suddenly in such a hurry that they did not even empty their glasses, even though it was not possible to hear any thunder. No drops fell. It was first the next morning when there was noise outside the windows, rustling through the leaves of the chestnut tree.

No night without storms and downpours.

The electrical power supply occasionally fails, as people are accustomed to in this valley; scarcely has a candle been found, finally the matches as well, when the power comes on again, light in the house while it continues to thunder.

It is not the inclement weather that is terrible.

The encyclopedia in twelve volumes, *DER GROSSE BROCKHAUS*, explains the origins of lightning and differentiates between line lightning, ball lightning, and string-of-pearls lightning, etc., though little can be learned about thunder; over the course of a night when one is not able to sleep it is thus necessary to distinguish at least nine kinds of thunder:

1.
The simple thunder crack.

2.
Stuttering or tantrum thunder, generally after a longer silence, dispersed throughout the valley, can last for minutes.

3.
Echoing thunder, jarring like a hammer blow on a piece of loose metal sheeting, which disperses a buzzing, wavering echo, whereby the echo is louder than the thunderclap.

4.
Rolling or rumbling thunder, comparatively pleasant, makes one think of rolling barrels bumping against one another.

5.
Timpani thunder.

6.
Sibilant or gravel thunder begins with a hissing, as if when a dump truck empties out a load of wet gravel, and ends dully.

7.
Bowling-pin thunder; as if when a pin, hit by the rolling ball, hurls into other pins and everything spins apart; there is a brief echo-confusion throughout the valley.

8.
Hesitant or snickering thunder (without a flash of lighting in the window) indicates that the storm is moving over the mountains.

9.
Blasting thunder (immediately after a flash of lightning in the window) does not evoke the idea of hard masses colliding; quite the contrary: an enormous mass is broken asunder and plummets apart toward both sides, whereby it frequently shatters; it then rains in gushes.

The power occasionally fails again.

Losing one's memories would be terrible—

. . .

At night it is otherwise also not possible to see many lights, two streetlamps (in the winter five, because no foliage obscures them then) and a couple of room lights in the village, in clear weather also a weak light from a solitary farmstead on the opposite slope, but now not a single light in the entire valley.

AT THE END OF THE ICE AGE THE SEA LEVEL WAS AT LEAST 100 METERS DEEPER.

EVERYTHING IS READY.

LIGHTNING SPEED:
100,000 KM PER SECOND.
AMPERAGE OF LIGHTNING:
20 TO 180,000 AMPERES

TRANSFORMATION OF
HUMAN BEINGS INTO
ANIMALS, TREES, STONES, ETC.
SEE: METAMORPHOSIS / MYTH

STONE AGE: 6000–4000 BC
LATER STONE AGE: UNTIL 1800 BC

Other kinds of thunder:

10.
Groaning or slat thunder; a brief and bright crash as if when one breaks a wooden slat, then a groaning, longer or shorter; slat thunder is generally the first thunder of a commencing storm.

11.
Sputter thunder.

12.
Pillow thunder, which has exactly the same sound that can be heard when a housewife thumps a pillow with her flat hand.

13.
Sliding thunder; its beginning leads one to expect rumbling thunder or timpani thunder, but before the windowpanes tremble, its roar slides away to the other side of the valley, where it so to say coughs itself out.

14.
Rattling thunder.

15.
Screeching or bottle thunder, often more frightening than blasting thunder, even though it does not make the windowpanes tremble, is one of the unexpected kinds of thunder, one has seen no flash of lightning, when suddenly there is a jarring rattling, as if when a crate full of empty bottles plunges down a flight of stairs.

16.
Rumoring thunder.
And so on.

Excerpt from Max Frisch,
Der Mensch erscheint im Holozän: Eine Erzählung
(Frankfurt am Main: Suhrkamp Verlag, 1979).
Translated by Amy Klement.

BEREIT SEIN IST ALLES.

BLITZGESCHWINDIGKEIT:
100.000 KM PRO SEKUNDE.
STROMSTÄRKE DER BLITZE:
20 BIS 180.000 AMPÈRE

VERWANDLUNG VON MENSCHEN IN
TIERE, BÄUME, STEINE ETC.
SIEHE: METAMORPHOSE / MYTHOS

STEINZEIT: 6000 – 4000 V. CHR.
JUNGSTEINZEIT: BIS 1800 V. CHR.

Weitere Arten von Donner:

10.
der ächzende oder Latten-Donner; ein kurzer und heller Krach, wie wenn man eine Holzlatte bricht, dann ein Ächzen länger oder kürzer; der Latten-Donner ist in der Regel der erste Donner eines beginnenden Gewitters.

11.
der Plapper-Donner.

12.
der Kissen-Donner hat genau den Ton, der zu

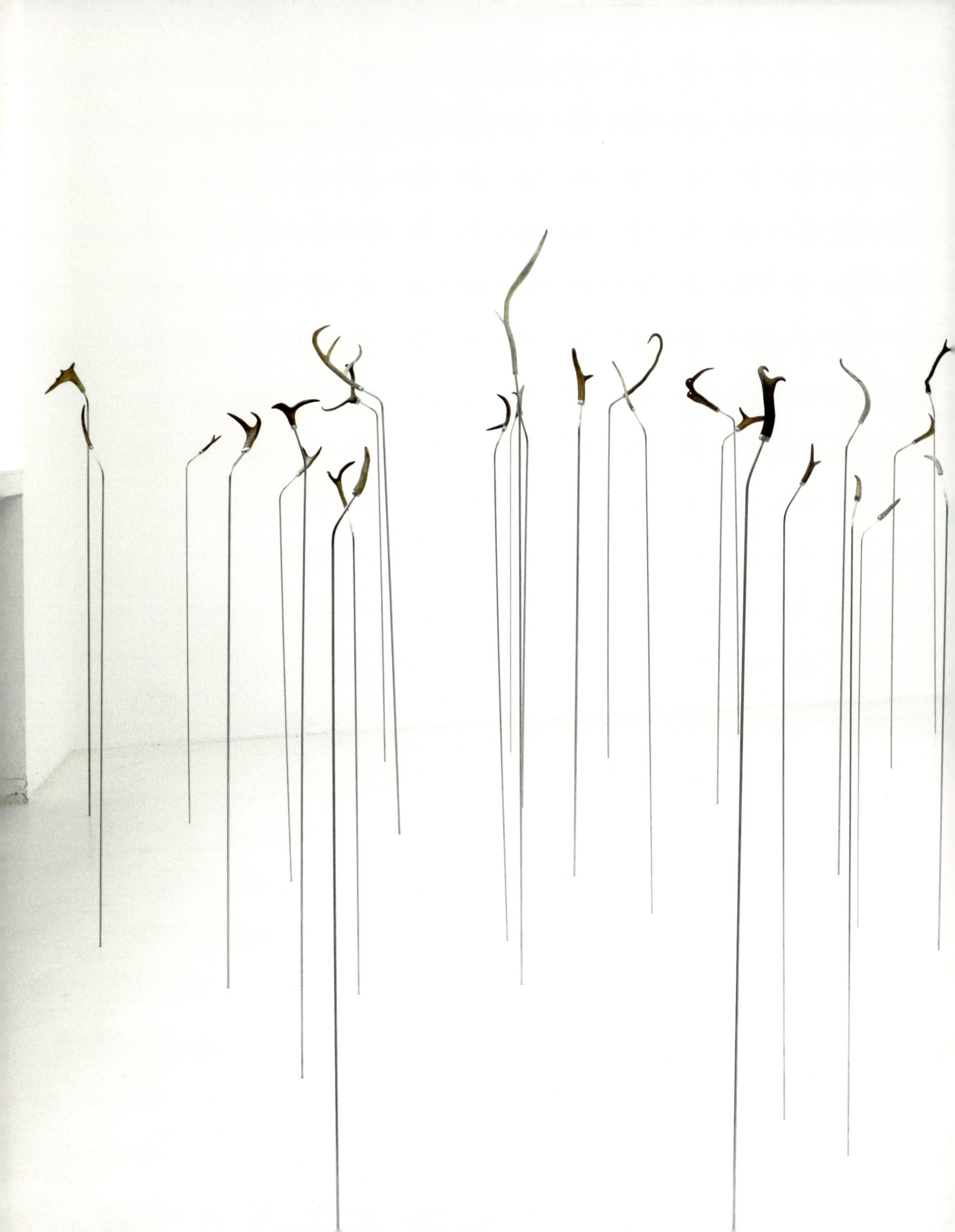

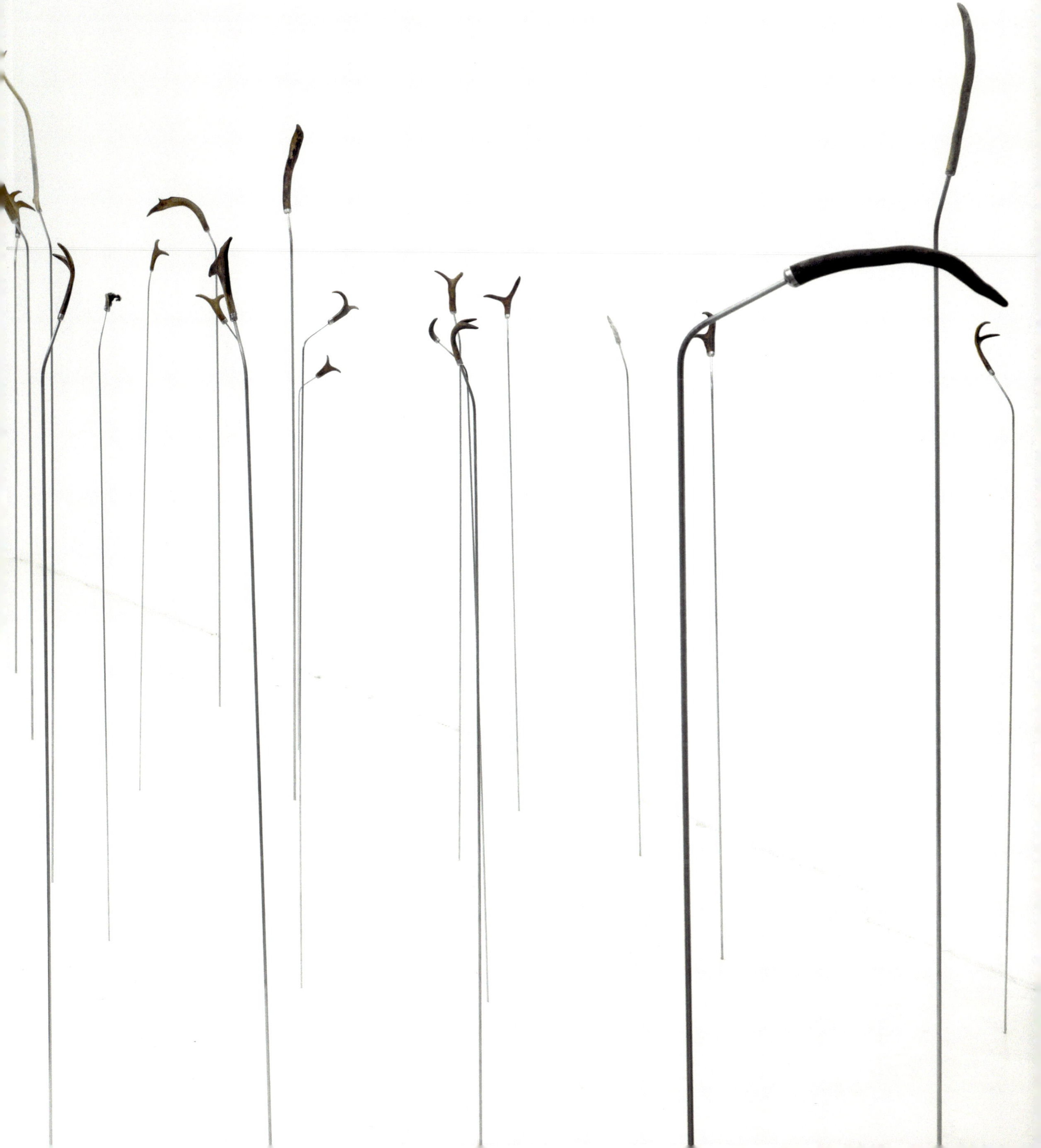

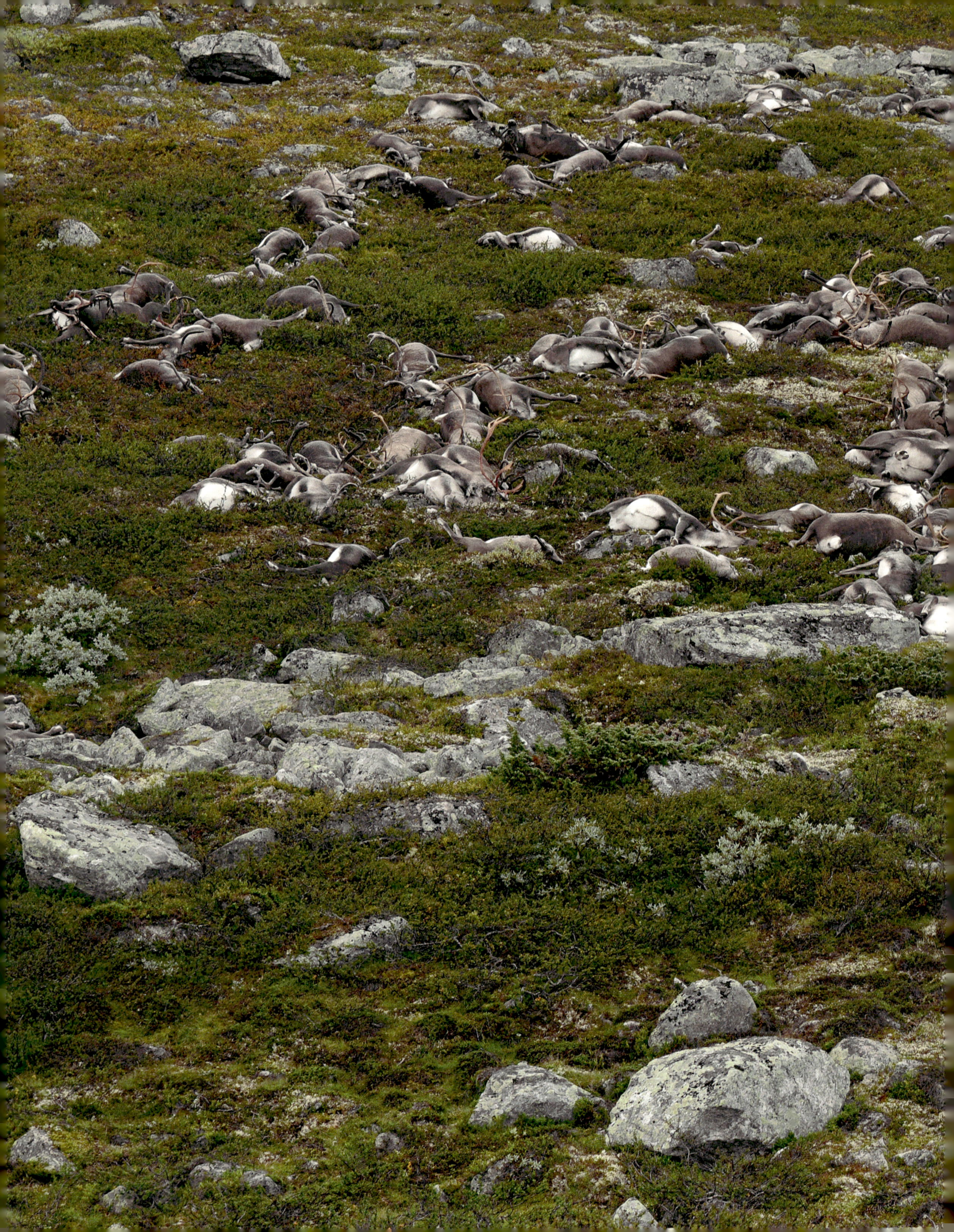

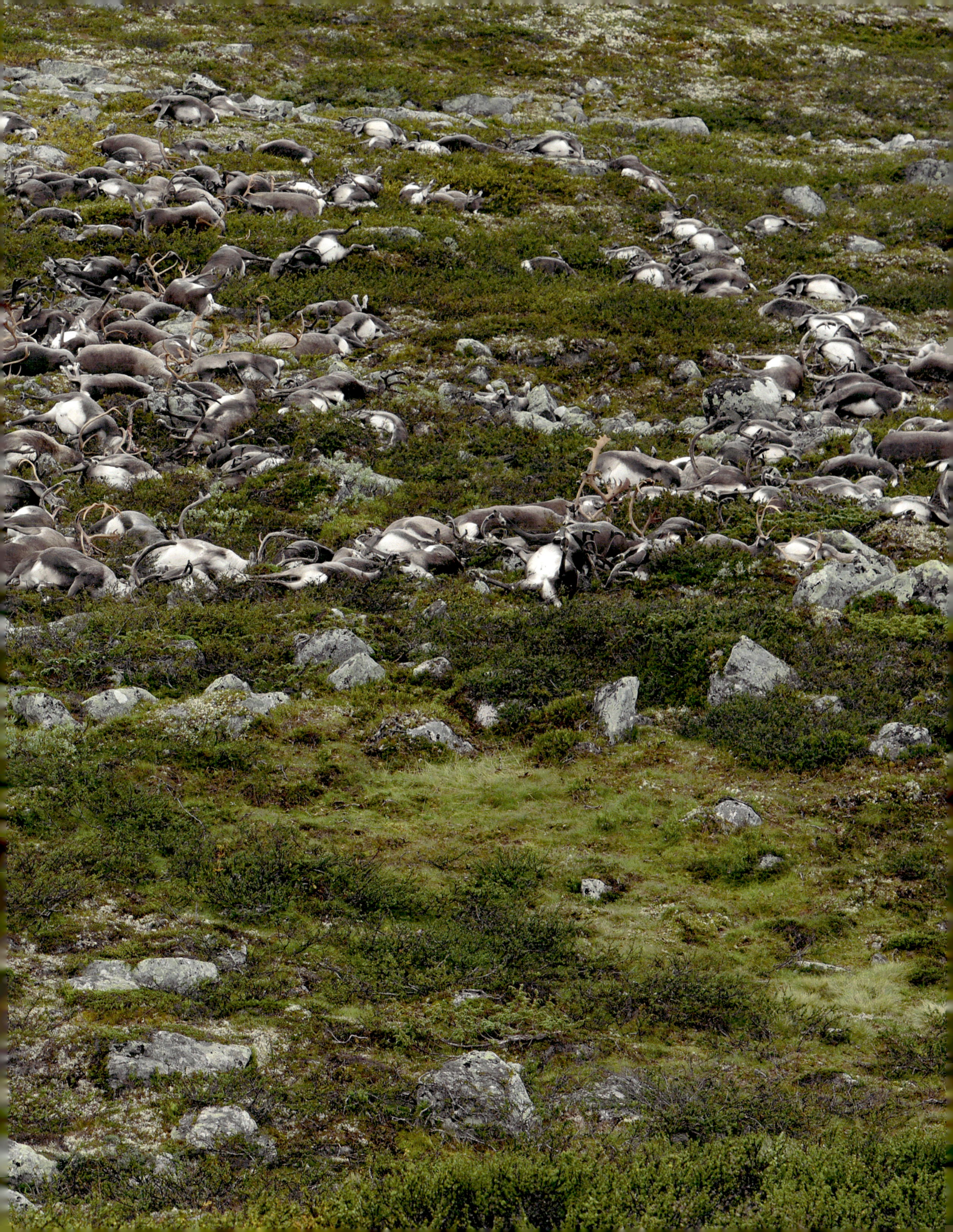

Taita Is Talking

Wiwa Shaman in Conversation with
Julius von Bismarck

On October 6, 2014, during an electrical storm, lightning struck a ceremonial hut in Santa Marta, in the remote Sierra Nevada mountains of Colombia. The villagers were engaged in an early morning ritual of the Wiwa community's government. Eleven people died. Fifteen were injured but managed to escape from the burning building. One of them was Taita.

Well, thunder is a spiritual person. They are spiritual, they live in a temple, but they talk; they live in the temple, but they breathe; their voice goes out. So He, that thunder, talks to us. When I settled on the side of this river He said to me:
—"You have to obey the law of the beginning, the real law."
I didn't understand very well. I started to learn with them and He said:
—"This basin is profane, they said: It is profane."
I didn't understand what profane meant. So He said,
—"You took out; you took all the gold and treasures out. You took bowls of pure crystal water. You took everything. That's why there is going to be drought, that's why your food is going to rot."

There is negative thunder and there is positive thunder. Some say thunder is an animal, an animal that has horns, that has a tail, that is inside a pond or a lake and that can also be sent: that's negative thunder. But positive thunder has no horns, no tail; it is like a person. It's in the temple. But negative thunder is in the lake, in the pond. So a lot of people say that thunder is that animal, the negative. Like us: there are positive people who want things to be good, everything. And there are some people who do harm. I hear that there is guerrilla; I don't know, I think, is it good? Like He has never talked to me, I say, "is He a good guerilla, how is He?" Here a lot of *paracos*[1] are born. We have to be very careful. When He does GRUU GRUU, it is the negative one, PUN CURURU, that is the positive one. So we do have to think that negative can't come, so that they don't let Him come, they stop Him, they send Him away. One has to remain positive; if one is negative it comes. You don't need to come here, if you are negative, what are you going to talk to me about. You see, there is no respect, there is too much disorder, too much negative things, a lot, thousands, millions of negative things.

If there is no thunder, there isn't any rain. He is the authority: He says, today it has to rain. He doesn't say rain, He says dance. So if they start dancing, there will be water. If they are still, summer will come. No rain, thunder, thunder, clouds, rain—because they are the authority that rules it all. They are a natural authority. From oxygen. A natural authority, like a government. Just like a shadow.

If they say, "pay us this," we have to pay it. If not, they can do a lot of harm. But they ask for gold, a green gold. What is the name of the gold? Black gold, green, reddish, yellow. They ask for it. We don't have it; we have very little. He takes it, it's his nurture.

That day the thunder was saying,
—"Pay us Conchemi. Today, today, today at midday, in the afternoon, pay Conchemi."
I started to say that the Conchemi Race didn't exist anymore, here on this side of the river, there are no Conchemi. Here, there are Sauna, Alberto, there is Gil, there is Mojica, but we don't have Conchemi. It was six, seven, when they said,
—"Ok, so in one minute you pay Conchemi. If you don't pay us Conchemi, we are not going to lift the sanction."
So everyone was reunited in the *Maloca*,[2] we were like forty, we said that the Conchemi did not exist. If there were Conchemi, we would have paid. We were all talking and like at twelve, at one, they said,
—"If you don't give us Conchemi, you are going to pay..."

... My son, my grandchildren, two, three, no, four José María was an assistant. My brother-in-law died,

1 Paramilitaries.

2 House of the indigenous community, where they engage in ceremonies.

Carricero. A *Mamo*,[3] Sauna, and another leader almost, almost. Authority. They died there, that's why we don't have any authorities now. We are looking for replacements, we want to install this one, and I am preparing Him. He doesn't speak Spanish like I do, but what is knowledge? To show some respect for the thunder. I'm teaching Him. How much time do we need? We have six months.

When I saw them all dead, I stood up, took the thunder, pulled Him outside and told Him I was going to denounce Him: "I'm going to denounce you."
And He said:
—"How are you going to denounce me? We told you, there is too much profanation in all the countries, there is sexual disorder, disorder of the psyche, disorder of desire, vice."
—"Then what should I do?"
—"You shut up. We are going to continue asking for what we deserve."
I said: "Like this? In such an ugly way?"
—"Somehow we need to charge you. A plague, diarrhea, vomit, blood, crash of small brother, country vs. country, bombs. We are the highest spiritual authority over nature, over everything there is on the planet: we are the authority. Over every planet: we are the authority. You are commissaries, a government; you are a government in a country. We are the highest spiritual authority of nature and of the spirits and planets. So you tell me: how are you going to sue us?"
So I told Him: "don't touch me anymore."
—"But your community, your people, owe us. When we say "attention" we are going to hit you. So you better give them some advice, teach your people, because they are doing a lot of harm. Disorder. We have to charge you. We have to charge; you have seen how they've excavated everything, the quartz. The four Mamos from *la sierra* are not connected; they are disorganized, in disagreement. And that is something we are also going to charge you for.

Thunder had warned us,
—"There is too much sexual disorder. Word: disorder. Thought: disorder. Disorder: a lot of desire, a lot of vice."
And He said,
—"You are responsible and you have to explain it to all the people."

But, the whole world is becoming profane. Here there is profanation; what is it? There is a girl of fourteen, and they are touching her, that is our profanation. And material profanation: they are still taking it away, they are taking the gold away.

So now, up there, the lightning struck, like three weeks ago. It strikes in the mountain, burns the tress and it says:
—"Be careful, we are going to make you pay, all the countries, other countries are going to pay with bullets, bombs."
Serancua[4] didn't say to finish with the people, but He doesn't know now. Five days ago He said,
—"You don't know what type of punishment is coming; you don't know, but there is a punishment for all the world."
They don't explain it. They say,
—"Be prepared, be ready, purify yourselves and pay your debt."
I ask: "What kind of debt?"
—"You drink water without buying it; you eat fruit without buying it; who buys it? You kill a *guaro*,[5] eat without buying, the owner of this *guaro* is not buying it; a banana, who buys it? You plant it but you are not the owners, the owner has to buy it, we all have to pay the debt, we breathe each second, we are sending thousands and thousands of gallons and you still don't know who pays the oxygen. You don't know how to pay. Well, the time to pay the debt has come."

Some pay with rocks, a little quartz. Today thunder doesn't need that. He wants another *pagamento*,[6] another quartz that we don't know. We have to study a lot so we know it; we are investigating it, to see what we can do. So that's why I said, we are not saints yet. We need antennas to stop the lightning. Because what if the lightning strikes when there are children at school; He fulminates everything.

3 Maximum spiritual authority/leader of the Wiwa and indigenous communities in general.

4 Son of God.
5 A bird.
6 Offerings to the gods.

And He is saying it.
—"You are going to pay. We are going to make you pay."
So maybe we do need help for up there; an antenna, where the town burnt. We are going to build again, down there, we are going to make a town again. We are thinking about it.

The lightning is a superior authority. If you make a mistake, it's ok, but if a superior authority makes a mistake He has to call for His attention. And like that, He is telling us,
—"If you don't make a mistake, if you have no debts, there is no thunder."
He talks, He says,
—"Ok I need this thing."
A *Mamo* with knowledge provides for them every day. They are authority, they send *aguacero*,[7] they send oxygen, and they take care of everything. They are authority; it's not only spiritual authority; they are like persons. He is in the temple but like this, He breathes, He goes out. Out. He clashes with that cloud over there. Thunder, He is talking there in the temple. So that is the knowledge of this. A lot of people don't understand the thunder. Here, there is one. They say He is someone who understands, who knew that it was going to happen. He said, "but the *Mamo* says, 'thunder says that . . . ,' but nobody pays attention." Just like the *Mamo*: He doesn't believe that He listens to the thunder. They don't believe it. Like they don't listen; they think He is telling lies. I listen, my people believe me, but not everything, so the thunder is hurt, a little. But some are impressed, because He burnt the house and why didn't He burn everything? Because when He lights a house, He destroys everything. Then why didn't He do it? Because I was there. I am paying my debt, I am positive, I don't hang around with negative people, and so the thunders respected me. But He announced it. What was going to happen? Some go drinking *chirrinchito*,[8] maybe they lie, maybe. So He is saying, "I have killed two here, some cows there." He was announcing, ". . . be careful, be prepared, pay your debts . . ."
Well it happened to us. They were like ten totally quiet, like dead, twenty . . . He killed cows, pigs, He is doing a lot of harm and here we are again and He continues asking for Conchemi . . . So we reunite the ones from here, we analyze, it was like a fruit. We analyze, we looked for that fruit, with nurture, with everything well-purified, and we gave it to Him. *No más*. The Conchemi is a race, here there are no Conchemi, we don't have any, they are done. So there were eleven dead people, I was there. And they came in, I looked Him in the face, big, red, and He said,
—"You didn't ask for what we wanted, we told you we wanted Conchemi."
I am investigating and I know that in the Cesar there is Conchemi. There is like five Conchemi; my plan is to take them and bring them here so we have Conchemi. The Conchemi means we have this arm, but it's not complete; here you cannot do anything. We have eyes. One good eye at least; but if you lose this, you cannot see anymore. We have like thirty teeth, we eat good, but if they finish there are no more teeth and we cannot eat good, the same for Serancua. He left us, so we could be complete, in accordance, with love for the race, for you, for the indigenous, any kind of people, people's race, for example Mojica, Sauna, Roberto, Gil, Barro: there are a lot of them, but some of them are vanishing. They cannot vanish, because if we don't have an arm, it cannot work. If you get your leg cut off, you cannot work well.

Originally published in
Gagarin 32 (2016), pp. 105–10.

7 Downpour.
8 Alcohol.

TALKING TO THUNDER

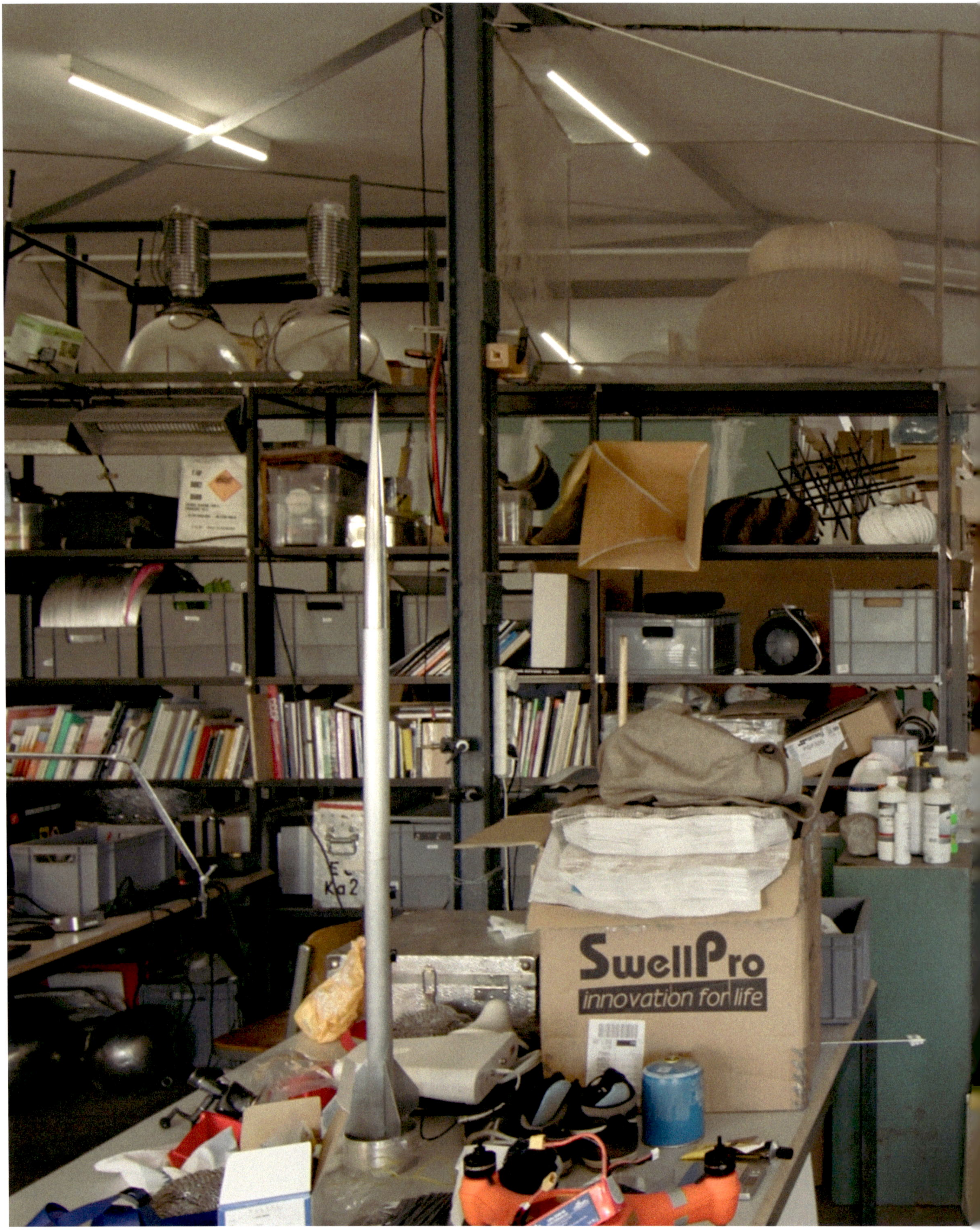
SwellPro
innovation for life

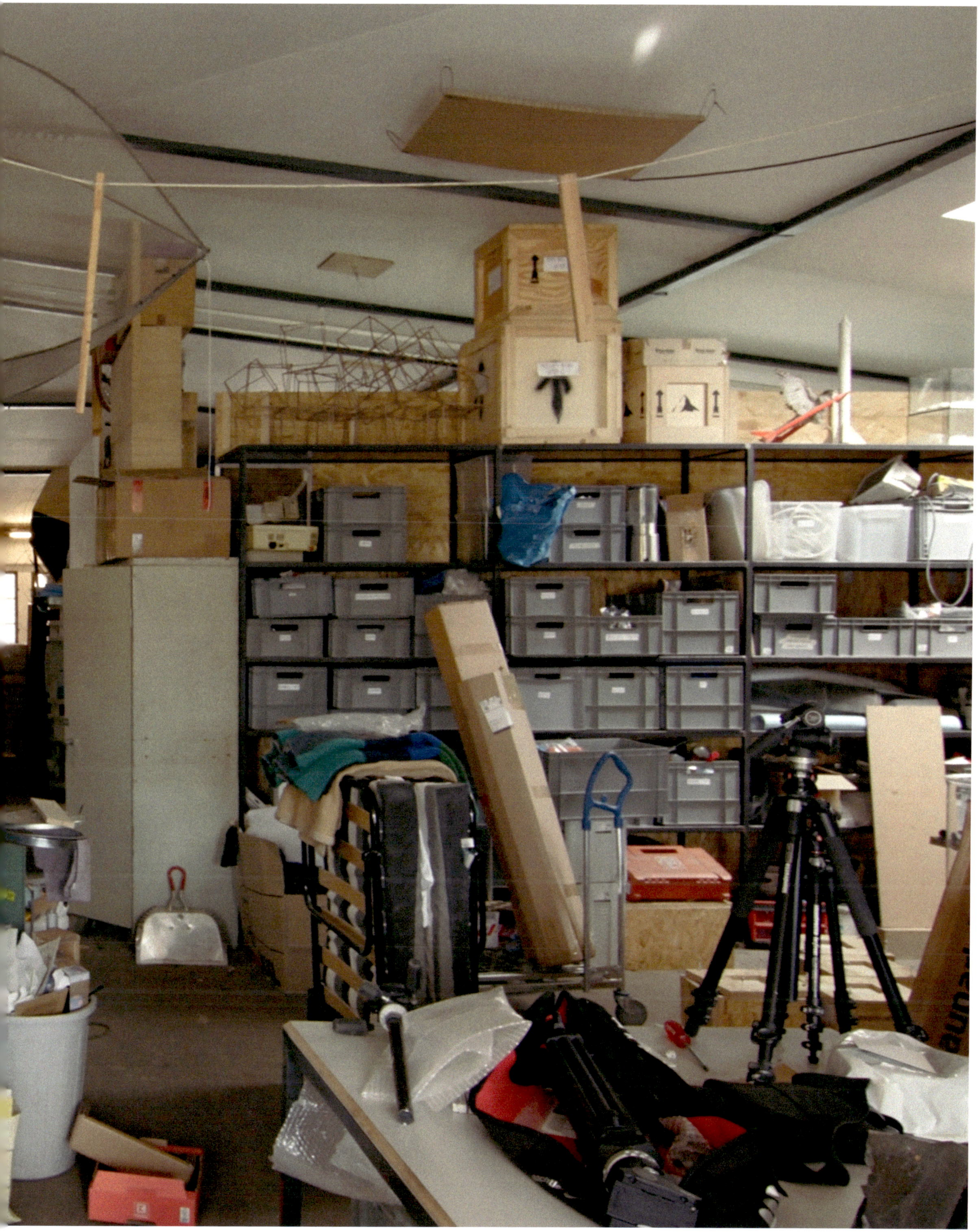

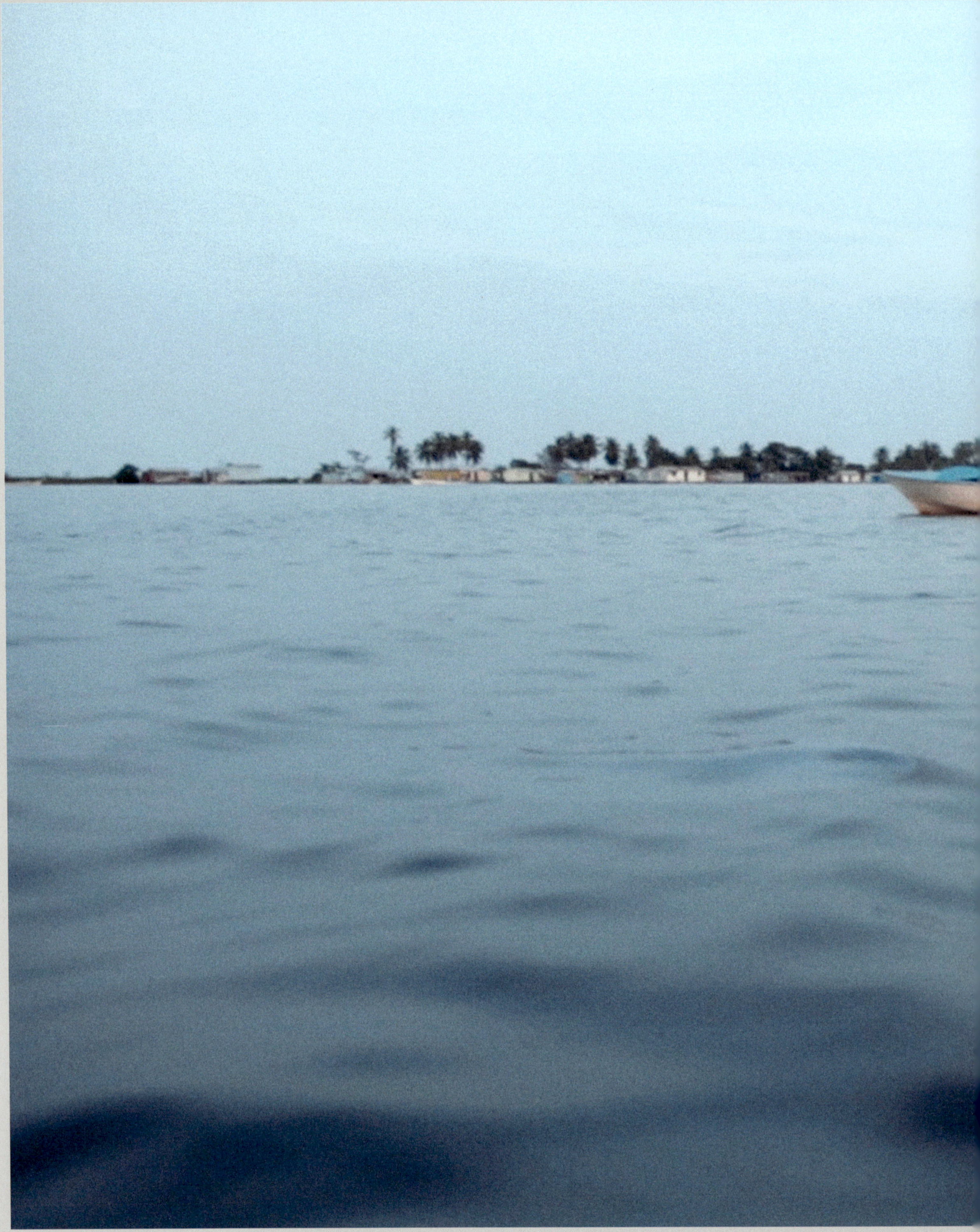

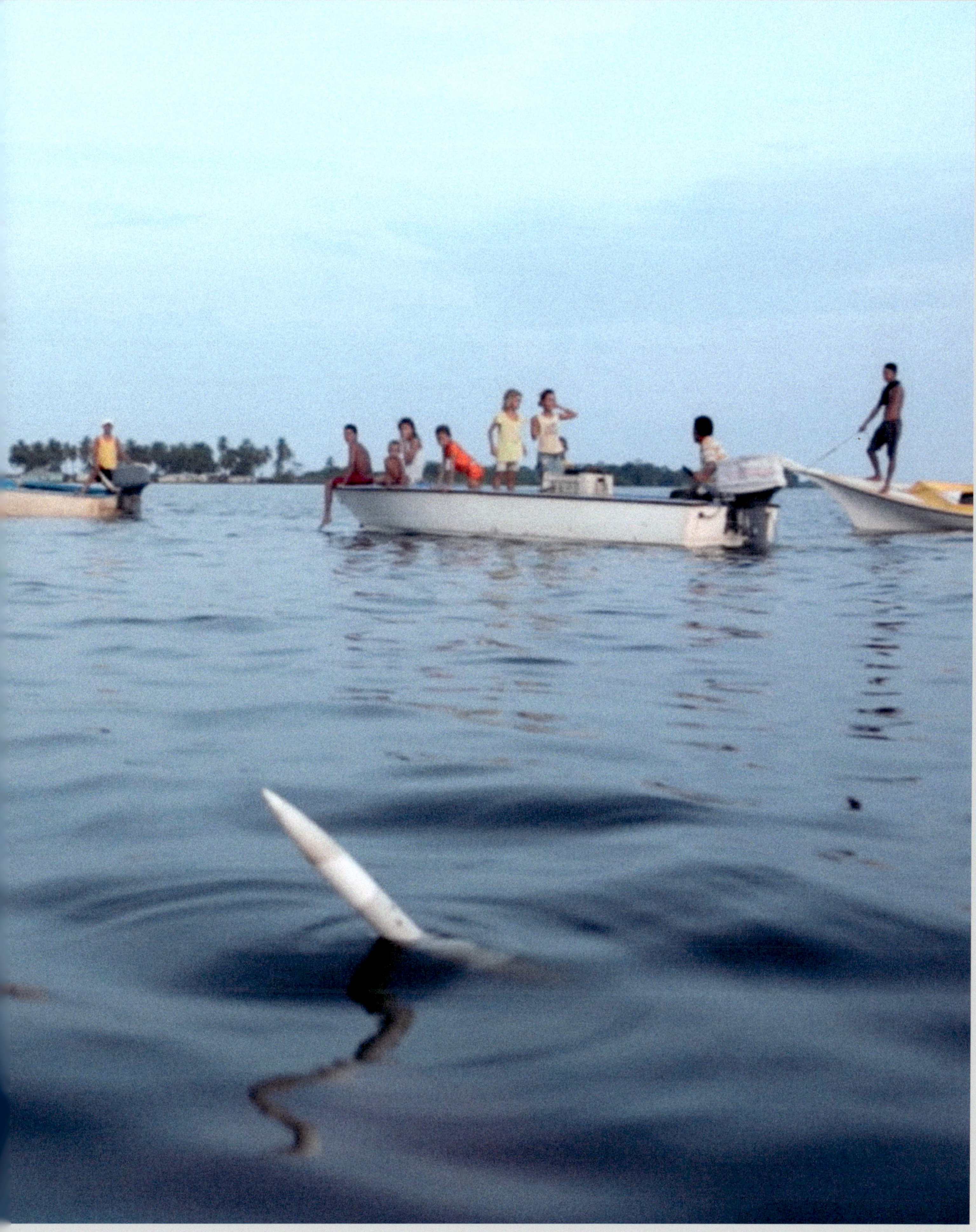

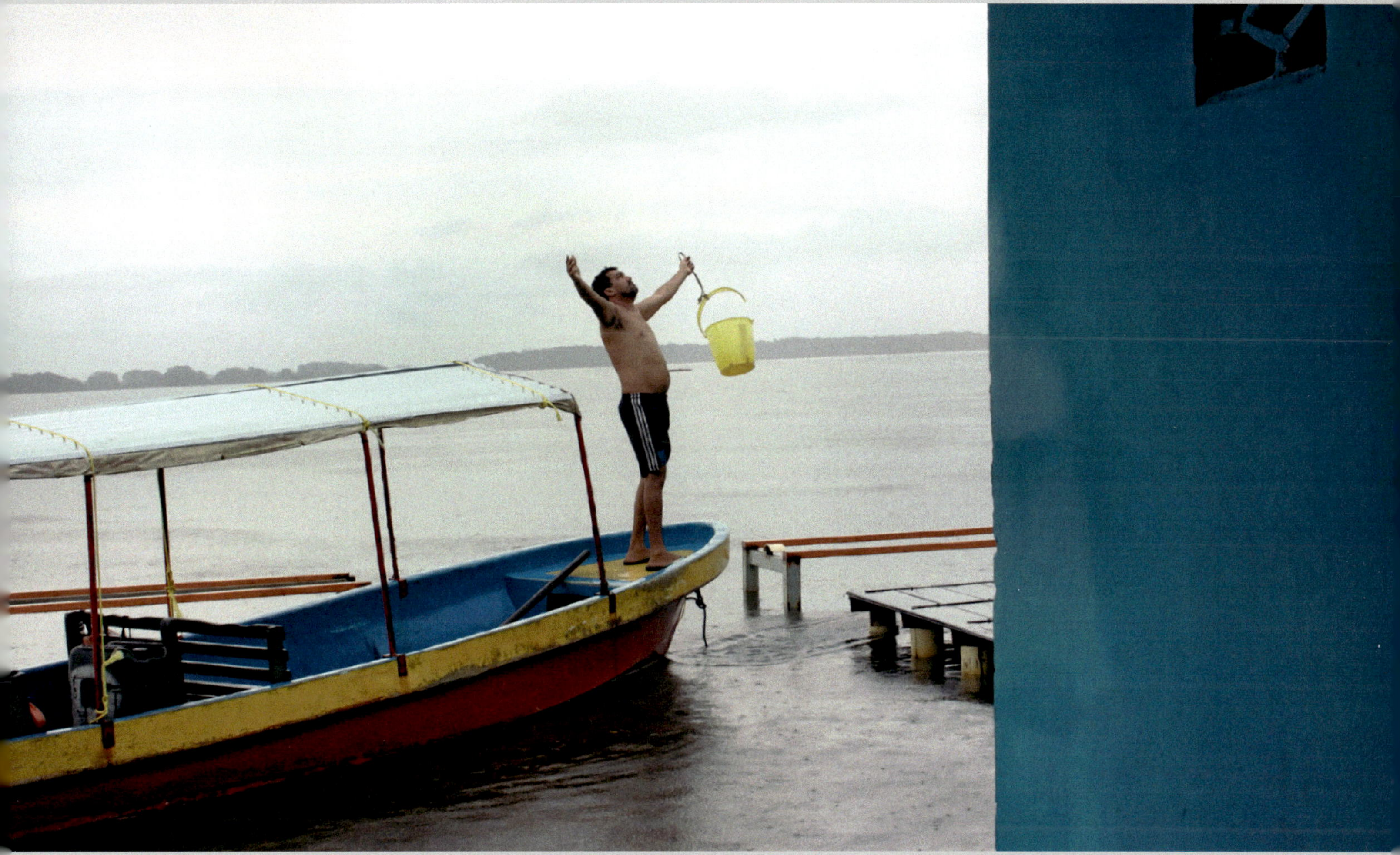

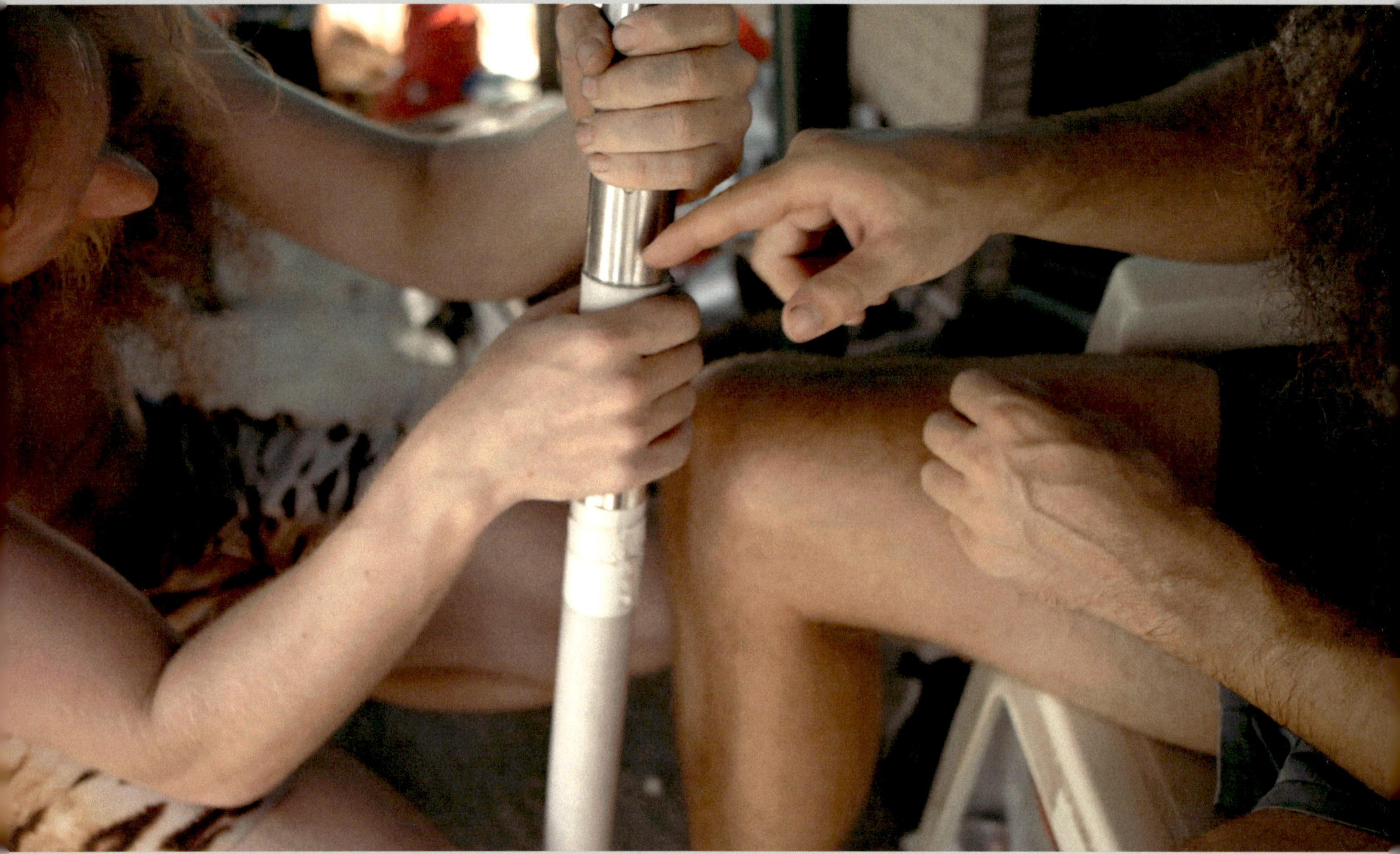

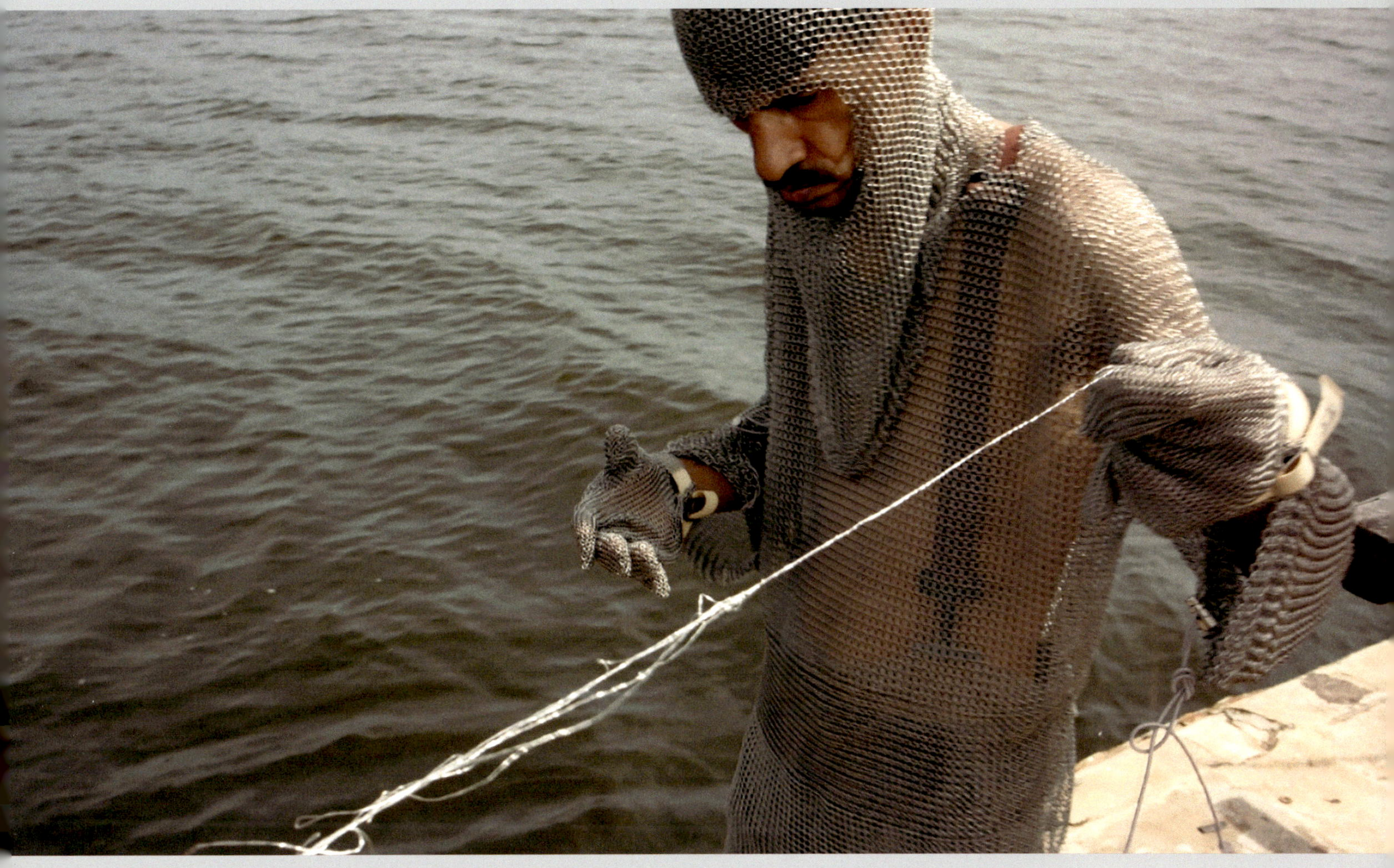

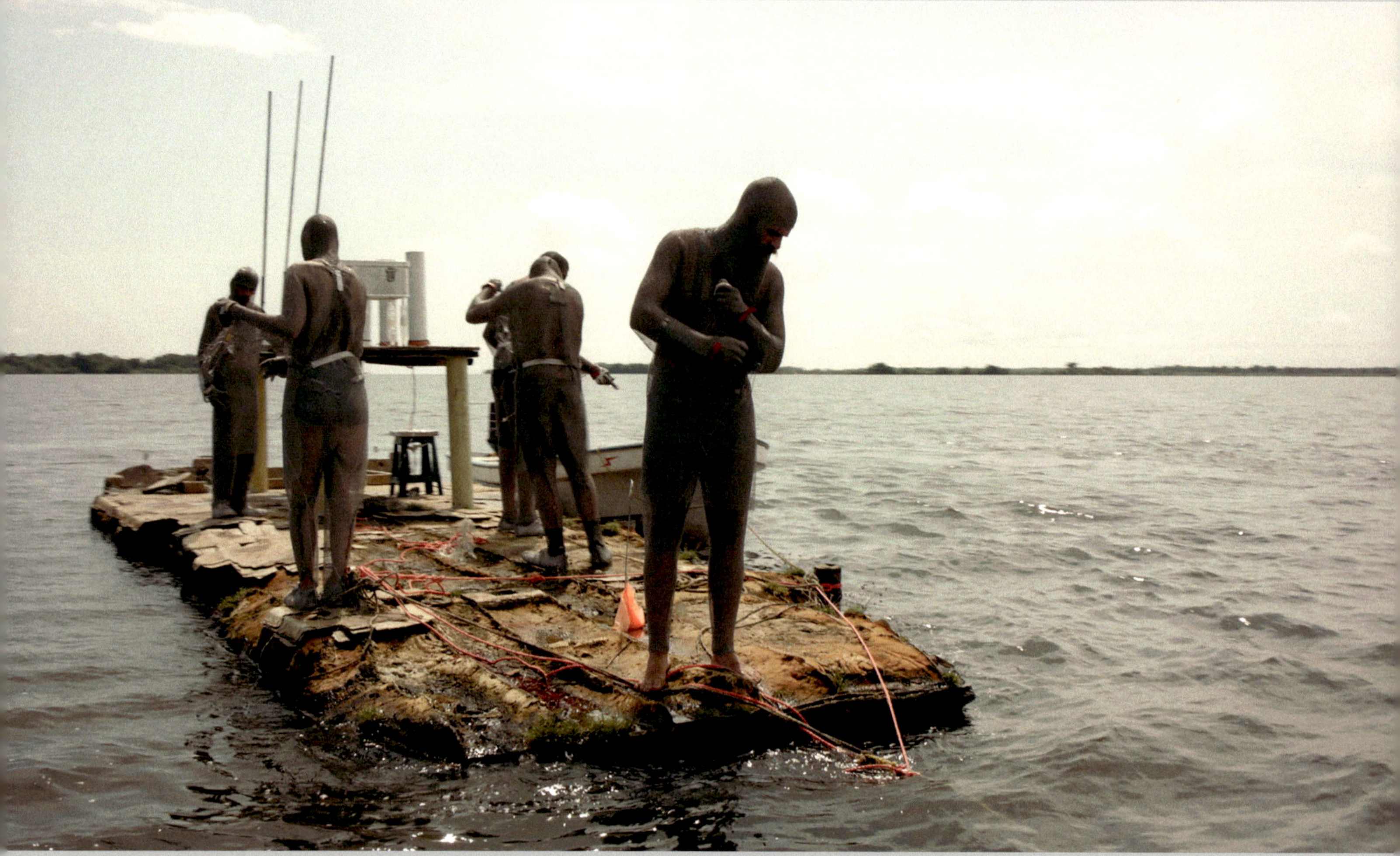

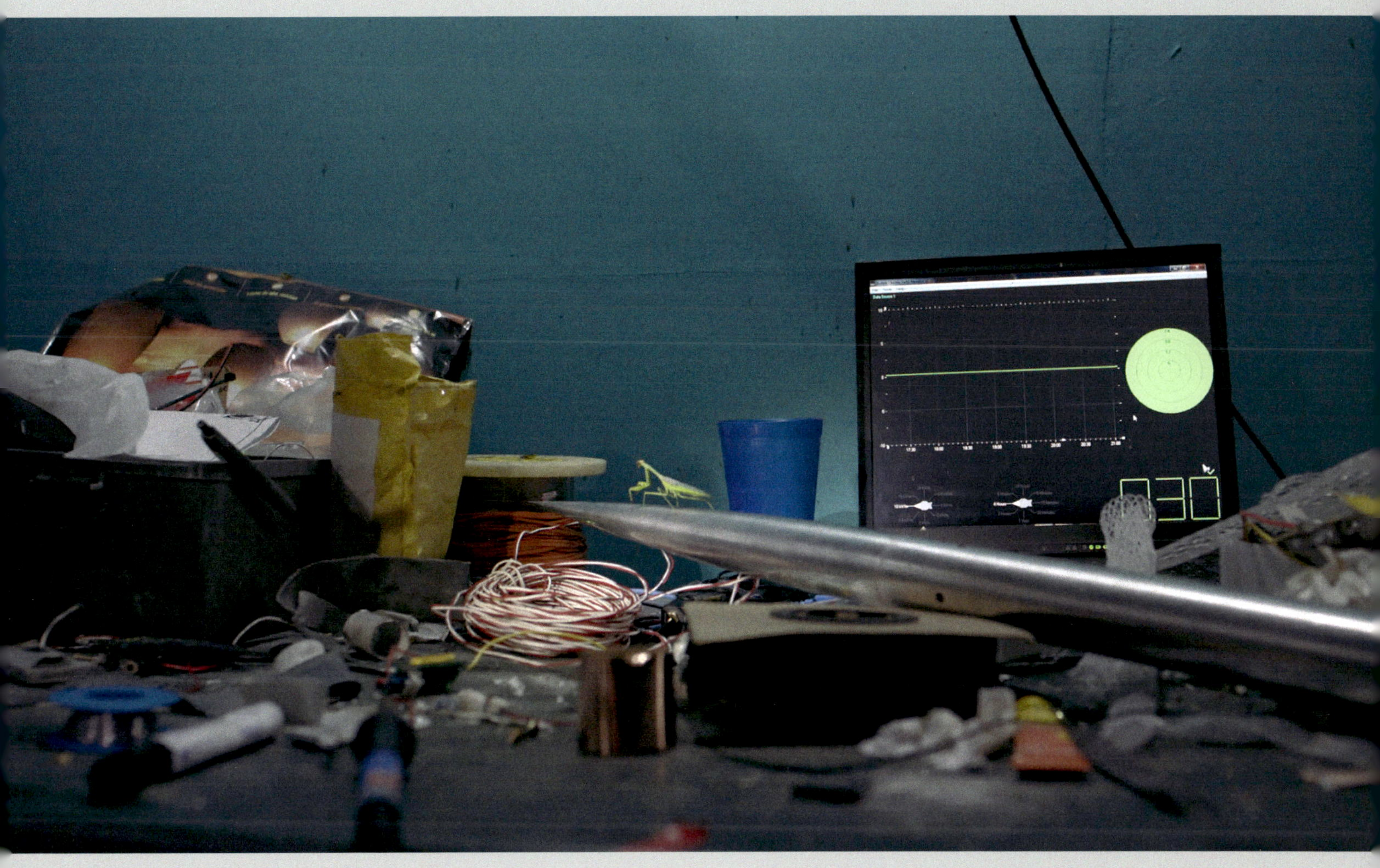

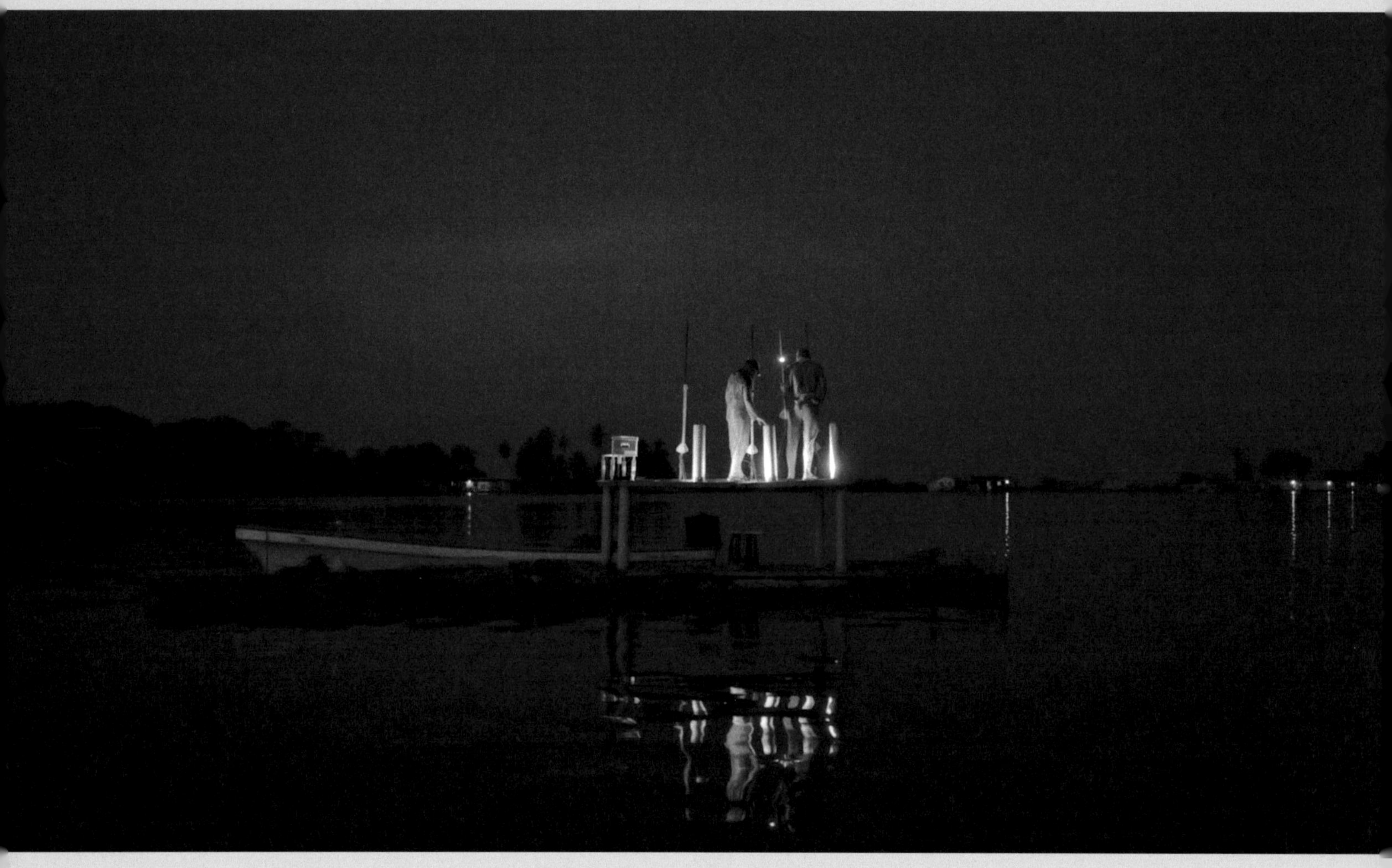

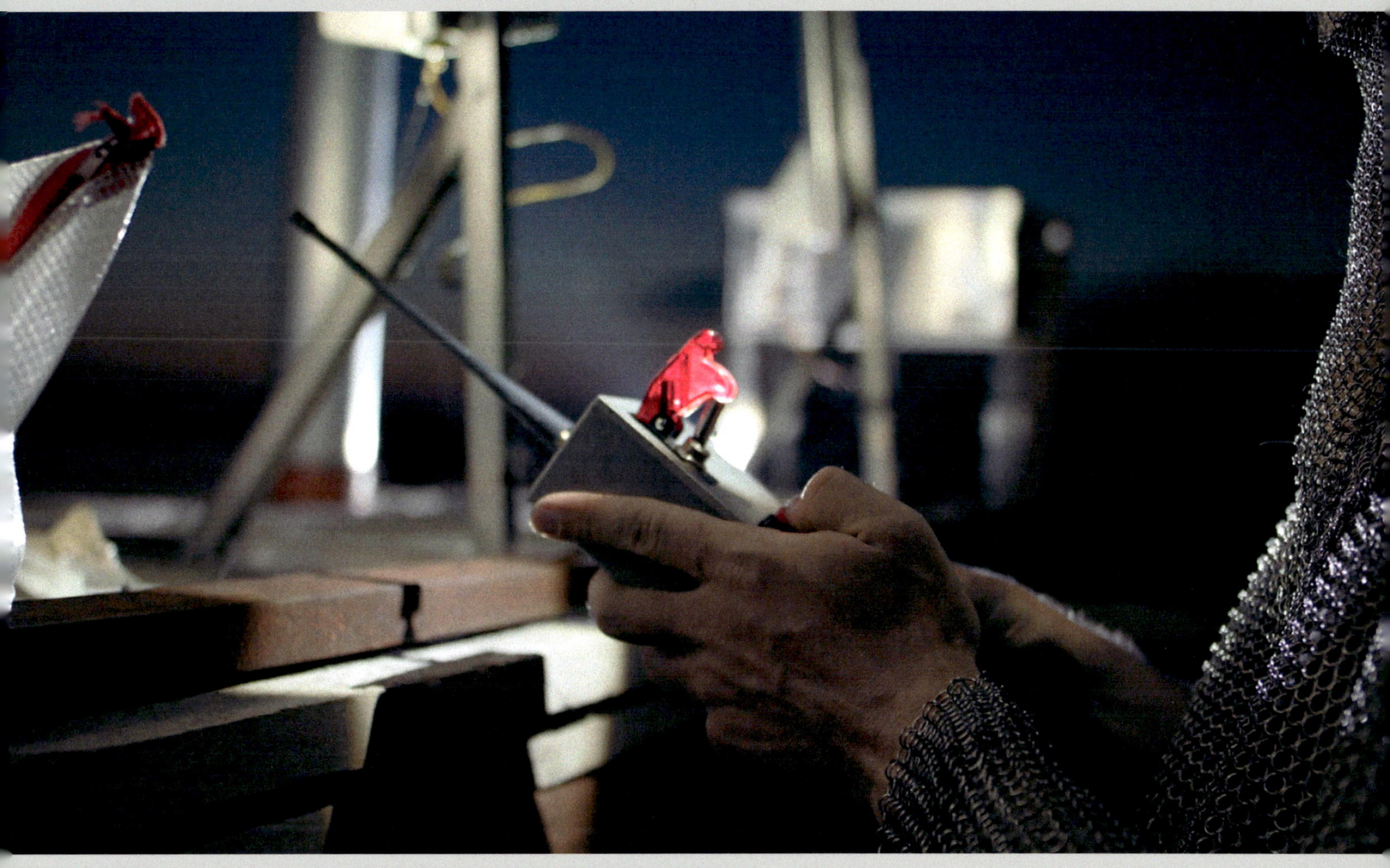

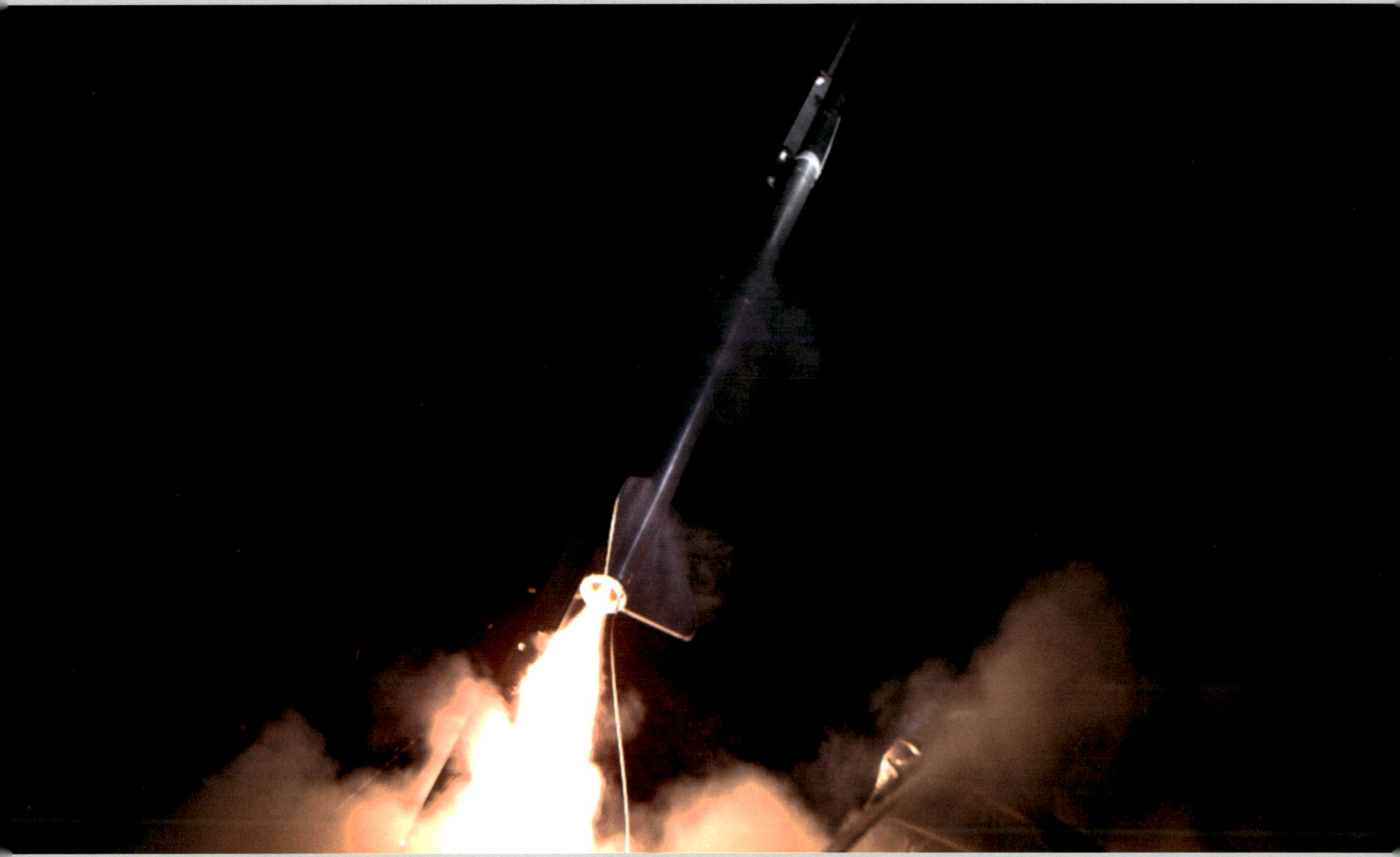

Talking to Thunder

2016–17

In late 2016 a large herd of reindeer was struck by lightning on the Hardangervidda mountain plateau in southern Norway. A day later Julius von Bismarck arrived to visit their corpses. The sad trophies of his journey comprise 130 antler tips harvested on the spot. Individually mounted on stainless-steel rods approximately the height of a reindeer's head, the array of different sized and shaped horns offer a monument to the relentless brutality of nature.

Talking to Thunder confronts the Western dogma of nature as a domain of innocence in need of protection with a competing image of nature as a punishing deity, a force which invariably devastates, which demands to be soothed and worshipped. In northern Colombia, a region of frequent and intense thunderstorms, the artist met a shaman named Taita of the Wiwa tribe, a survivor of a lightning strike that killed eleven members of his community. As is common in indigenous cosmologies of the Americas, the Wiwa speak of thunder as a person.

Ever since he was struck by lightning while camping in his car, years ago, Bismarck has been attempting to tame lightning bolts. He traveled to an atmospheric research lab in New Mexico, to a Navy base in Florida, and he visited a remote area of Venezuela where there are particularly frequent electrical storms time and again. With a slow-motion camera, he filmed intense thunderstorms: lightning perforates the sky, plants sway heavily in the storm, gushes of rain whip the surface of a lake. These silent recordings have been set to a score of the artist imitating the sounds of a rain, thunderstorm, and wind.

The electric current between the ground and the sky can be measured. If it is particularly high, an electrical discharge can be provoked by building a bridge, for example, in the form of a Kevlar-spun copper thread shot into the sky by a sounding rocket. In a fishing village in the middle of the Venezuelan jungle, after many experiments, Bismarck succeeded in capturing several lightning bolts and guiding them toward the ground. In a series of photographs that show the lightning striking palm trees, tropical plants, and the lake, the lightning bolt itself becomes almost tangible as a sculptural object.

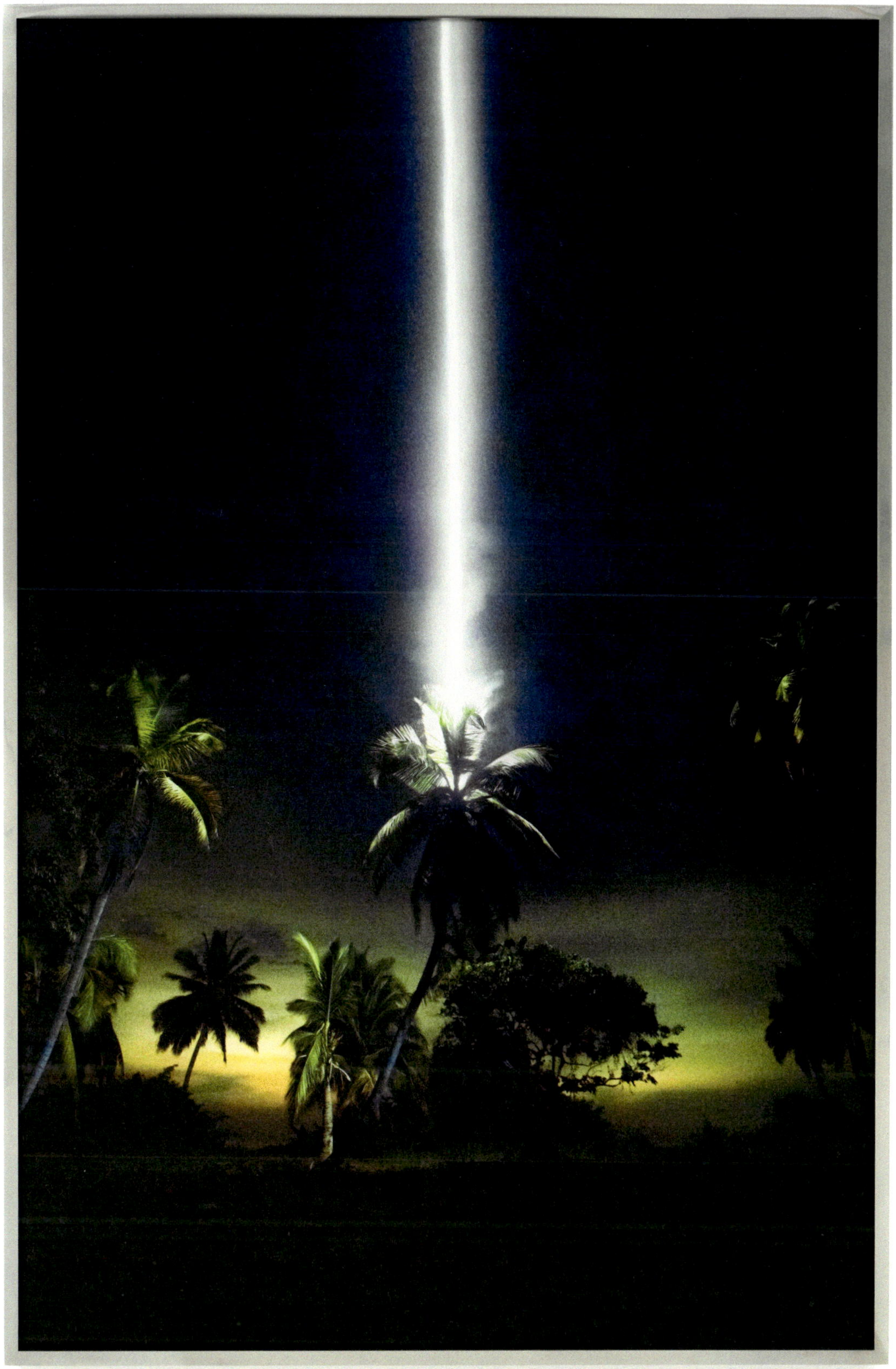

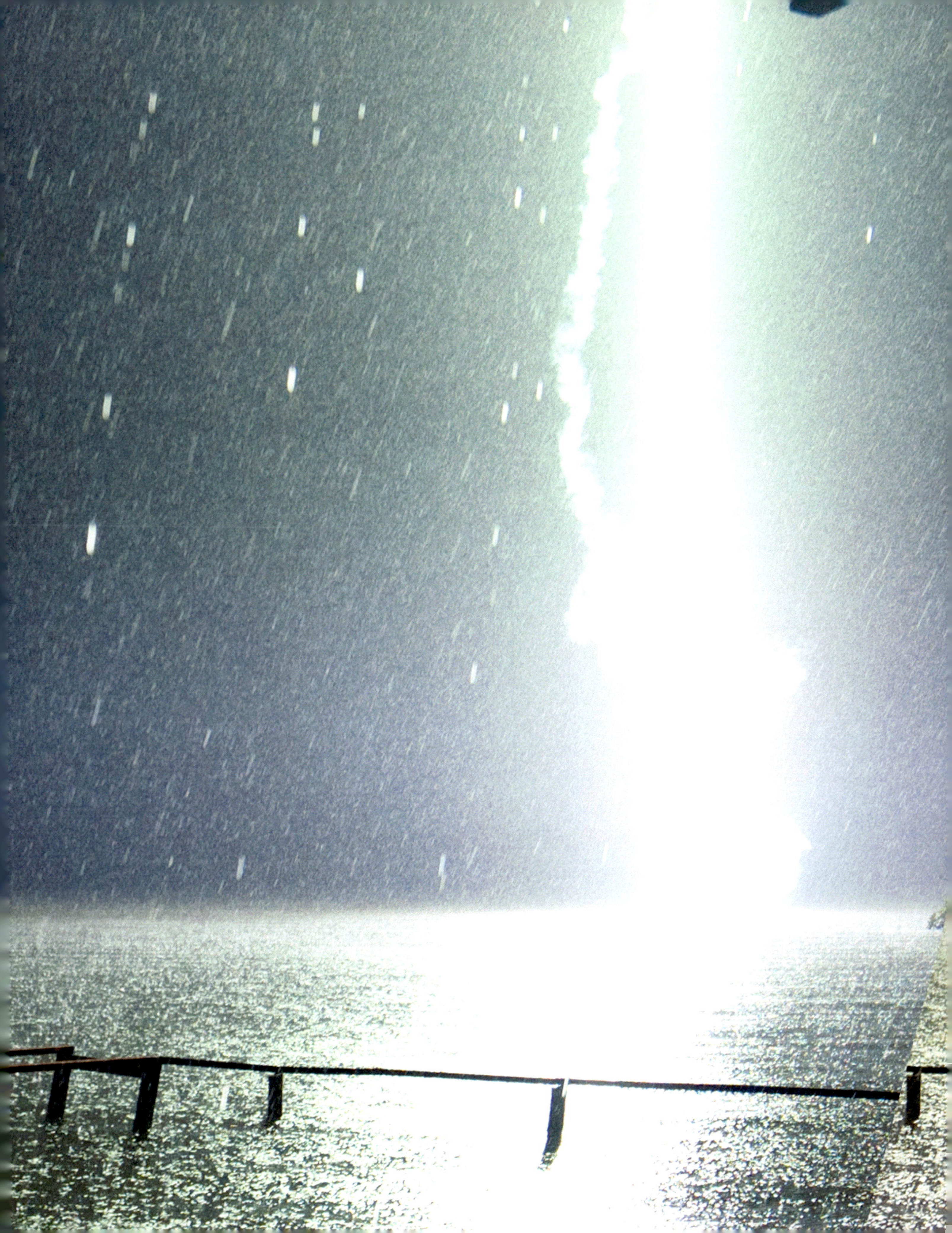

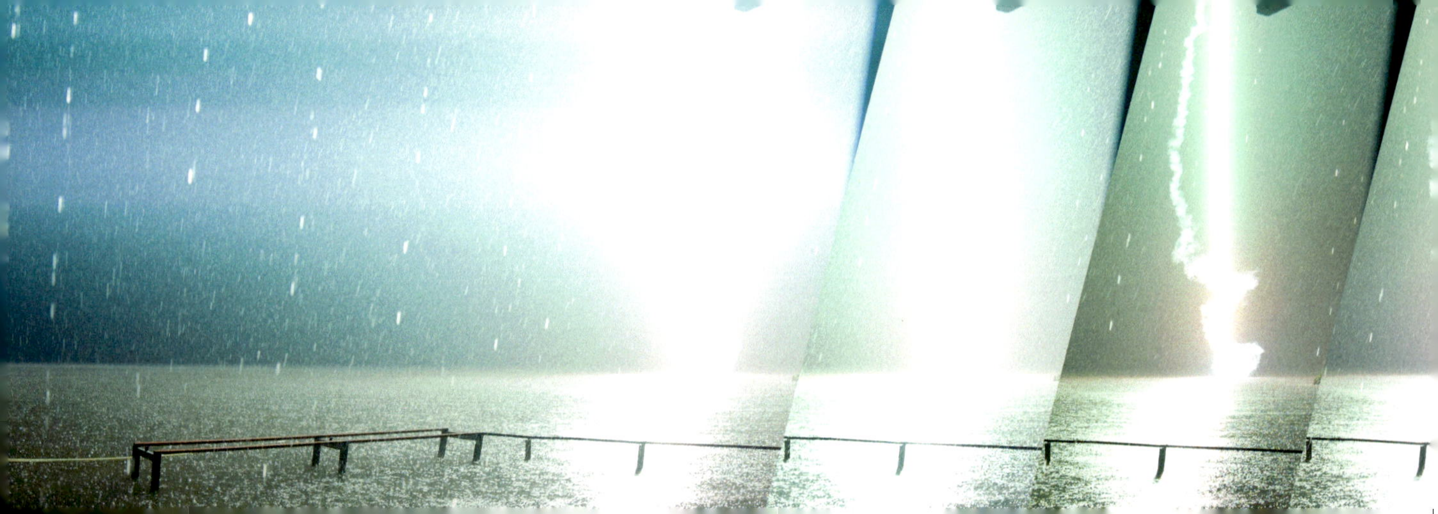

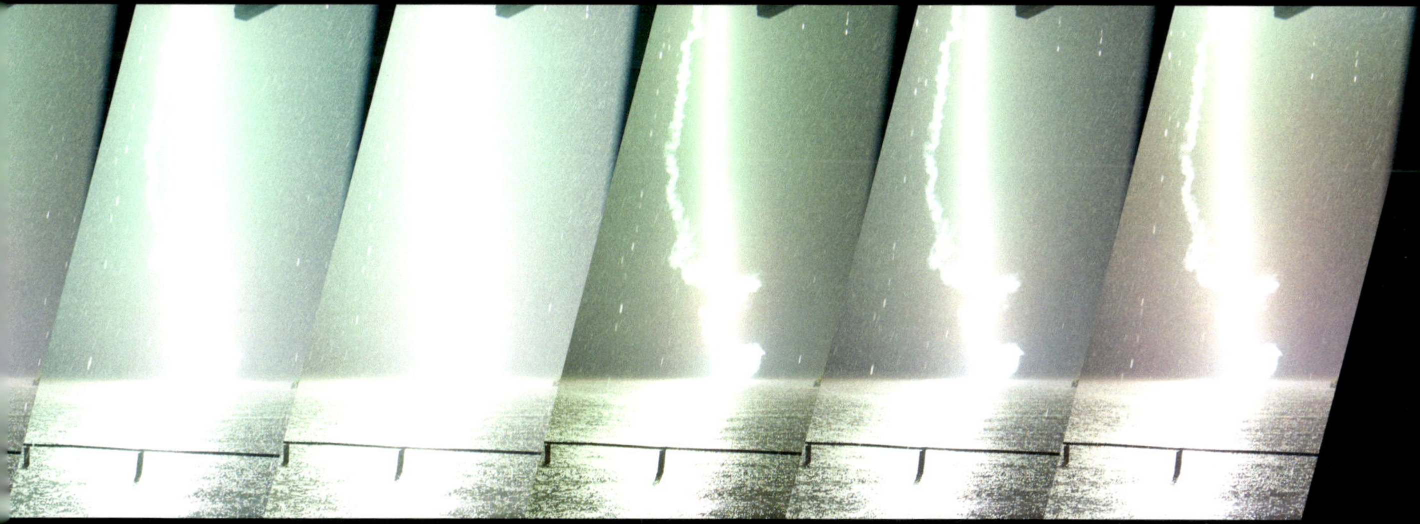

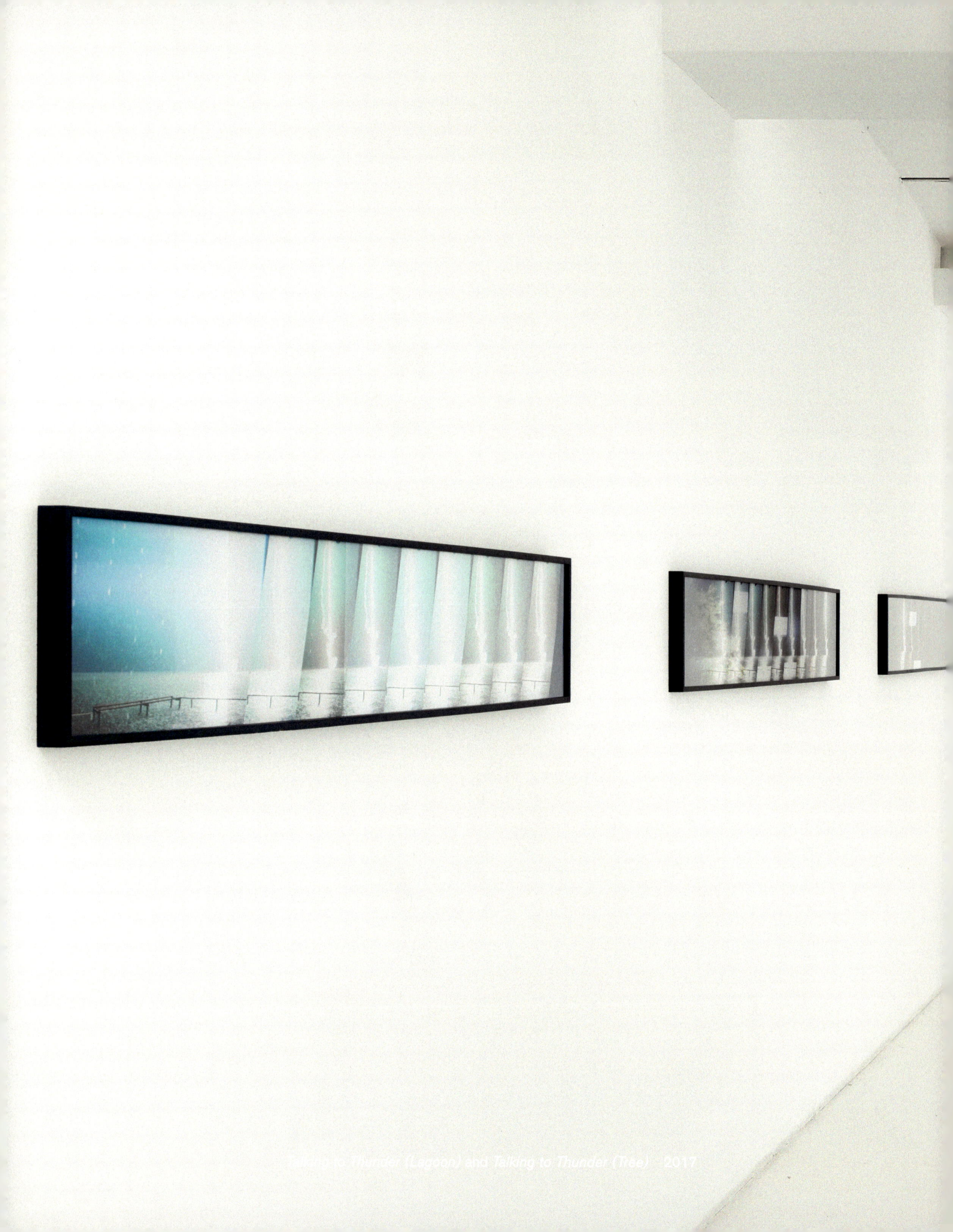

Talking to Thunder (Lagoon) and *Talking to Thunder (Tree)*, 2017

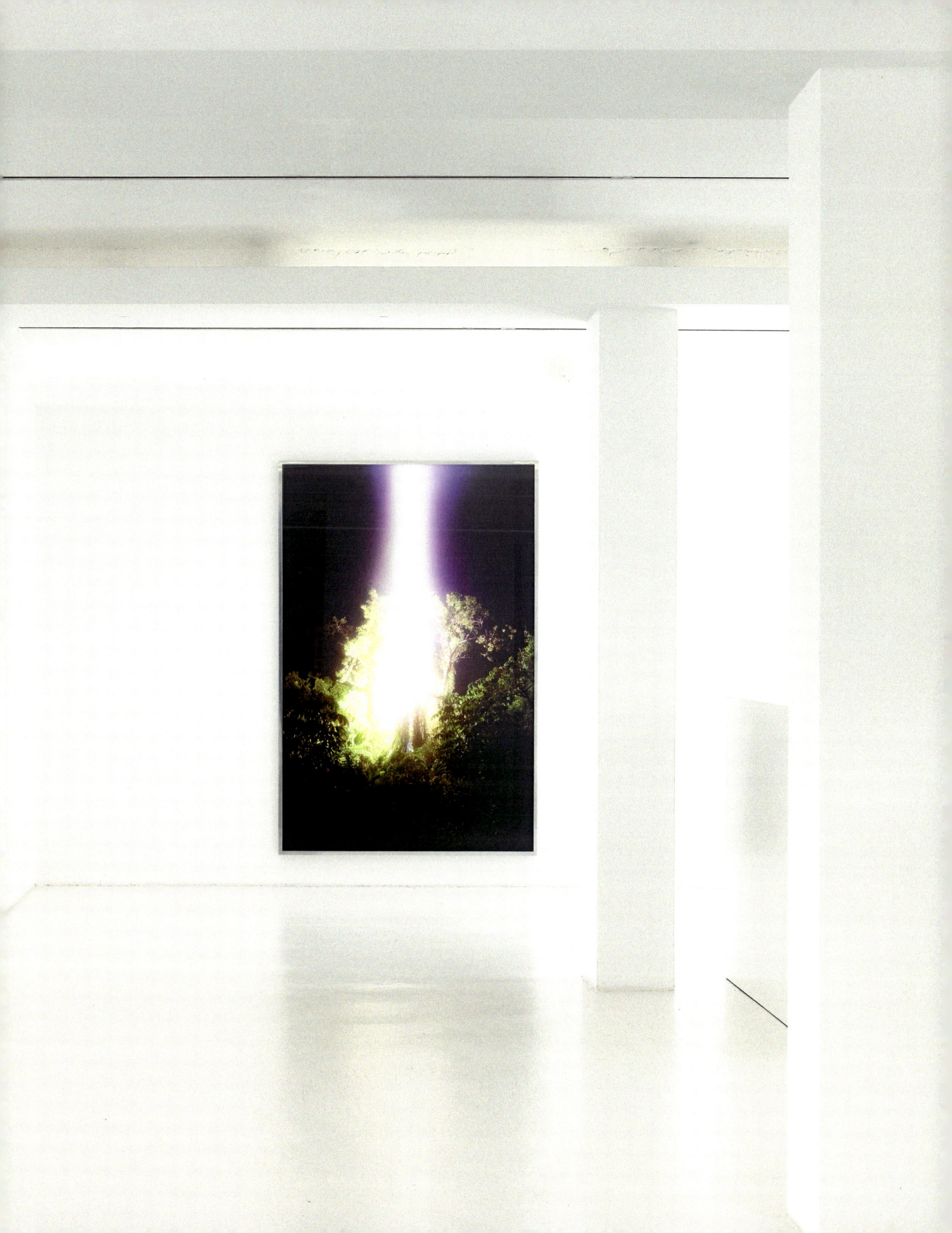

Talking to Thunder (Bright Tree) 2017

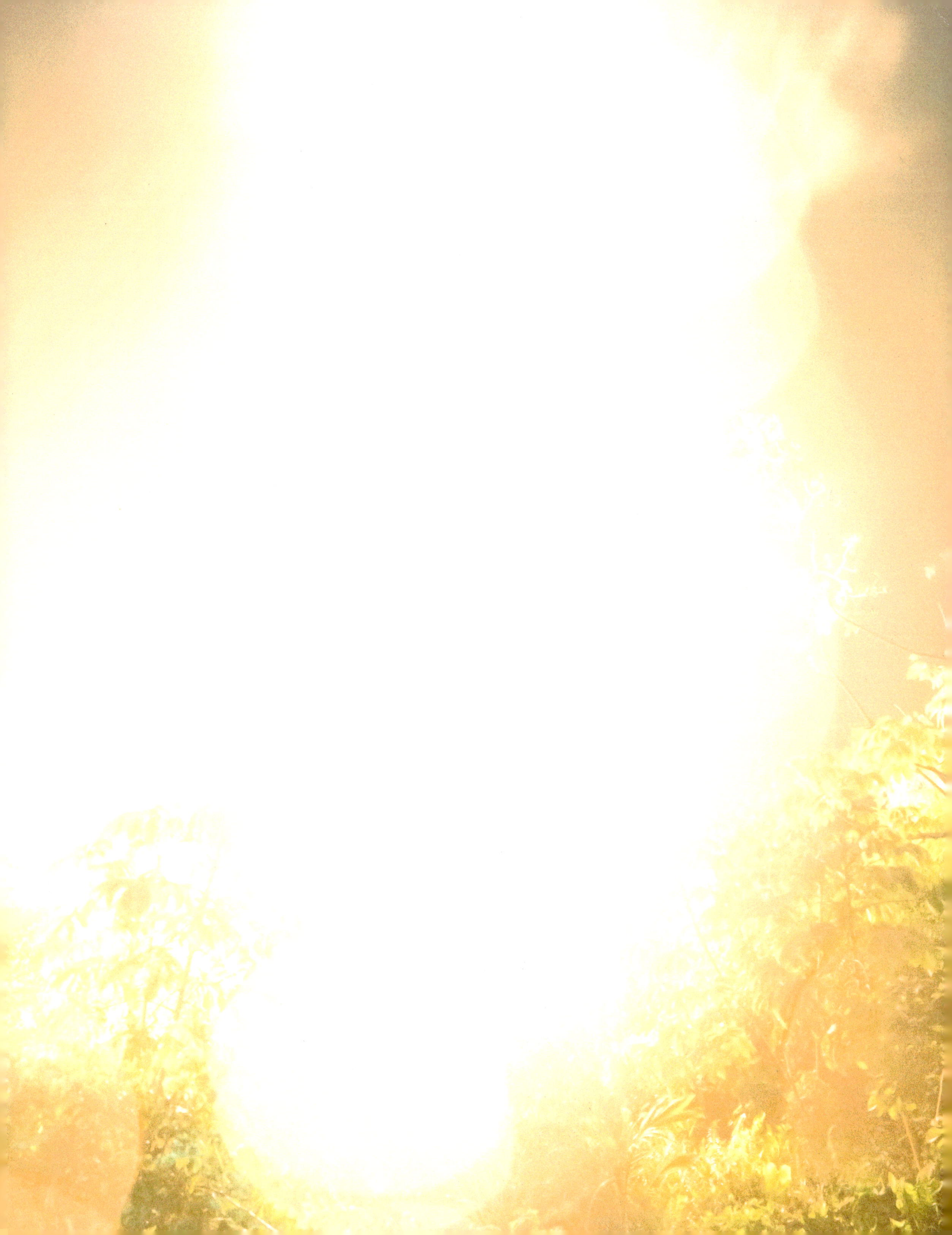

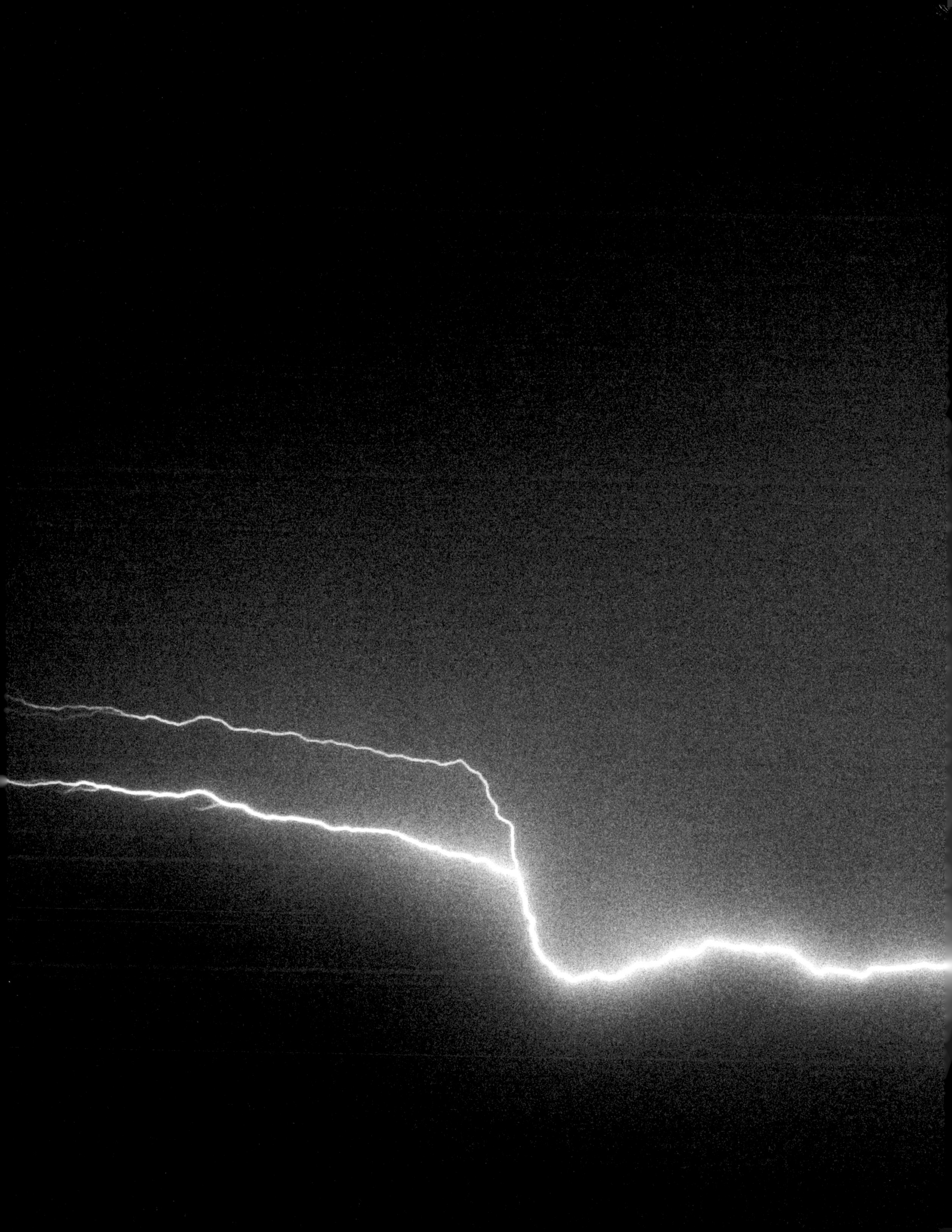

Lightning Rockets 2017

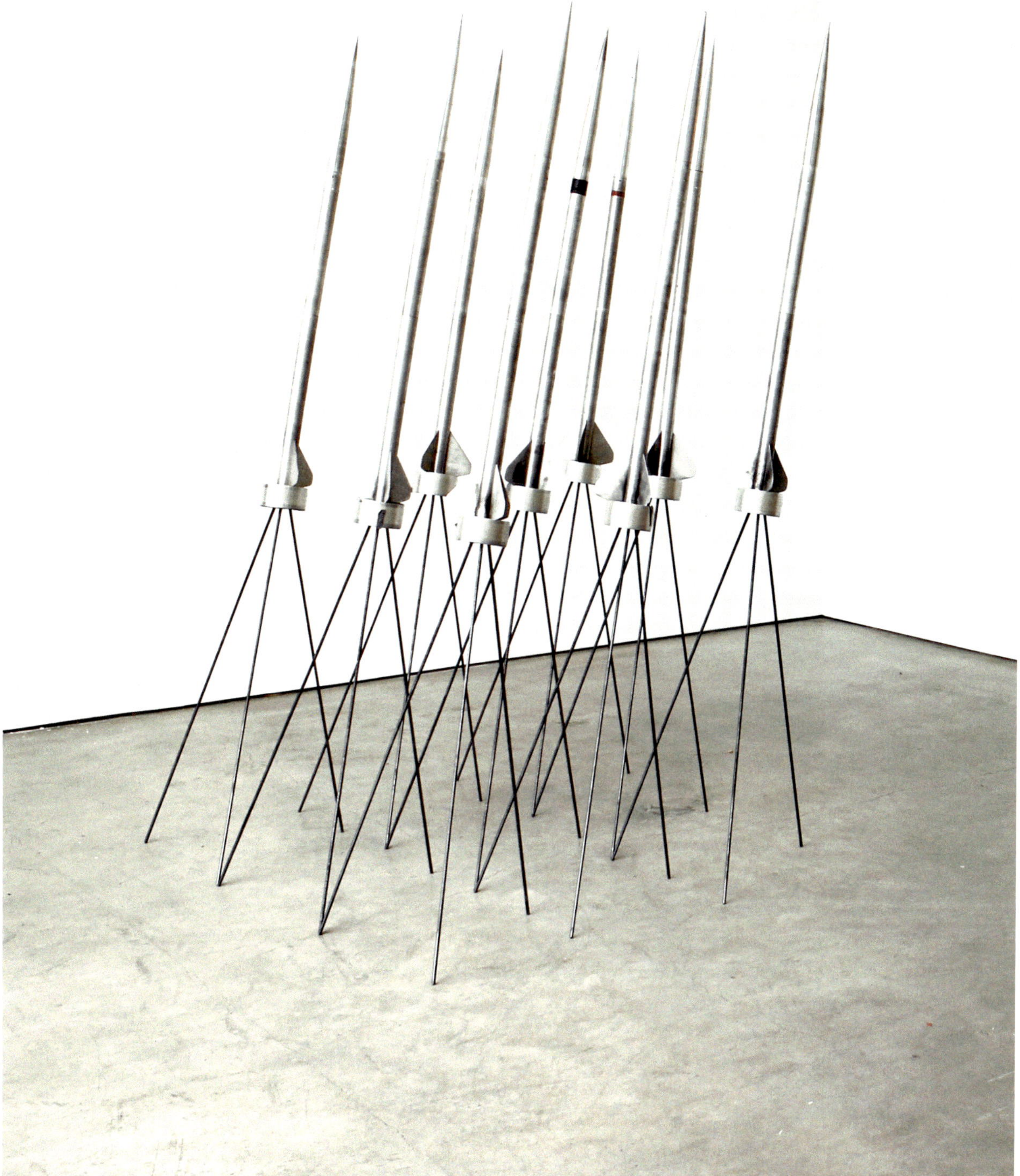

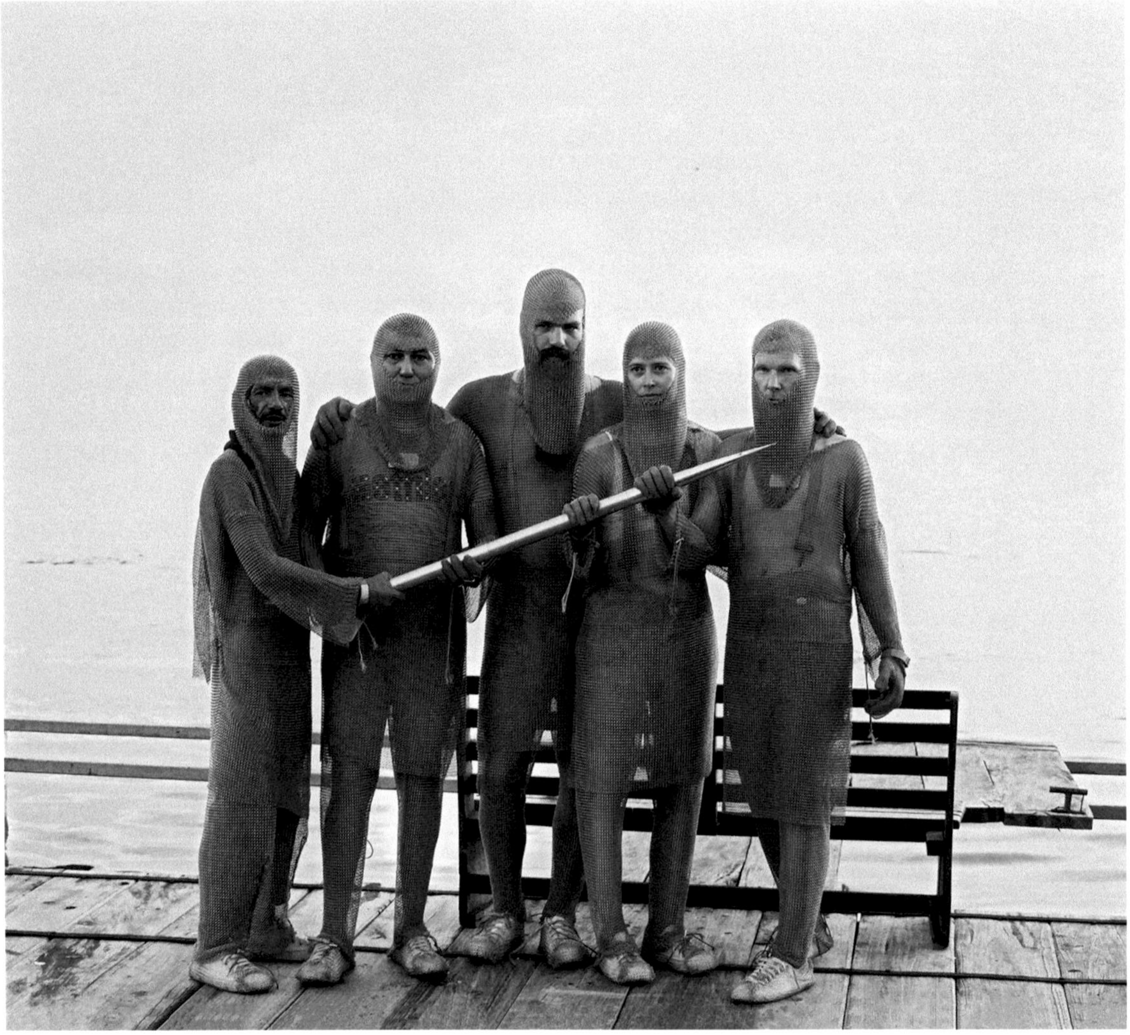

Ologa, Venezuela 2016

Struck by Lightning (in His Car)

Nadim Samman

Julius von Bismarck's account of being struck by lightning while asleep in his car has the quality of a barroom tale. But when set alongside his other creative work, featuring thunderbolts, fire, and crashing waves, its symbolic potential becomes apparent. In fact, this found work of autobiography illuminates the images that appear throughout this volume.

To be struck by lightning is a unique occurrence. There is something miraculous about it. Within a classical frame it conjures up the grandiloquent hand of god—massive power issuing from the heavens, for good or ill. Being struck by a thunderbolt sets up an origin story; a kind of mythical beginning. Conversely, a spectacular conclusion—Zeus sending down his wrath from the heavens in order to smite a fool or would-be foe. Bismarck's vignette certainly leverages both polarities; apparent inspiration for his projects concerning lightning—the spark that inspired him to pursue others touched in a like manner: a group of shamans taken down by a bolt from the blue, or a herd of Norwegian deer, struck off this mortal coil in an instant. Indeed, Bismarck's origin story underpins his pursuit of these others' literal endings. All the while, a fact of the matter remains: Bismarck was struck by lightning *in his car*. His automobile might have been on top of a mountain but it drove there. He was no *wanderer above the mist* but a man asleep in a European sedan. Cocooned in its profane shell, parked on a dirt road, his body was prone, his eyes shut, and his mind absent, when the sublime came to meet him. And in that moment, when it did, the prosaic interface of a Volvo would mediate between his person and the live wire of a paradigmatically higher power. He was asleep at the wheel of romance.

Lightning doesn't strike twice—at least, not in the same place. Blink and it is over. When Bismarck awoke he thought his vehicle blasted by artillery. It took some time for him to understand the situation. He was *late* for his own experience. The shock of missing it seems to have been burned into his artistic psyche. In later years Bismarck would begin working on a mechanism capable of bringing a lightning bolt to him; so that he could, we imagine, stage another rendezvous—this time, on his own terms. Deploying a kind of celestial fishing line—a metal wire shot up into storm clouds by a rocket, its spool drawing down electrical energy to a chosen location. Retooling Benjamin Franklin's kite experiment of 1752, Bismarck's enterprise seeks to catch and harness potency. The exact destination; the bull's-eye: his own body, clad in a bespoke metal suit (looking, suspiciously, like chain mail for a medieval knight on a grail quest); a protective outfit to *conduct* the charge around but not through his self. The project continues. Lighting has been summoned in test events, striking the ground and palm trees. Bismarck believes his carapace is nearly ready.

In the meantime, he chases down other situations where people and beasts have truly seen the light. Before his future showdown, or duel, Bismarck plays a knight errant, impatiently *following* where electrical storms lead. Coming hot on the heels of others' (fatal) dealings with the sky, he arrives late (like thunder) to survey their fallen bodies. Then he effects an image-making, or taking, from the scene (the horns of each dead deer, for instance, a story), manifesting the deadly event's echo *in his authorship* or artistic voice. Close but so far, Bismarck speaks to the decisive moment, and *for* it, in place of the dumb (the deceased), as if there can ever be real dialogue with a power too quick for human, animal or machine. A power *once here, already gone . . .*

Throughout such dealings, these schemes, Bismarck seems to live as Echo to lightning's plenitude and indifference; its Narcissus. The latter arrived when the artist wasn't ready, charging him with a reverie that he, Bismarck, might really have, hold, or become It. A reverie that would order his working life hence—that he might revalue his initial encounter by casting aside the bathos of automobile armor for more heroic accoutrements and dramaturgy. The shamans met their fate with eyes open, while performing a ceremony. So, too, the deer, huddled together in a field. There was pathos. Speaking to the surviving shamans Bismarck draws out their confession: they take the blast as evidencing their own guilt; punishment by a bigger magic than their own. There is something innocent about this speculative relation, in as much as it is resolved. By contrast, Bismarck labors under a repetition compulsion—his actions asserting the incomplete aspect of his experience, perhaps because he was not punished enough for sleeping, or surviving. Now, in as much as he wants to have the lightning, he welcomes being taken by it. Persons who have been directly struck by hundreds of millions of volts and lived to tell the tale bear extreme mental and physical scars. Bismarck's trauma, at least in part, obtains in the prosaic mediators between him and such a superlative burden.

Indeed, the contemporary poetics of the automobile are not what they once were, when the latter was a key figure for modernism; ancillary to the new Prometheus, facilitating his world making agenda and rhapsody. Filippo Tommaso Marinetti's "racing car whose hood is adorned with great pipes, like serpents of explosive breath," drove the Futurist agenda.[1] Then, the poet could demand a "hymn to the man at the wheel." The vehicle was dangerous, intoxicating, and magical. From such rhetorical heights, "erect at the summit of the world," the automobile's total victory (covering the globe in asphalt) could only roll downhill in song. Indeed, the ubiquity and hence banality of its power is such that while cars summit ever more actual mountains

1 Filippo Tommaso Marinetti, *Initial Manifesto of Futurism.* English translation published in *Le Figaro,* February 20, 1909.

(saving today's Nietzscheans from hiking) a contemporary artist like Bismarck feels compelled to turn towards the unalloyed thunderbolt, even as the first electric vehicles enter mass production.

With this in mind, it is necessary to consider *Unfall am Mittlepunkt Deutschlands* (2013), in which the artist staged a crash by a black VW Golf into the Imperial Linden Tree (famously marking the geographical center of Germany).[2] In this work, as with the coming together of automobile and lightning in the artist's experience, confrontation between an emblematic "natural" figure and the car's banality obtains. In fact, the symbolic nature of the state (the German state) appears at issue in the slippage between tree, vehicle, animal, and (the artist's own) person. The prosaic aspect of the contemporary car casts symbolic shade over the matter; over lightning, mountains, *roots*, and prospects for Bismarckian heroism. The romance of nature was central to the Prussian imaginary; a vision that was later incorporated into the Nazi "natural order." After World War II, this state, and its antecedent image-ground, was put into question. Its soil, Wagner's theater, its *Sturm und Drang*, indeed, the whole *nature* of the German imaginary, had to be rethought. The wanderer had to get down from the mountaintop, and the very topic of triumph became suspicious. Suspicious, that is, until *das Auto* made a plausible case for German excellence on the world stage. In ostensibly neutral language an engineer chorus professed a vehicle for pride in *Vorsprung durch Technik*. But this pride was, at all times, to be measured; and emanating from reasons *measurable*—the aesthetic against sublimity; an anti-romance of brakes and airbags. Was this a real U-turn—we must ask—or just better sublimated *overcoming*?

In such traffic with romantic and postwar vehicles for the German-nature Bismarck is playing with fire. But *the incendiary* is precisely at issue. It is only a small step from a metaphorical wildfire, and Promethean mythopoesis (with its attendant topic of punishment) to the burning fact of our time: Marinetti's fascist racer and today's family car are related—weapons of an unrelenting war against nonhuman nature; *die Umwelt*. The deer were fried by the sky but they had a better chance of being run over. Every spew from an exhaust pipe stokes the flames of forest fires, burning all the more frequently; helps the hurricanes that whip the roofs from houses. Climate change, punishing *everything*, and everyone, is the thunderous reply to our narcissism.

---

2 The description of the project on the artist's website states, "The car had clearly suffered substantial damage, yet the tree remained unharmed. The accident was protocolled on April 15, 2013, by the police, and press reports followed. All expressed astonishment about the accident, since it seemed almost impossible that the VW could have swerved from the street to impact this central tree, considering the bushes and large boulders in its path. Only after some detective work did the police find out that the car was crashed prior to its encounter with the tree and then lifted into place at the site of the supposed accident by the artist and his team during the night of April 14, 2013." See http://juliusvonbismarck.com/bank/index.php?/projects/unfall-am-mittelpunkt-deutschlands/.

The picture of Bismarck's material preparations for a conscious showdown with lightning clads the topic in a costume that best describes our historical hubris: Modern technical, rhetorical surface-engagements have dissembled about our dealings with the environment. They promised the receipt of *power* and the mitigation of risk. *If there are conflicting interests* (an anthropocentric term) *then we will be victorious; If we have done wrong, we can make it right—the error of our ways merely a prelude to some kind of en*lightenment *or success*. Within this Kantian frame the world remains enchanted, if only through humankind's moral vocation. But Bismarck's work appears to cast this stance as errant; *quixotic*. As his travel to disaster zones suggest—*Because it is too late*. A Christian kernel (that you may be forgiven if you confess) underpins the thought that we can look at horrible scenes and be redeemed through the appropriate affordance of our egos—indeed, that this affordance provides a *reason* to look. But such a reason is beginning to ring hollow: the heroism of the gaze frays around the edges when we encounter visions of communities displaced by hurricanes, and the gigantic flames of forest fires, knowing what we do about the ecological facts and (lack of) political will. Knowing what to do does not mean it will ever get done: running around in rhetorical suits of armor does nothing to stop lightning striking. In a like manner, King Xerxes could not stay the tide, even by ordering the sea to be whipped. Perhaps a thought like this is at work in Bismarck's iconographic choices.

But what if Bismarck's imagery taps into something else altogether? What if the project in question is more a channeling of recent disaster movies? Arguably registering popular anxieties attending our climate crisis, mainstream cinema revels in destruction. Parallels would seem to obtain between the artist's footage of Hurricane Irma's aftermath and such films. This may be the point. But the structure of his video work manifests some divergence: commercial films have beginnings and endings, each arriving at some sort of conclusion or narrative reckoning with the nature of the disaster in question. Bismarck's work does nothing of the sort. Within his art, at least, there is no neat summary of causes, blame, and/or prescriptions. This lack of conclusion is significant as, when it comes to our present ecological emergency, calls to action predominate. Avoiding any call, or conclusion, it is as if Bismarck's footage delivers images *from the dream of the sleeper* in his comfortable car. There is no drama in this place, only a floating eye, sliding impassively across desolation in the manner of a god (or, at the very least, a nonperson). Drama, we suspect, can only obtain with the emergence of the character, the ego, upon waking—out of the dream, into self-awareness and a moral universe.

A will to aestheticize hurricanes and forest fires, today, is the dream of *a time before waking* that lingers on, illicit, in our reveries. It is the errant dream of a fair fight (between a man and a thunderbolt; a deer and a car; dreams and action; knight and windmill). It is the dream of a conflict that concludes with a reasonable outcome, perhaps, even, a graceful one: it is the dream of a space and time in which to talk to thunder, directly, and come to some reasonable compact. It is the dream of meditation in the midst of an emergency; philosophy and poetry—clear-eyed and world-making—withstanding the heat of the moment and all that is to come. What is most disturbing about this vision is that we, along with Bismarck, are coming to suspect that it can only be dreamt at the end of the road, windows up, with only airbags and a little metal standing between us and *a rude awakening.*

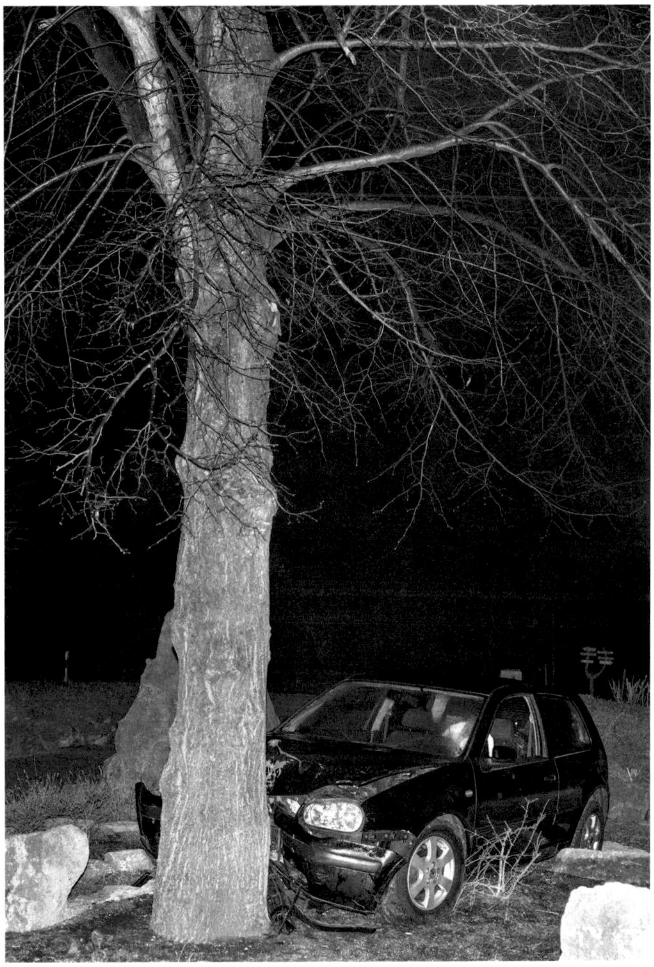

Unfall am Mittelpunkt Deutschlands #1 2013

Apocalypsoid

2017
Flint stone, granite, stainless steel, pigment ink, tables, apparatuses, prints

The *Apocalypsoid* series documents an impossible attempt to reassemble the remains of flint and granite boulders shattered by explosions engineered by the artist. Prior to their detonation, an alphanumeric quadrant system was painstakingly mapped onto each stone, dividing its surface into a longitudes and latitudes so that fragments could be reassembled later. The labeled stones were analyzed by a computed tomography (CT) scanner, and the explosions filmed with a slow-motion camera, capturing fleeting moments of destruction. The fractured remains were subsequently X-rayed to return countless splinters to their original positions. A digital model was used to facilitate sculptural reconstructions of the process of transformation. Held together by stainless-steel struts as if floating in midair, the original cometlike shapes of the boulders remain clearly visible. The construction captures the moment of explosion, freezing in time a moment not perceived by the naked eye. The final work preserves not only the stone and all its states, but also the labor and apparatuses involved in its making. Despite use of the best available technologies, the complex process of the planetoid's reconstruction can only fail.

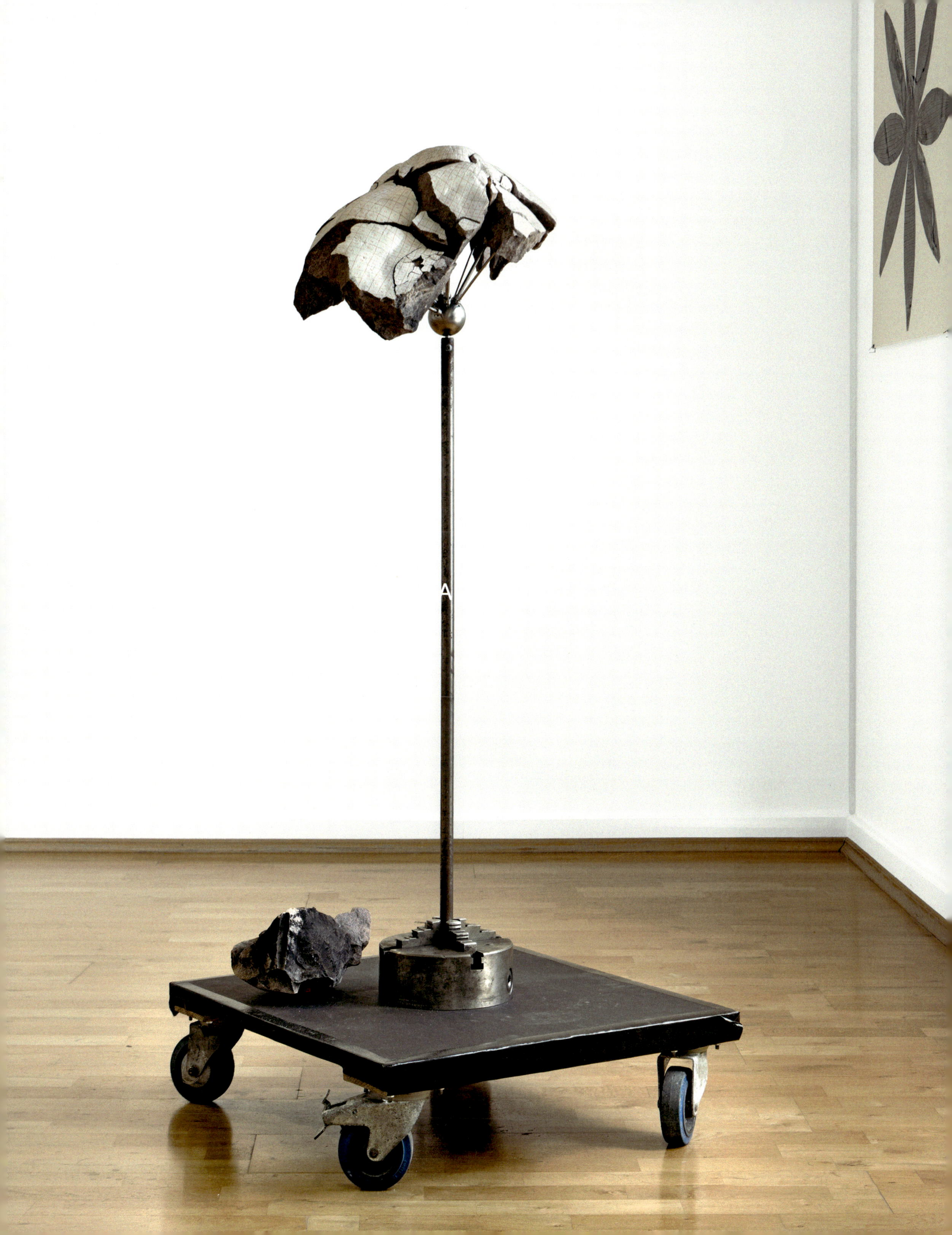
A

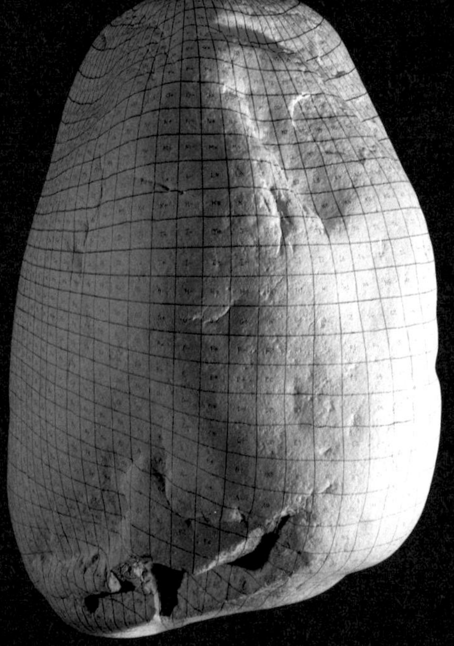

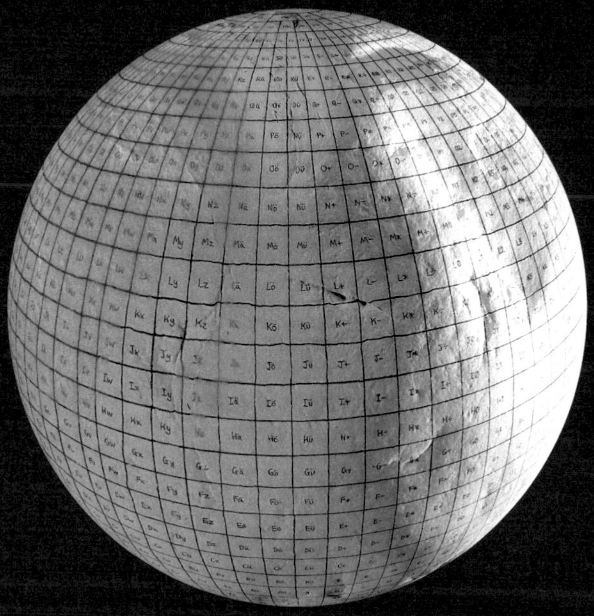

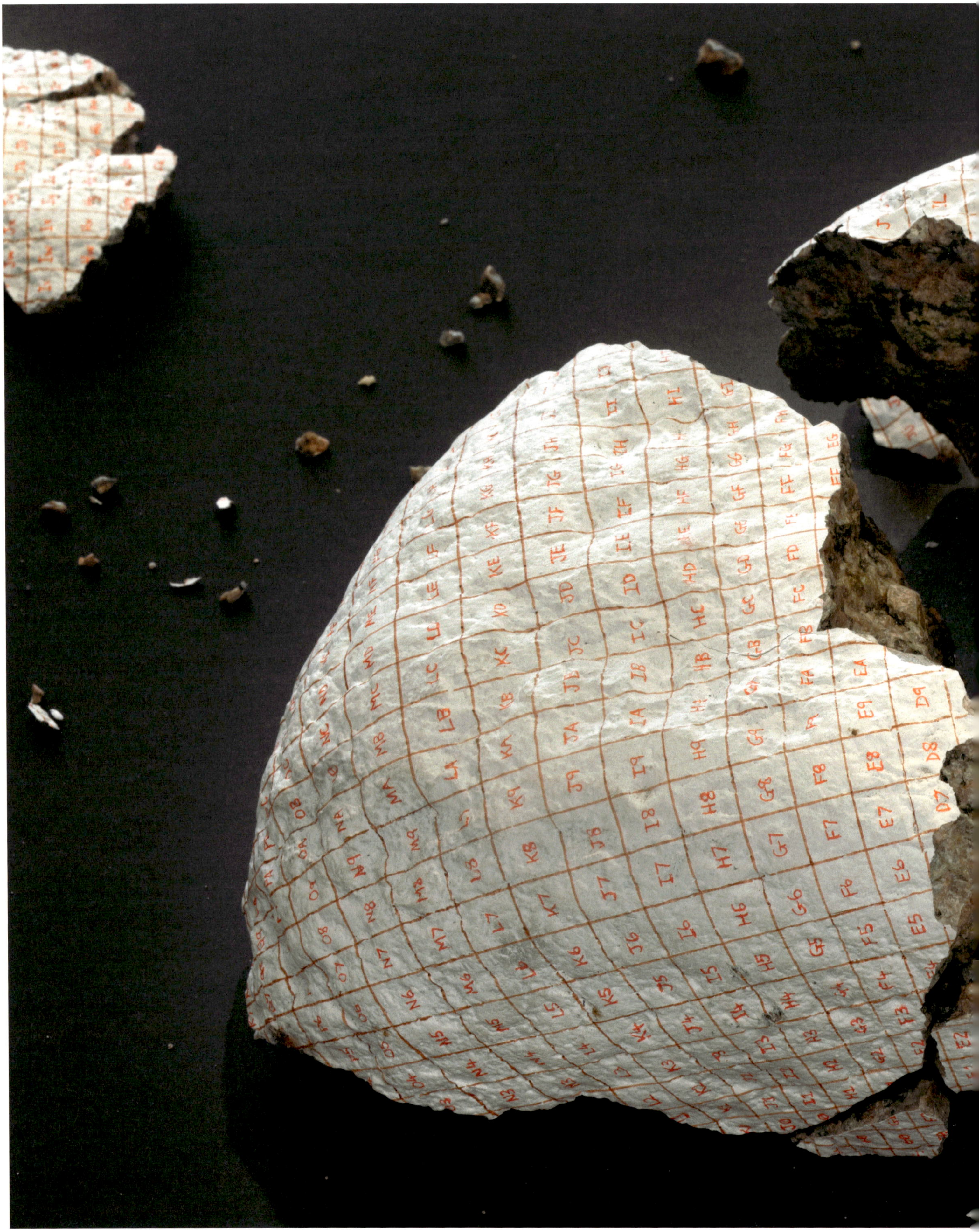

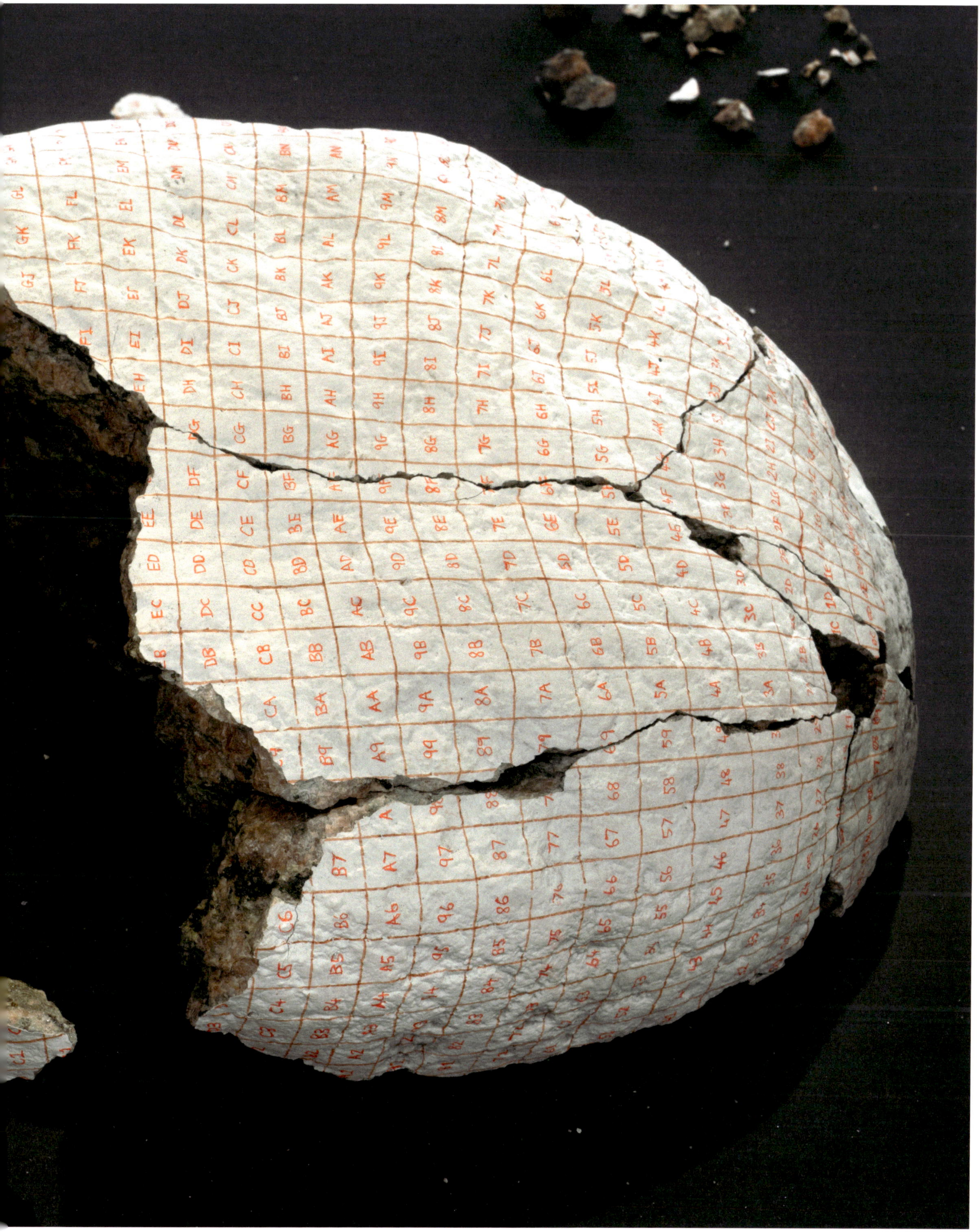

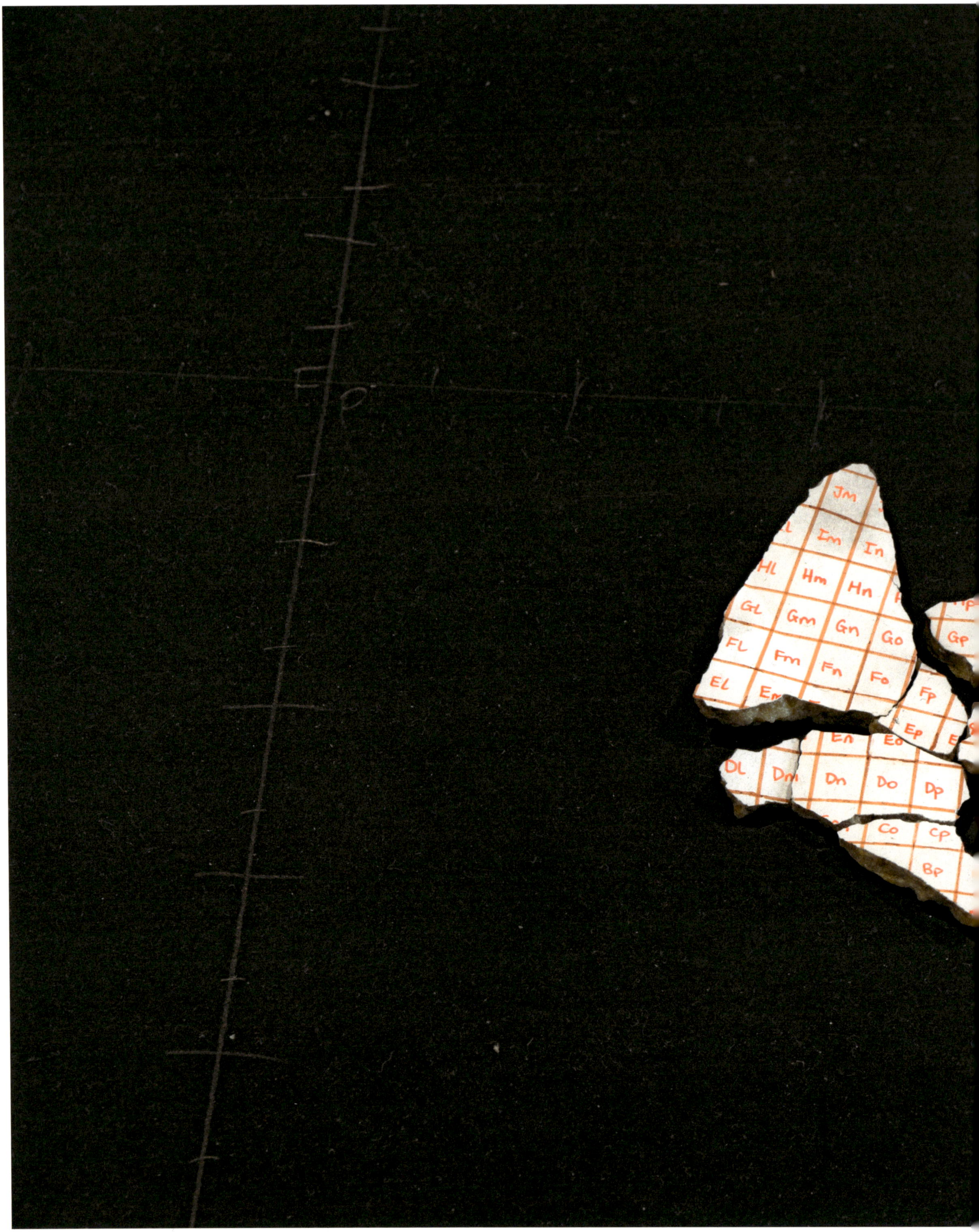
Fp
Jm
Im
In
Hl
Hm
Hn
Gl
Gm
Gn
Go
Gp
Fl
Fm
Fn
Fo
Fp
El
Ep
En
Eo
Dl
Dn
Do
Dp
Co
Cp
Bp

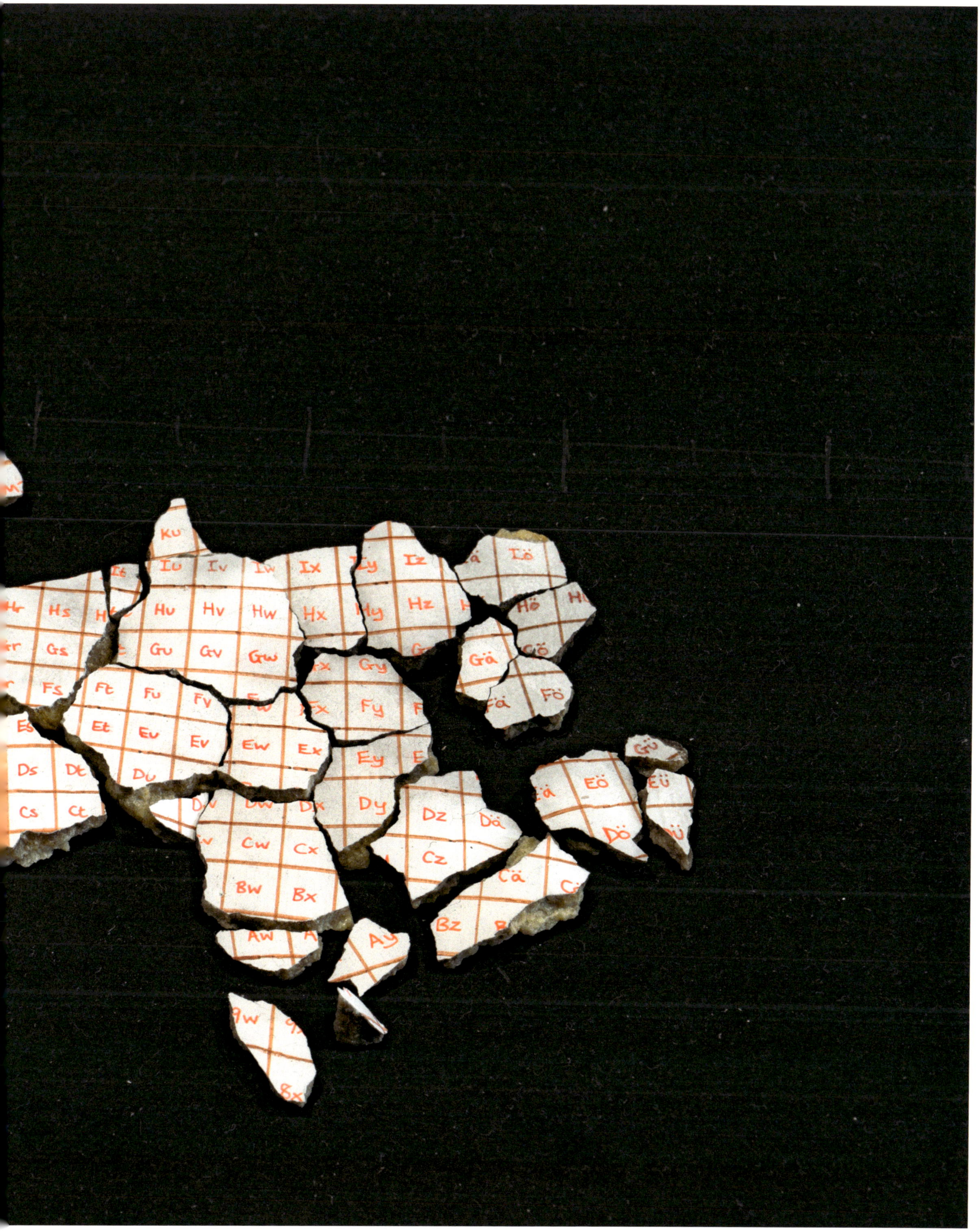

Ku
Iu
Iv
Ix
Iz
Iö
Hs
Hu
Hv
Hw
Hx
Hz
Hö
Gs
Gu
Gv
Gw
Gy
Gä
Gö
Fs
Ft
Fu
Fy
Fx
Fä
Fö
Et
Eu
Ev
Ew
Ex
Ey
Eö
Eü
Ds
Dt
Du
Dw
Dy
Dz
Dä
Dö
Cs
Ct
Cw
Cx
Cz
Cä
Bw
Bx
Bz
Aw
Ay

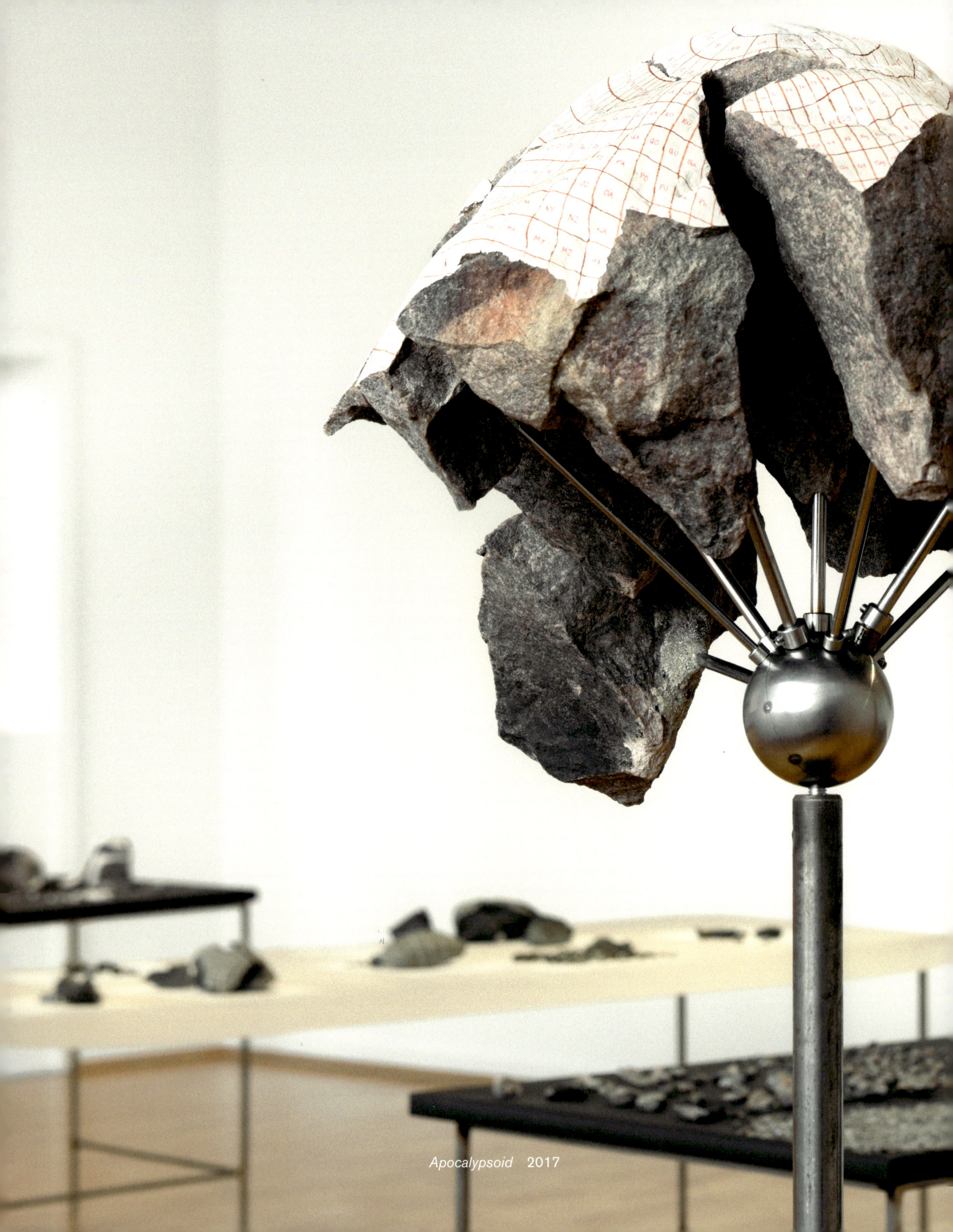

Apocalypsoid 2017

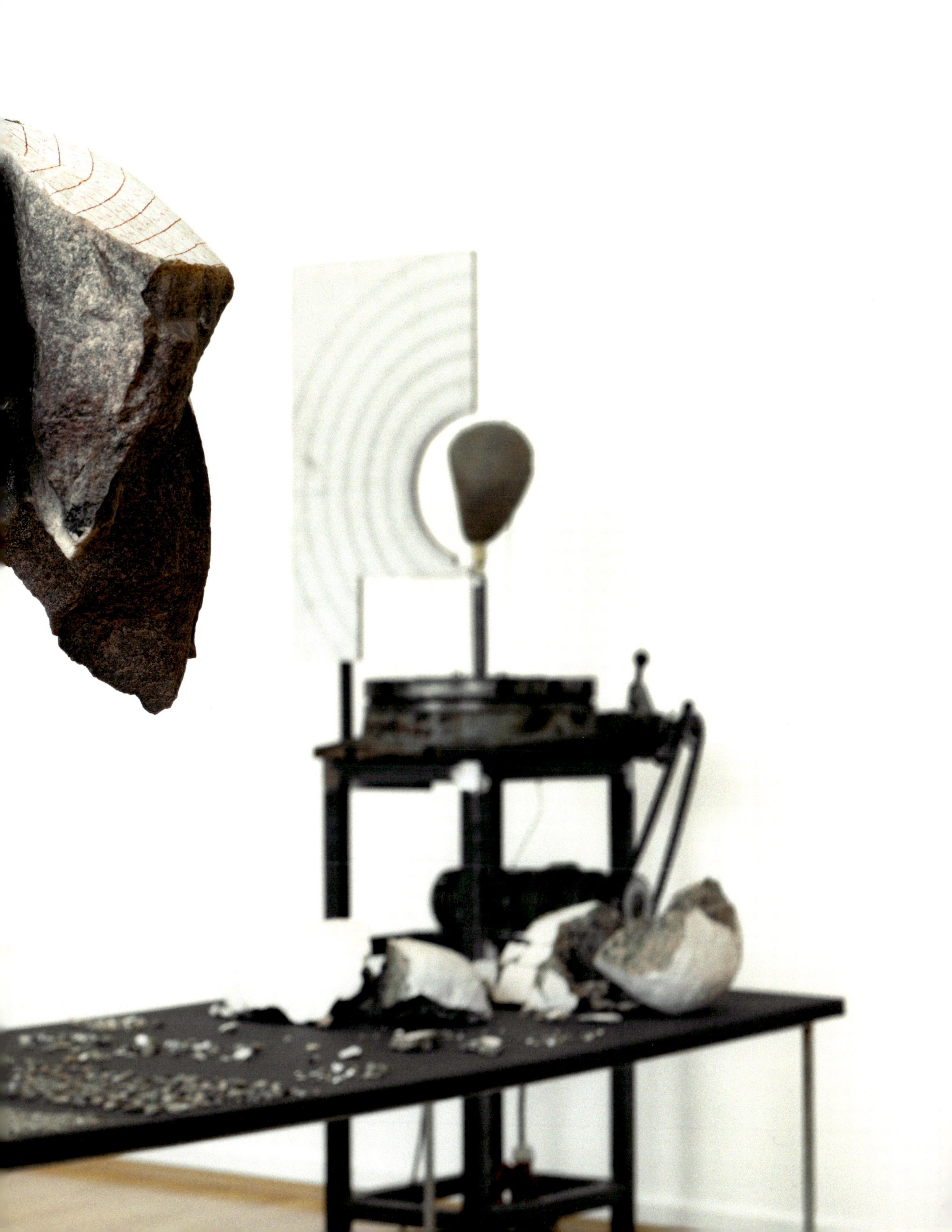

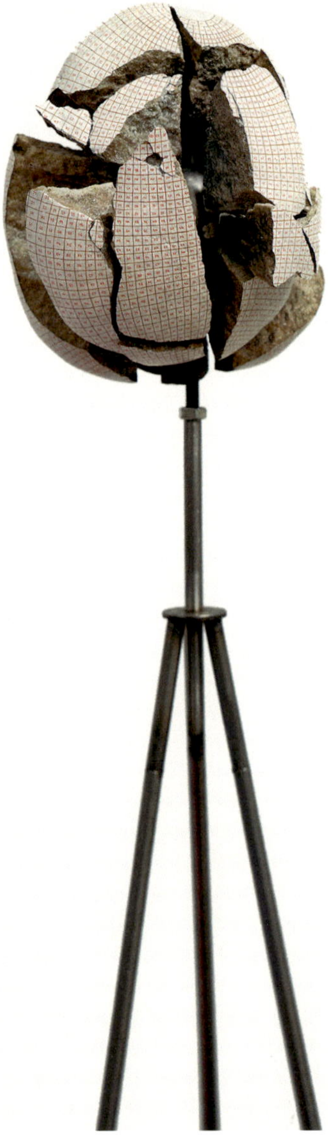

66

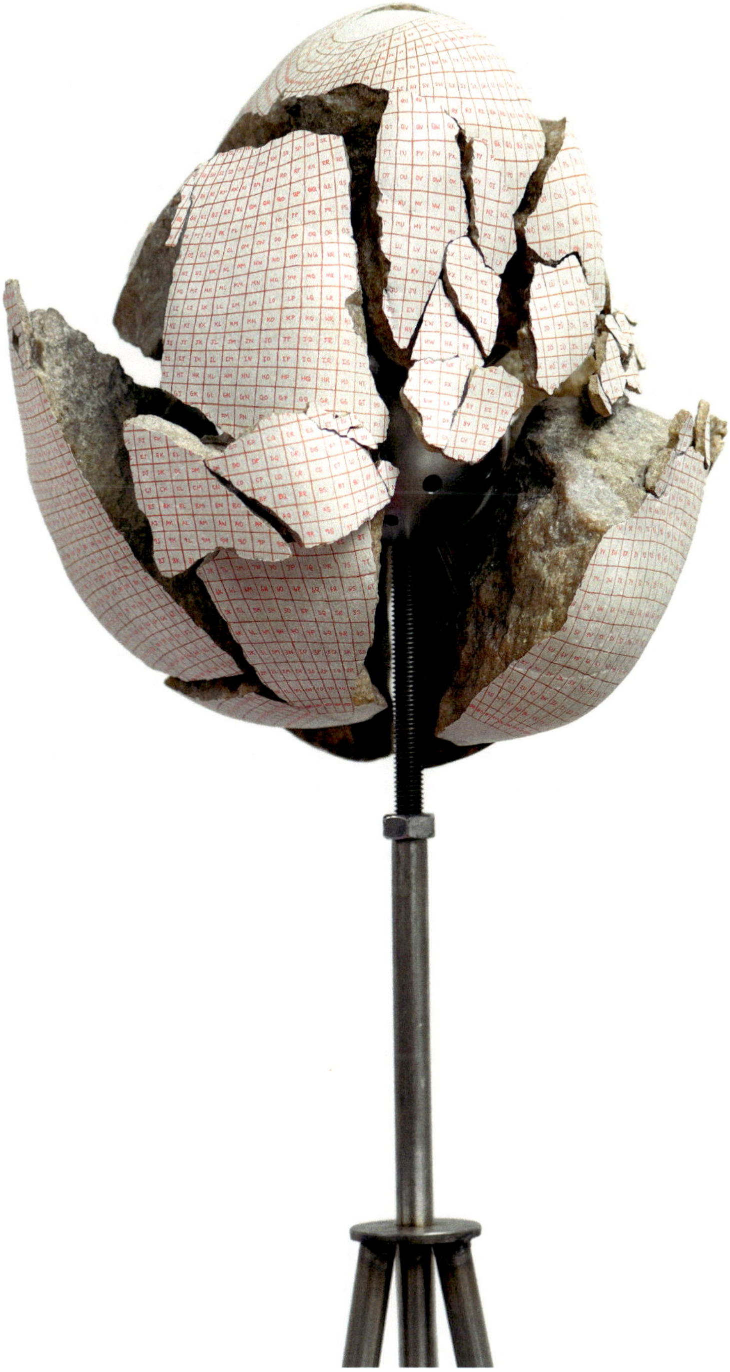

Apocalypsoid c 2018

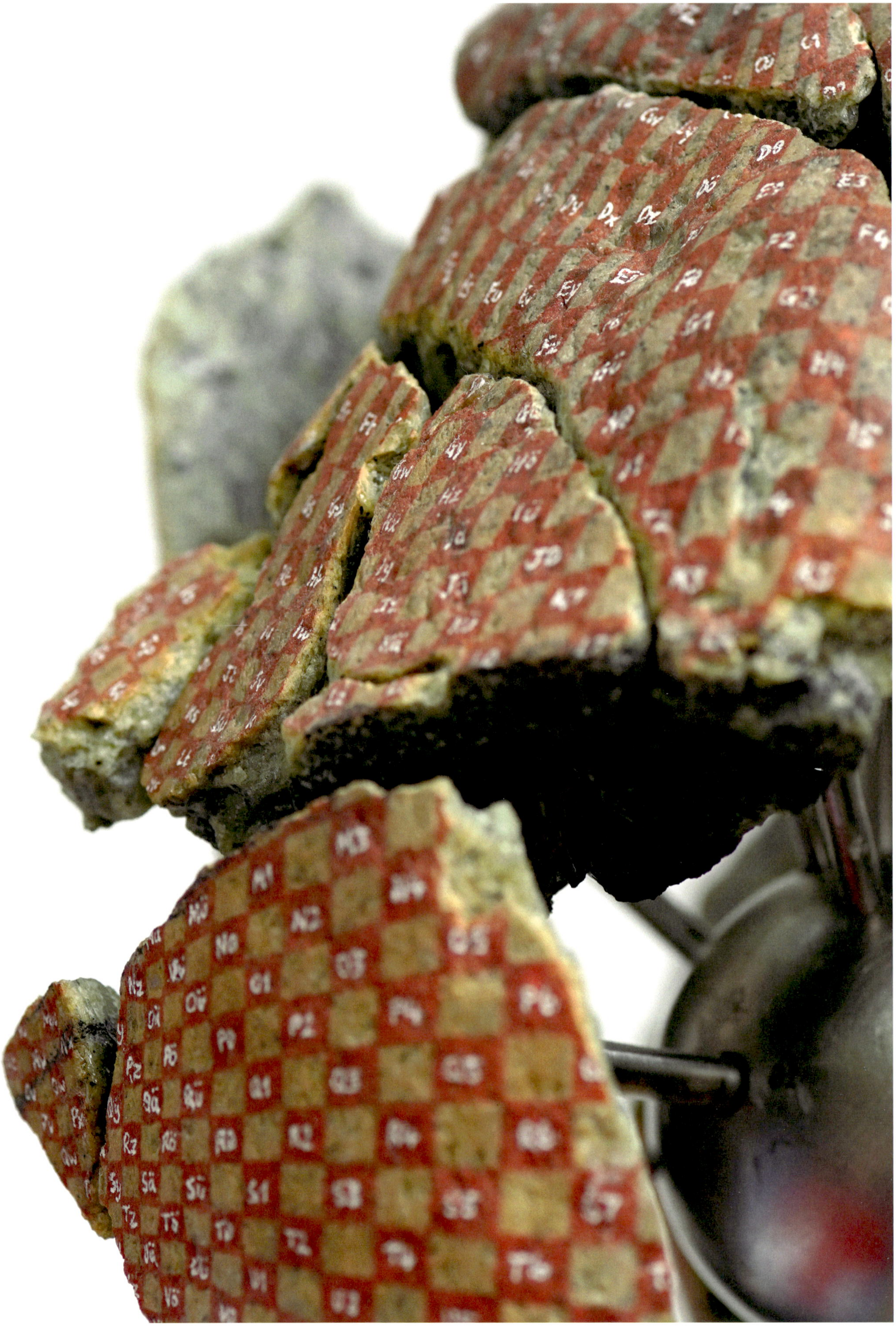

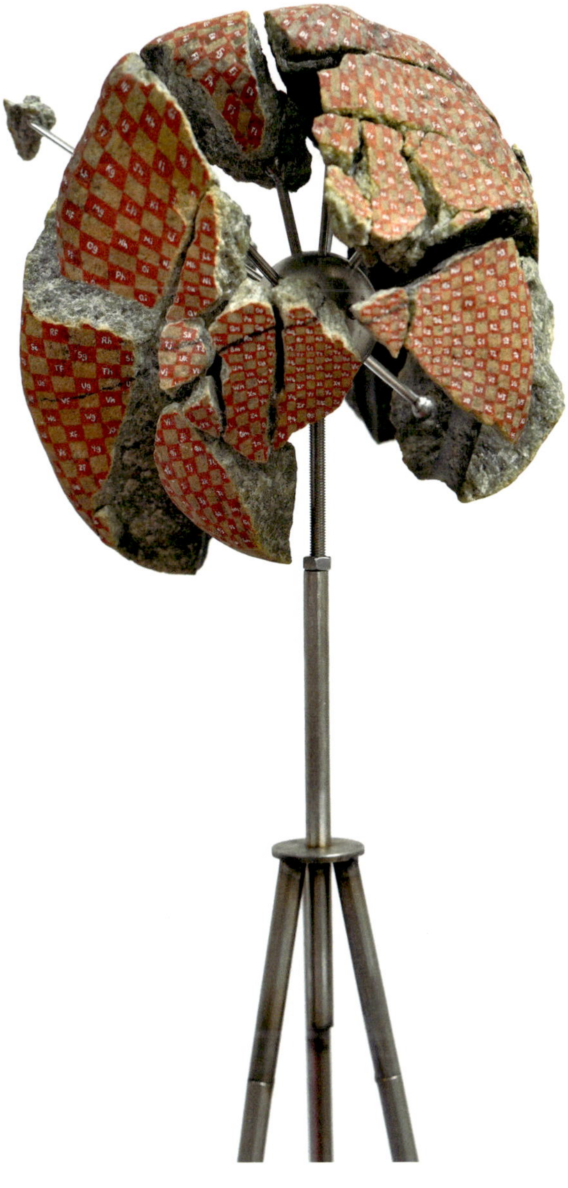

Apocalypsoid b 2018

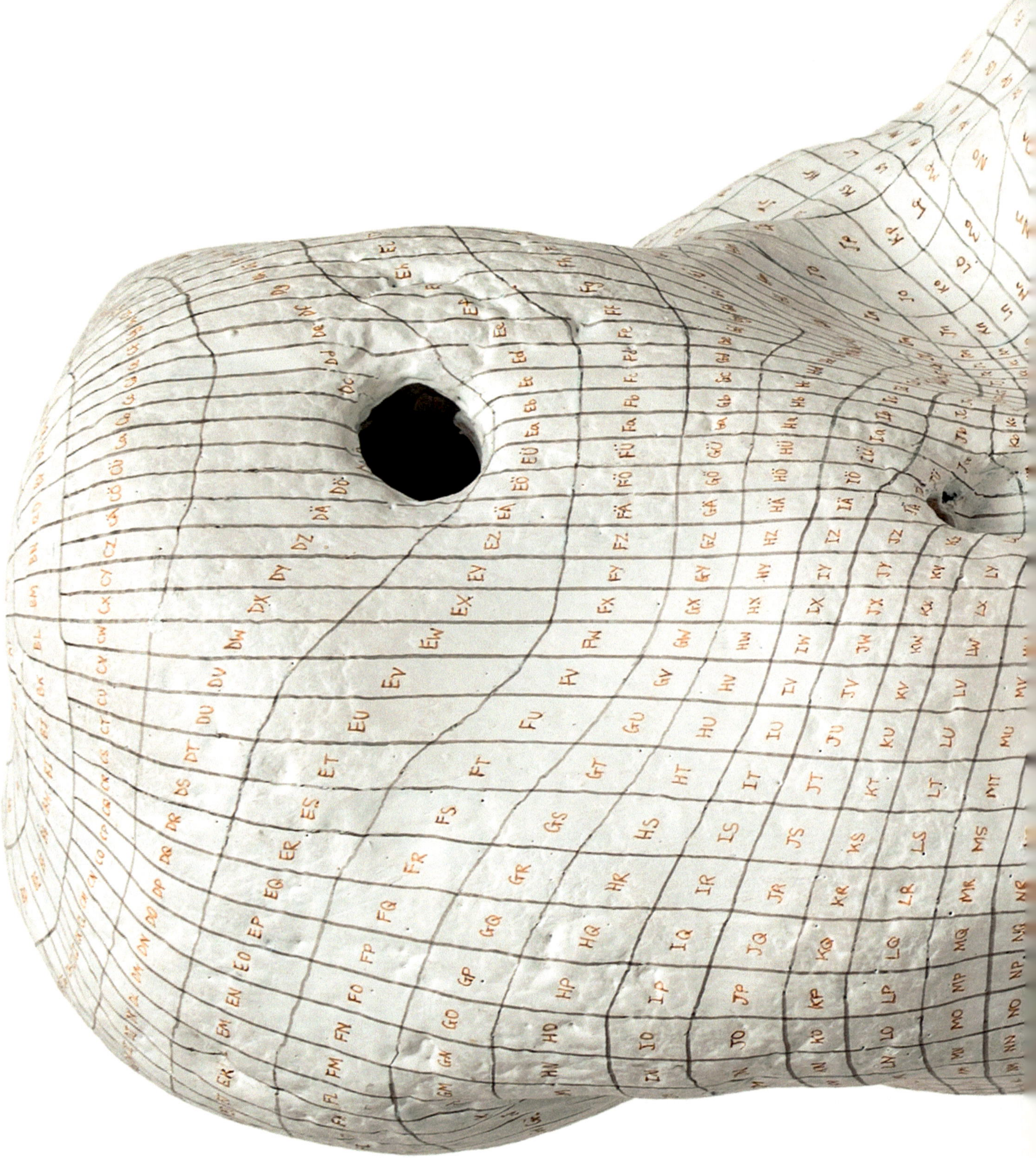

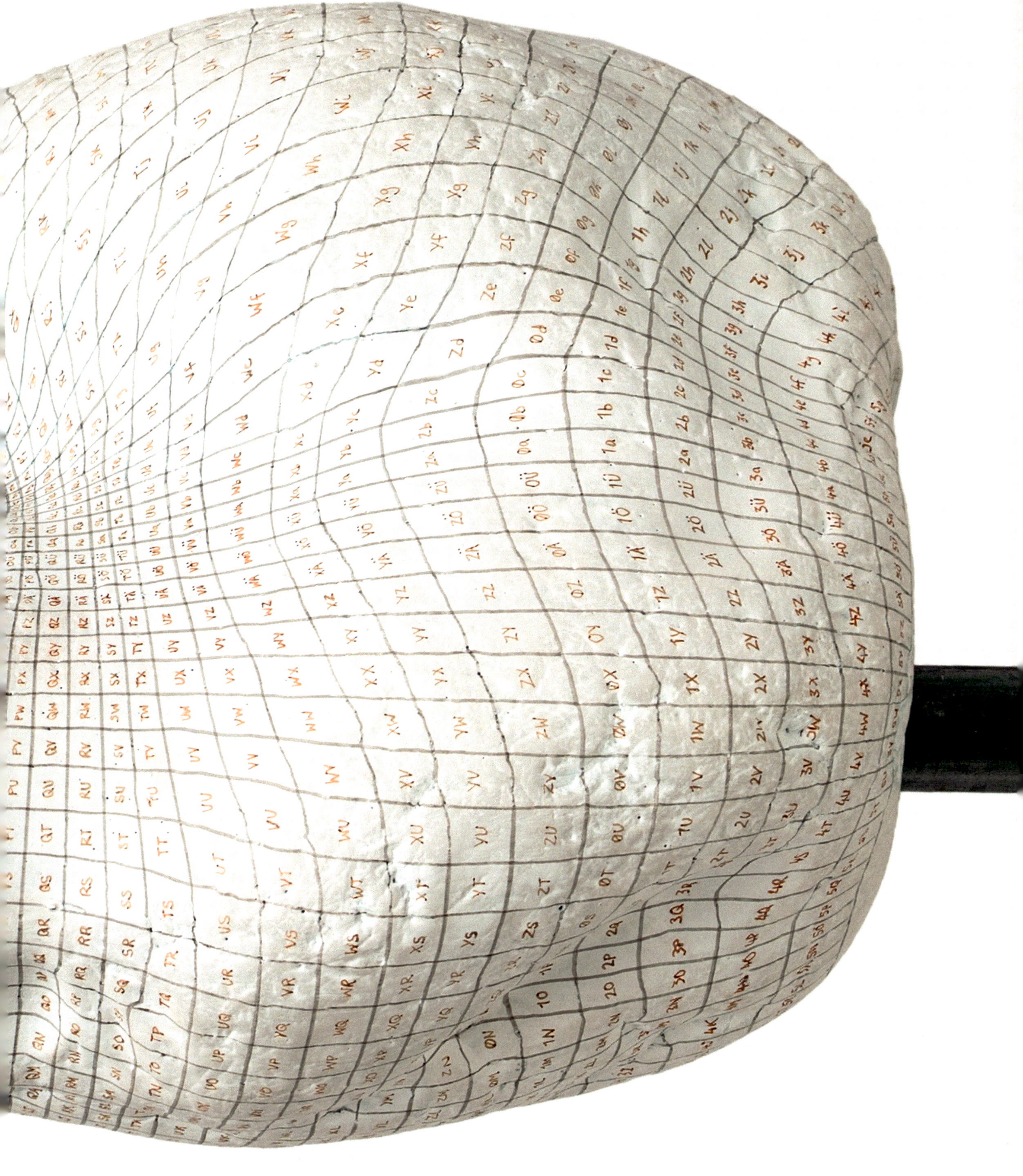

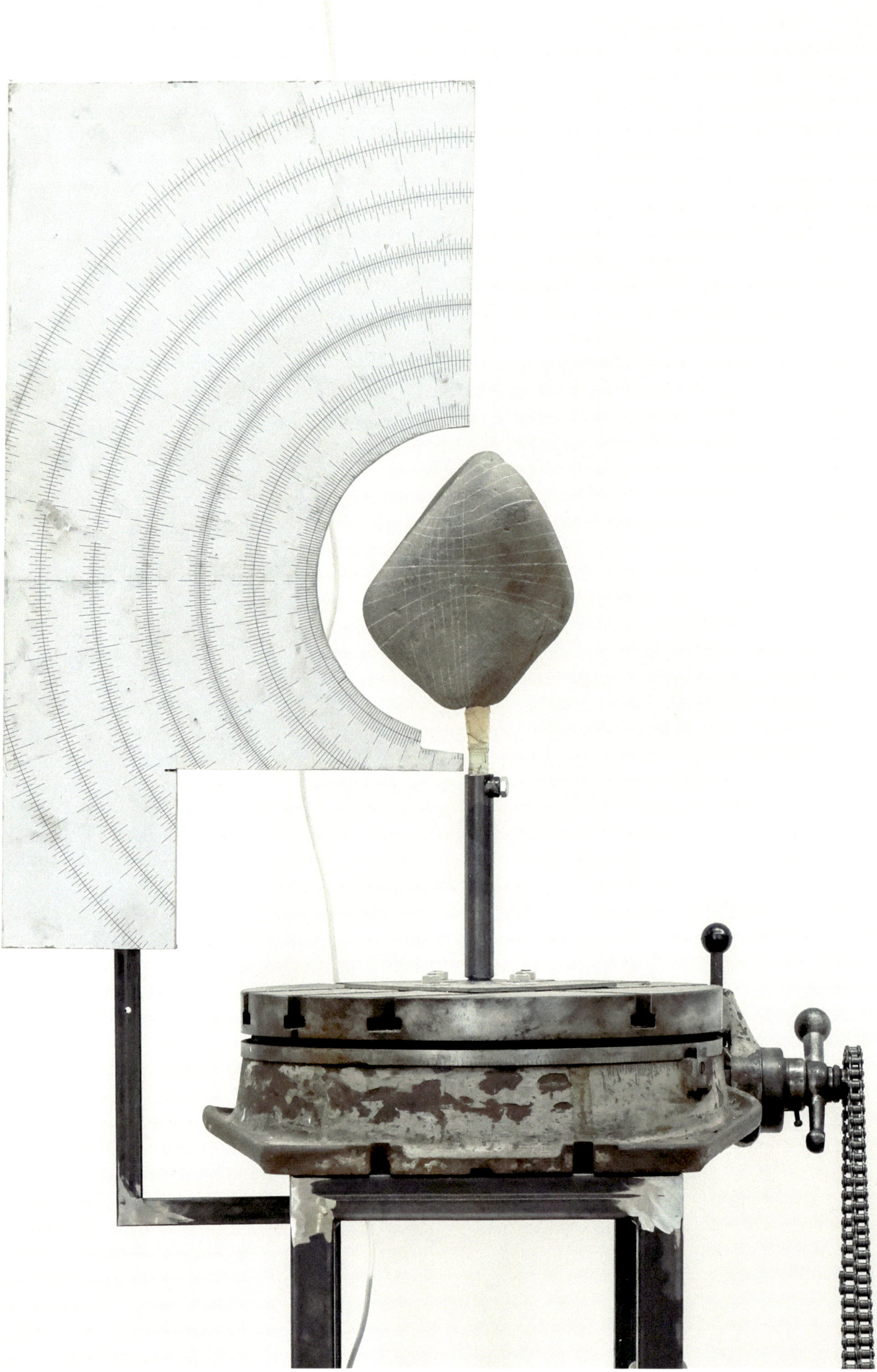

The State of Nature

Dehlia Hannah

It was something formidable and swift, like the sudden smashing of a vial of wrath. It seemed to explode all round . . . with an overpowering concussion and a rush of great waters, as if an immense dam had been blown up . . . This is the disintegrating power of a great wind: it isolates one from one's kind. An earthquake, a landslip, an avalanche, overtake a man incidentally, as it were—without passion. A furious gale attacks him like a personal enemy, tries to grasp his limbs, fastens upon his mind, seeks to rout his very spirit out of him.
—Joseph Conrad, *Typhoon*, 1902

A streak of lightning stretches its tentacles across the sky. Rain droplets hang in midair. Shards of stone lie arrayed on a table, ordered by size and shape like puzzle pieces. A great wave of hurricane-churned ocean fills the room, stilled in its tracks. Moments to be reassembled. Palms strain to hold themselves erect against their sharply inclined fronds, whose gentle fluttering betrays the camera's slow-motion deception. A line of flames rises slowly at the edge of a forest, trailing the drip torch of a firefighter like a dog on a leash. Smoke rises through the leaf canopy as burning embers creep across the ground. Out of hollow tree trunks, a glow emanates. The air thickens. Continuing apace, the maelstrom gives way to scenes of destruction: overturned cars, fallen branches, flooded streets, beleaguered residents, emergency services and news crews there to survey the aftermaths of disaster. A tattered American flag waves against a clear sky.

In a series of recent projects, Julius von Bismarck explores encounters with elemental forces that exceed the perceptual capacities of the naked eye and body, on account of their scale, pace, and the danger that they pose. By turns disorienting and enchanting, his investigations open up crevices in the well-trodden ground of *nature*, shaking the foundations of lifeworlds that we have erected upon this time-worn idea. As a source of norms and familiar patterns—of intuitive human sentiments, the cyclical return of the seasons, and the guiding light of stars—nature offers a regulative ideal, a vision of how things *are* and how they *should* be. Storms, floods, wildfires—the sorts of environmental phenomena that occupy Bismarck—tend to challenge cultural imagination as aberrations to be explained away, or omens to be heeded. Though they may be as natural as the tides in physical terms, apparent states of disarray offer provocations to all-too-human constructions of concerning the order of nature. Today, in an era in which we are conscious of the role of Anthropos (or particular representatives thereof) in exacerbating the destructive power of natural forces, to meditate on their violence of borders on complicity. To stare too long into the roiling abyss is to risk romanticizing what it means to lose oneself in a furious gale. Crimes *against* nature give way to crimes committed *with* environs denatured by our own hands—to perversions of the orders of nature. At the risk of losing firm footing and forsaking a sure grasp on the moral high ground, one follows Bismarck deeper into the storm.

Irma and Ophelia, sisters in making the 2017 hurricane season among the worst on record, embody persistent uncertainties about the relative significance of anthropogenic climate change against a baseline of natural variation in weather patterns. In this regard, they are symptomatic of an epistemological paradox that has long plagued philosophical aspirations—to find legitimation in nature. In classical political philosophy, an original *state of nature* is proposed as the precondition for political society. Just as it is difficult to gage the degree to which any particular storm or wildfire is due to human impact on the climate (the attribution problem), we cannot know how much images of the state of nature are merely projections of contemporary social relations into the past. Reasoning from speculations about inherent human dispositions and psychologies, the philosopher endeavors to reconstruct how our basic needs found fulfillment in relation to the environment and the other creatures inhabiting it. As the hypothetical kernel latent within every contemporary social order, these accounts envision the potentiality of our relations with plants, other people, and animals; with earth, water, wind, and the elusive element of fire—control over which constitutes a decisive achievement in every narrative of human evolution. And yet, the philosophical concept of the state of nature is not a historical-anthropological hypothesis but a thought experiment, one that seeks to explain and correct the condition we find ourselves in today.

Visions of the state of nature range from halcyon to dystopian, with profound consequences for the forms of government founded thereupon. Thomas Hobbes proffers a fearsome tale of competition over scarce resources, in which the naturally querulous human animal struggles for existence amid perpetual "war of all against all," where life is "nasty, brutish and short."[1] Thus, for Hobbes, a society ruled by a tyrant capable of suppressing the aggressive instincts of the masses constitutes a significant improvement over our natural condition, however unpalatable it might appear. By contrast, John Locke envisions an original state

1 Thomas Hobbes, *Leviathan* (1651), ed. C. B. MacPherson (Harmondsworth, 1982).

of freedom, equality, and a nascent form of private property.[2] This delicate equilibrium is regulated by natural laws known intuitively to each person, laws that supervene on established political orders and whose violation may even justify revolution. Still more idyllic are Jean-Jacques Rousseau's fantasies of abundance in which "noble savages" find easy subsistence and peaceful coexistence within felicitous environs.[3] Our exit from this simple existence is a fall from grace, redeemed only by a democratic society that promotes higher forms of human flourishing. As the limit case of civilization, barbarism serves to naturalize the political order, indicating what is possible and desirable in modern societies.

Not to be consigned to a fictive past, the state of nature persists beneath the cobblestones, waiting to reappear at the interstices of governmental control. In the absence of a supervening international governing apparatus, nation-states remain in this condition with respect to one another; at best mutually avoidant and noninterfering, at worst factious—a condition not unlike that of the confederation of small Prussian states prior to their 1871 unification into the German Empire by the artist's paterfamilias, Otto von Bismarck. A resurgence of such tendencies also manifests in moments of societal breakdown such as those occasioned by natural disasters, which become case studies for reassessing competing versions of the state of nature. When storms sweep through communities, breaking down infrastructure, compromising electricity grids, transportation, police, and emergency services, news media are flooded with heroic tales of altruism and self-reliance; elsewhere, brutishness and opportunism. Catastrophes provide opportunities for restructuring the apparatuses of state: for the reconsolidation of government control through militarization, curfews, surveillance, and the suspension of rights and freedoms—or, for dismantling the state under the terms of disaster capitalism: deregulation, privatization, and austerity measures.[4] As in classical political theory, estimations of the state of nature function prescriptively to legitimize certain political-economic forms over others, allowing them to appear inevitable, even if unpalatable to a vulnerable public. And yet, where "nature" functions to both destabilize the state and to naturalize its reconsolidation, the presence of vested interests on both sides of the equation offers cause for suspicion.

---

2 See the *Second Treatise on Government* (1689) in John Locke, *Two Treatises of Government and A Letter Concerning Toleration*, ed. Ian Shapiro (New Haven, CT, and London, 2003).

3 Jean-Jacques Rousseau and James Miller, *Discourse on the Origin of Inequality* (1755), trans. Donald A. Cress (Indianapolis, 1992).

4 Naomi Klein, *The Shock Doctrine: The Rise of Disaster Capitalism* (London, 2008).

In the wake of Hurricane Katrina, it has become a truism that *there is no such thing as a natural disaster.*[5] The category-five hurricane, which hit Florida and Louisiana in 2005, killed over 1,800 people and displaced over two million for years to come. In spite of accurate meteorological forecasts of the severity of the impending storm, American emergency management agencies failed spectacularly in their evacuation and rescue efforts. The tragedy of Katrina spurred international outrage as a transparent instance of corruption, environmental racism, and class stratification in one of the wealthiest countries in the world—caused by a storm whose severity was very likely exacerbated by climate change. One must distinguish between natural and anthropogenic *causes* of environmental phenomena, and, secondly, between dangerous events themselves and their *effects* on human well-being, property, and the social order. As much was evident to Rousseau, who, in his nostalgia for a prelapsarian condition, blamed the built environment and human reactions to the great Lisbon earthquake of 1755 for its catastrophic effects. Since then, we are increasingly capable of moderating our exposure to environmental hazards. The development of environmental monitoring and communications infrastructure in the twentieth century dramatically expanded our capacities for prediction—of weather, earthquakes, tsunamis, volcanic eruptions, as well as long-term changes in climate caused by our own activities. If such phenomena were once natural, today, activities like mining, fracking, and burning fossil fuels are implicated in triggering them, increasing their frequency and intensity.[6] Even in those rare instances where hazards are entirely natural in origin, our vulnerability usually is not. The naturalization of disasters thus involves double disavowal of responsibility—one that indulges a desire for moral innocence and self-affirming expressions of virtue, feelings compromised by awareness of our complicity in or willful ignorance of the quotidian disasters of environmental injustice and the myriad ecological catastrophes of the Anthropocene. If a certain ideological fantasy promises that we can return to the wilderness when society falls apart under the pressure of a tsunami or hurricane, then a critical understanding reminds us that we are "getting back to the wrong nature"—a nature that never existed historically, but rather was envisioned to justify a social order.[7]

---

5 Gregory Squires and Chester Hartman, eds., *There Is No Such Thing as a Natural Disaster: Race, Class and Hurricane Katrina* (Milton Park, Abingdon, 2006).

6 See, for example, Bill McGuire, *Waking the Giant: How a Changing Climate Triggers Earthquakes, Tsunamis, and Volcanoes* (Oxford and New York, 2013).

7 William Cronon, "The Trouble with Wilderness; Or, Getting Back to the Wrong Nature," *Environmental History* 1, no. 1 (January 1, 1996).

We must ponder the anomaly that it is only in the most completely humanized environment, the one the most fully and obviously the end product of human labor, production, and transformation, that life becomes meaningless, and that existential despair first appears as such in direct proportion to the elimination of nature, the non- or antihuman, to the increasing rollback of everything that threatens human life and the prospect of well-nigh limitless control over the external universe.
—Frederic Jameson, *The Political Unconscious*[8]

Our motivations for naturalizing disasters are not only political but also aesthetic. In its classic formulations by Edmund Burke and Immanuel Kant, the sublime is a feeling of pleasure that arises from a delicate combination of safety and proximity to danger, from which position terror transforms into a peculiar pleasure. In eighteenth- and nineteenth-century aesthetic theory, the sublime applies primarily to natural phenomena of vast magnitude or power; mountain peaks, violent storms at sea, erupting volcanoes. In the twentieth century, human-inflicted catastrophes dwarfed the damage inflicted by nature, displacing nature as a privileged site of encounter with terror and incomprehensibility. The notion that nature is amoral and that natural disasters are therefore blameless is central to the aesthetic enjoyment of nature's violent extremes. By contrast with genocide, spectacular acts of terrorism, and the banality of poverty, natural disasters offer rare affirmation of the solidarity of humanity against the universally threatening *otherness* of nature. Yet the horizons of the natural sublime are receding in direct proportion with our ability to predict and insulate ourselves from hazards—even as their tragic impacts are visited upon natural sites and creatures themselves. From a safe position in front of the television, we face an overwhelming temptation to aestheticize environmental disasters *as natural*, or, rather, to naturalize either their causes or our vulnerability to them—and in turn the state of nature that their havoc allows us to glimpse. This is all the more reason to be mindful of T. J. Demos's admonition, in the context of a critical media ecology of wildfire imagery, that "Even more perverse than using evidence itself (of drought, megafires, devastation) to negate causality (global warming, climate change, petrocapitalist agency) is the aesthetic delectation of images of beautiful destruction, where the photographer, or more likely cellphone user, positions themselves in the thick of things, so that the viewer, distanced, protected—at least temporarily so—can witness destruction as a sublime aesthetic object."[9] A comprehensive reassessment of the state of nature in this postnatural era must take account of the aesthetic dispositions that organize social relations within dangerous environs. It is here that the artist has an opportunity to intervene.

---

8 Fredric Jameson, *The Political Unconscious: Narrative as a Socially Symbolic Act*, (Ithaca, NY, 1982), p. 251.

9 T. J. Demos, "The Agency of Fire: Burning Aesthetics," *E-Flux Journal* 98 (February 2019), https://www.e-flux.com/journal/98/256882/the-agency-of-fire-burning-aesthetics/ (accessed March 18, 2019).

When we want everything to be changed we call on fire.
—Gaston Bachelard, *The Psychoanalysis of Fire*[10]

Natural disasters are a rare species, of which Bismarck is a connoisseur. Moved by his own unlikely encounter with lightning (albeit within the metal frame of an automobile insulated by rubber tires), he hastens to the scene of a lightning strike that annihilates a herd of reindeer in southern Norway. Memorializing the instant in which electricity coursed between their huddled bodies, Bismarck's ghastly harvest yields a set of reindeer horn-tipped steel lightning rods, as if to offer an image of the herd from the indifferent perspective of lightning itself. He travels to the Sierra Nevada mountains of Colombia to interview the eldest shaman of the indigenous Wiwa tribe, Taita, survivor of a preternatural lightning strike that hit a ceremonial building during an annual ritual designed to restore community harmony with nature. Killing eleven shamans present, the strike was understood as message from Thunder (a being, in many Amerindian cosmologies) to "obey the law," repay debts for the overuse of water, plants, and animals, and refrain from sexual vice. Bismarck's identification with others who have experienced radical vulnerability to this elemental force goes well beyond vicarious thrill-seeking; against Romantic enchantment, he posits a reassertion of control over narratives—if not forces—of nature in its capacity for destruction. In a region of Venezuela prone to the most intense electrical storms in the world, in consultation with scientific experts and residents familiar with the local ecology, he deploys a series of rockets designed to harness lightning in a determinate trajectory. This technological intervention constitutes a form of direct address to Thunder *personified*—an electrical initiation of a conversation that reverberates sonically through disturbances of the air.

As the title work of this book, *Talking to Thunder* amplifies a tension between vulnerability to and provocation of nature's wrath, elaborated through Bismarck's wranglings with hurricane-force winds, ocean waves, stone boulders, and wildfires. Every poetic mind, according to the philosopher Gaston Bachelard, is animated by an affinity with one of the four classical elements: air, water, earth, and fire. Less a preference for a certain form of matter than a sensual resonance with its dynamics, a poet or artist's material orientation (like sexual orientation) expresses itself formally as well as thematically. The work, a product of material-inspired reveries, presents an intensification of primitive or archetypal human dispositions towards the elements. Of the four, fire does not survive scientific analysis as a material to be resolved into ever-smaller components; in contrast to water, air, and earth, it is reclassified as a process, one which transforms—indeed consumes—other elements.

---

10 Gaston Bachelard and Northrop Frye, *The Psychoanalysis of Fire*, trans. Alan C. M. Ross, revised ed. (Boston, 1987), p. 57.

As a basis for reverie, its motif is self-destruction—or rather, a self-immolation. While all are drawn to the warmth and light of the hearth (the bonfire, or the candle), the temperament of one who dreams with fire finds no satisfaction at a safe distance. Like Prometheus, he needs to steal fire, even at the risk of losing control over it—a nearly universal theme of origin myths of human exceptionalism. Whether courting lightning bolts or masquerading as a scientist to film in wildfires, Bismarck manifests symptoms of the archetypal Novalis complex, in which "the need to feel dominates the need to see."[11]

Even when he is working with water, wind, and stone, Bismarck operates under the logic of fire. *Irma to Come in Earnest* (see pages 82–109) is a double entendre announcing not just the arrival of the storm but her climax. Slowed to one fiftieth of real-time speed and repeated in an infinite loop, the video draws viewers into a shared space of deliberation *within* the furious gale—a space normally foreclosed by the all-encompassing urgencies of the situation itself. Aestheticization operates here in the service of disclosing compromised infrastructure and exhibiting news media's role in constructing the image of disaster, even as dynamism of wind and rain sustains a feeling of being engulfed in the storm. We meditate here upon quantified and insured environmental futures; unevenly born individual and societal costs of our exposure to environmental risk.

Apocalypsoid (see pages 56–72) embodies the paradox of our contemporary culture of prediction even more acutely. A granite boulder, vaguely planet shaped, is digitally scanned and mapped according to a system of longitudes and latitudes, with each quadrant carefully numbered—only to be shattered by a stick of dynamite. The explosion is filmed in order to facilitate a painstaking process of reassembly (only partially possible), freezing an imperceptible moment of the stone's violent fragmentation. Bearing visual resemblance to the General Circulation Models of the earth's atmosphere used to model different scenarios of climate change, the work offers a dark proxy for the work of the Intergovernmental Panel on Climate Change (IPCC), which, despite overwhelming scientific consensus, sees its warnings largely unheeded. We rush towards certain catastrophe with open eyes, and a set of instruments at the ready to measure the wreckage. The data collected is used, in turn, to recalibrate the models and refine their predictions to a statistical minimum of uncertainty. The edition of boulders, subtly varied in shape and color, is reminiscent of the Coupled Model Intercomparison Project, working since 1995 to improve regional and national forecasting. Paralysis in the face of disaster combines with a fascinated compulsion to take inventory—symptoms of a failure to *feel* antithetical to the fire temperament.

---

11 Bachelard and Frye 1987, p. 41.

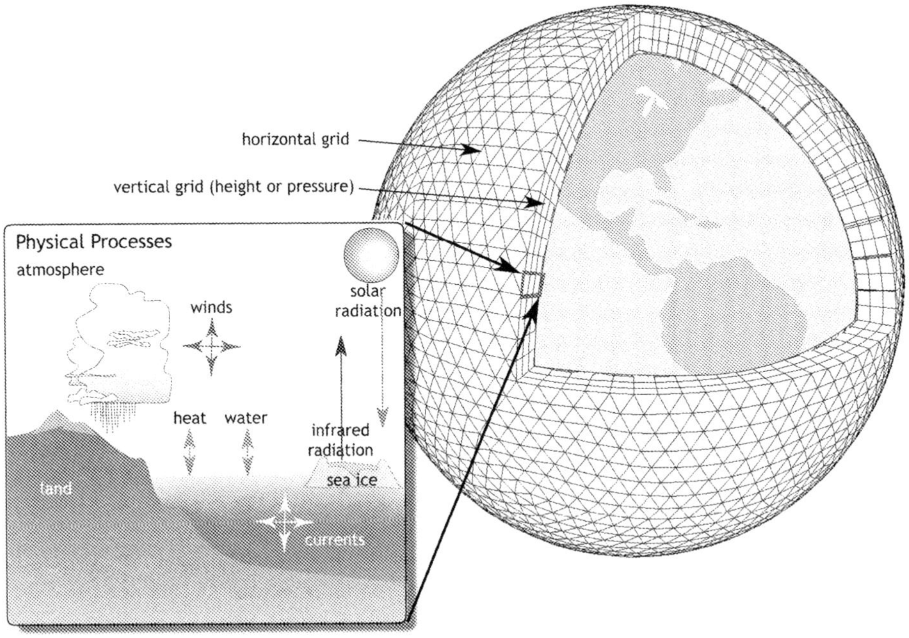

General Circulation Model of the Atmosphere

In place of data *visualizations*, Bismarck offers two alternative modes of engagement with data-driven descriptions of the turbulent surface of the ocean. Highlighting the paucity of scientific diagrams, *Die Luft muss man sich wegdenken* (One Must Think Away the Air; see pages 116–23) offers a sculptural translation, at scale, of a digital scan of a wave off the coast of Ireland during Hurricane Ophelia. The topography of the wave is traced by hundreds of bent steel wires, filling a large room almost completely. The static snapshot portends movement but offers no position of distance from which to survey the scene. One crouches beneath it, or surfaces between the wires, moving *in* rather than on the sea. *Die Mimik der Tethys* (The Expressions of Tethys; see pages 124–35) likewise offers an immersive and dynamic experience in place of an image, in this case positioning the viewer below the surface of the water. A deep-ocean buoy sweeps through the gallery on a precarious looking system of pulleys, its four-dimensional path driven by data streaming in real time from a buoy deployed at sea. Tossing and tumbling above, the buoy induces a vague sense of sea sickness born of a failure of haptic coordination between the eyes and the feet. Rather than affirming a position outside the phenomena, or proffering trite reality effects like the weather forecaster's blowing umbrella, the imperative to map and control is deployed in order to open the turbulent elements to experience from within.

If Bismarck is guilty of aestheticizing environmental hazards, his guilt goes beyond that of producing sublime spectacle to be viewed from a safe distance. What is at stake in his indulgence of a psychically and politically fraught desire to be in the midst of ecological disasters? Now, with the keen awareness that they are neither natural nor innocent? In excavating a place for the aesthetic within the political fiction of the state of nature, we find ample material in Bachelard's account of primitive human reveries toward the elements: the fireside, the candle, the gently moving waters of a country stream. Today we must inquire as to the reveries inspired by the elements in their agonistic interplay with thoroughly anthropogenic environs. Indeed, we must consider whether the aesthetic attraction exerted by such dangers compounds other drivers towards destruction. Envisioning the magnification of our attraction to fire, Bachelard quotes George Sand in asking, "Why have I not the eyes of an ant in order to admire this burning birch log? With what transports of blind joy and of love's frenzy these swarms of little white moths come to hurl themselves into it! For them this is the volcano in all its majesty. This is the spectacle of an immense conflagration. This dazzling light intoxicates and exalts them as the sight of the whole forest on fire would do for me."[12] Plunging into wildfires burning near the Arctic Circle in Sweden, near Berlin, and in California, Bismarck entrains our gaze upon the ecological conflagrations that ensue from our contemporary relationship with fire, in which the cozy glow of domestic hearth is outsourced to the power plant beyond city limits. If human nature resurfaces in moments of societal breakdown, moments of environmental breakdown rekindle the embers of the state of nature itself—forcing us to rethink a social order that has set the world ablaze.

12 Bachelard and Frye 1987, p. 17

Irma to Come in Earnest

2017
Video (1920 × 1080), stereo sound, 44 min.

"Irma to Come in Earnest" warned a news headline of September 2017, as the category-five hurricane swept through the Caribbean and bore down on Florida. Its arrival is the subject of Bismarck's eponymous film, shot in Miami amid gale-force winds, flooding, and desolation. In an attempt to fathom the essence of a hurricane beyond the media spectacle, the black-and-white footage is drastically slowed down, taking in rain and debris swirling through empty streets, submerged cars, and houses in disarray. A haunting ambient soundtrack pieced together from news reports is slowed to the same pace as the moving image, rendering it unintelligible. In the first part of the film, the camera stands still; the only thing that moves is the hurricane itself. The slow-motion effect brings the violent event back to a speed perceptible to the human eye, allowing the viewer to perceive the union of the storm with the suburban environs—the actual invisibility of moving air overcome by an interplay of raindrops and blowing objects. In the second part, the storm has moved on, allowing humans to move again amid the destruction. For the first time people, not least media representatives, appear in the frame. For the viewer, the pleasure of watching the constructed image dovetails with the perverse implications of witnessing a catastrophe. By shifting the speed of image and sound, the film attempts to transcend familiar images of disaster, capturing both the nature of the storm and the media presentation of the catastrophe in an otherworldly atmosphere.

IRMA TO COME IN EARNEST

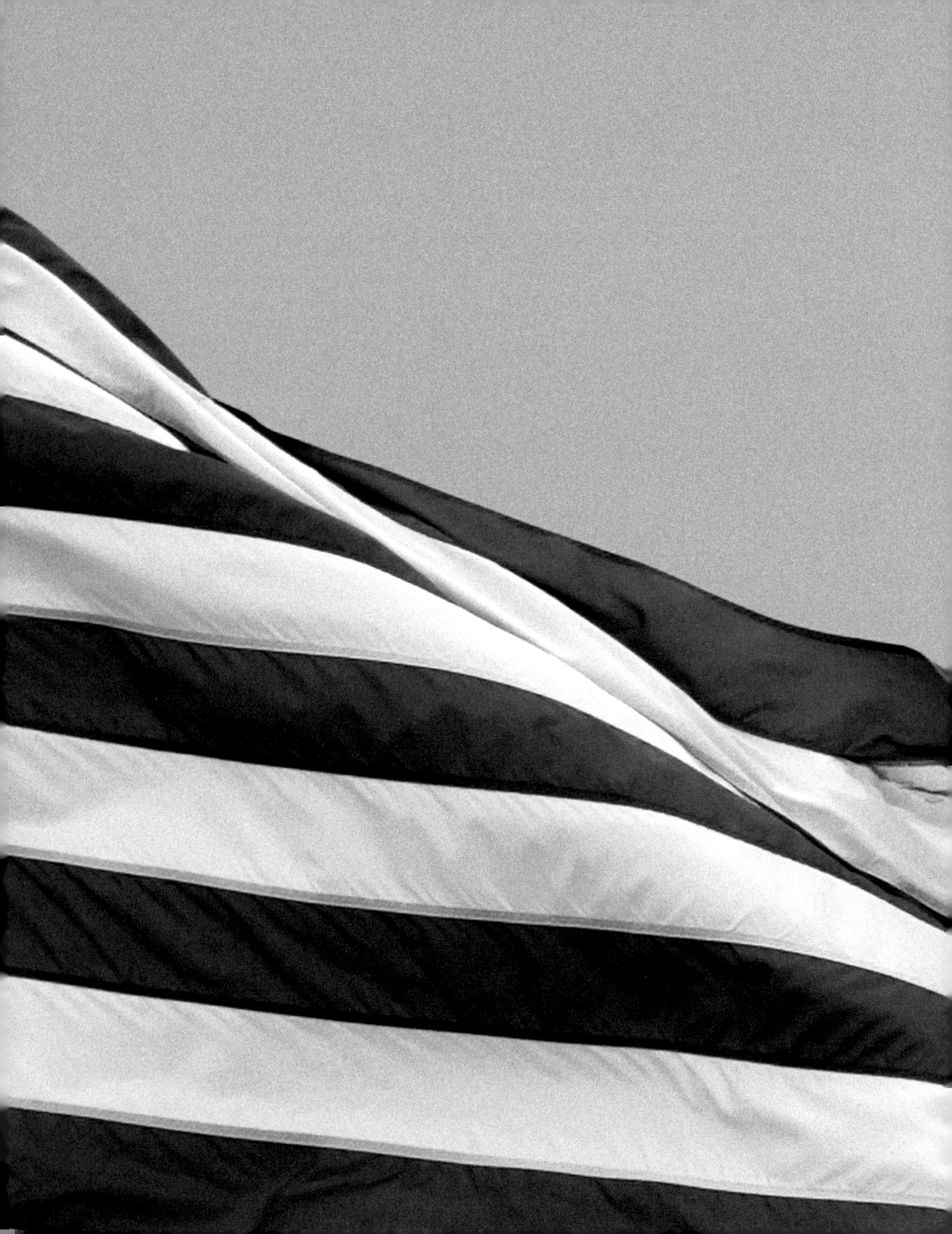

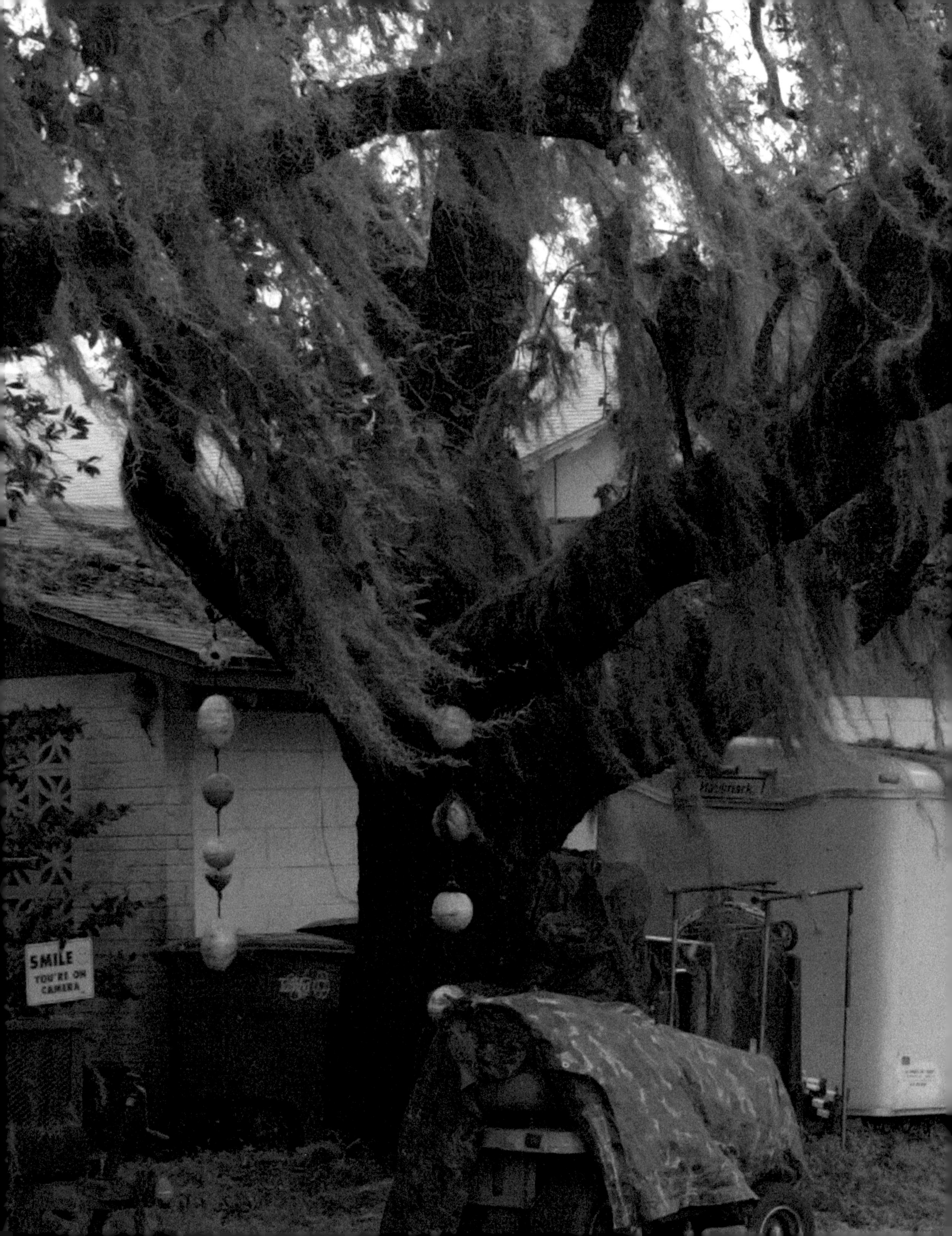
SMILE
YOU'RE ON
CAMERA

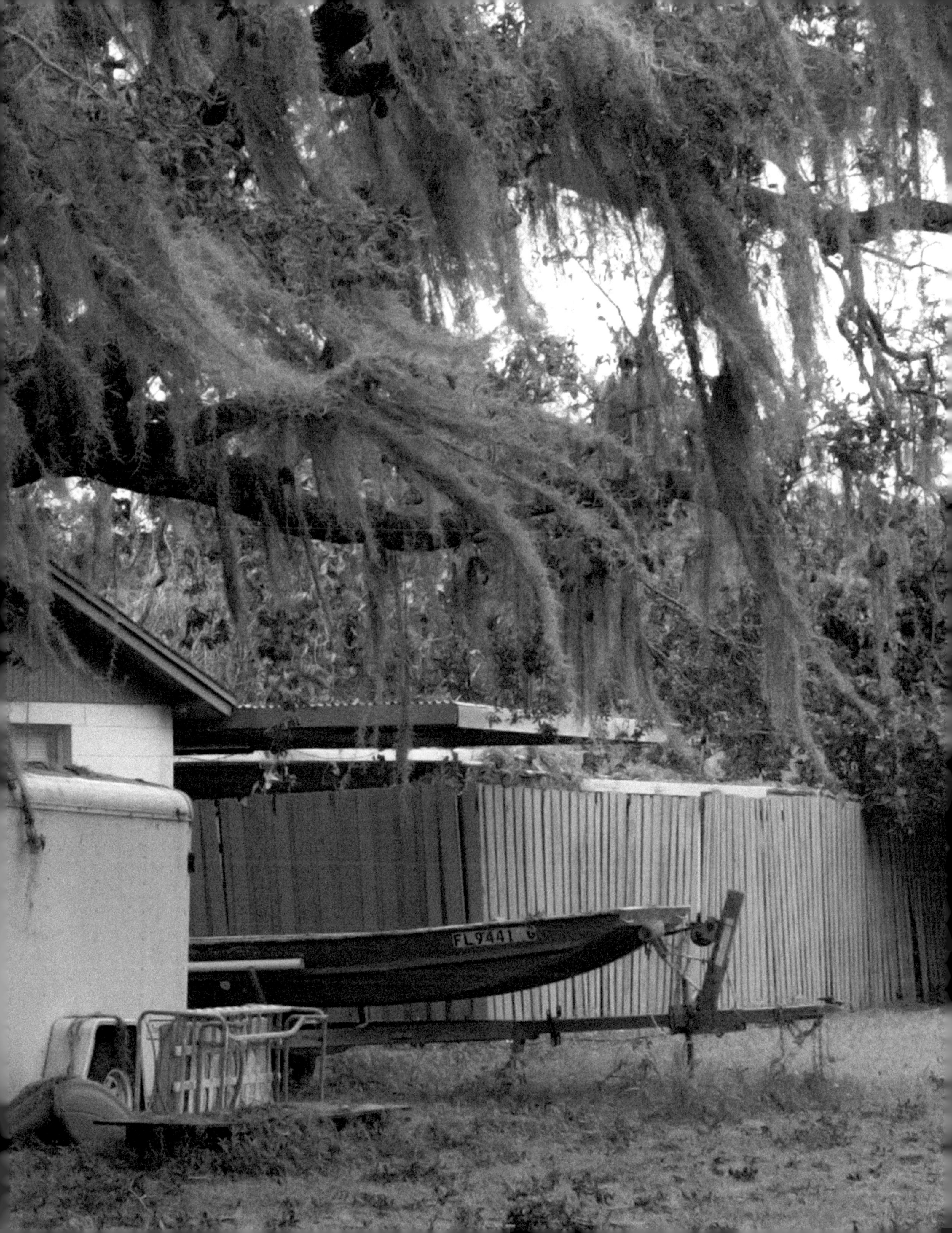
FL9441 G

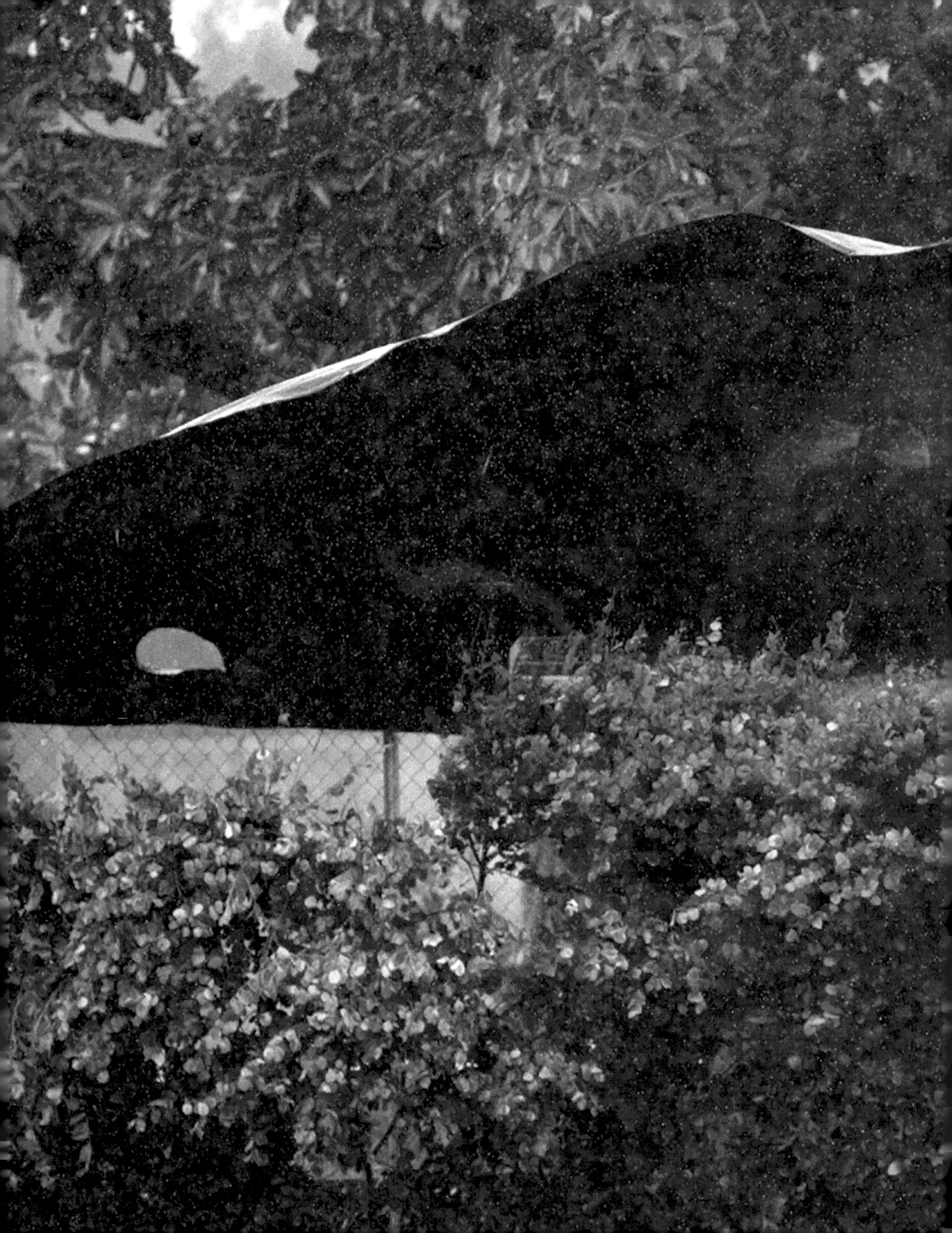

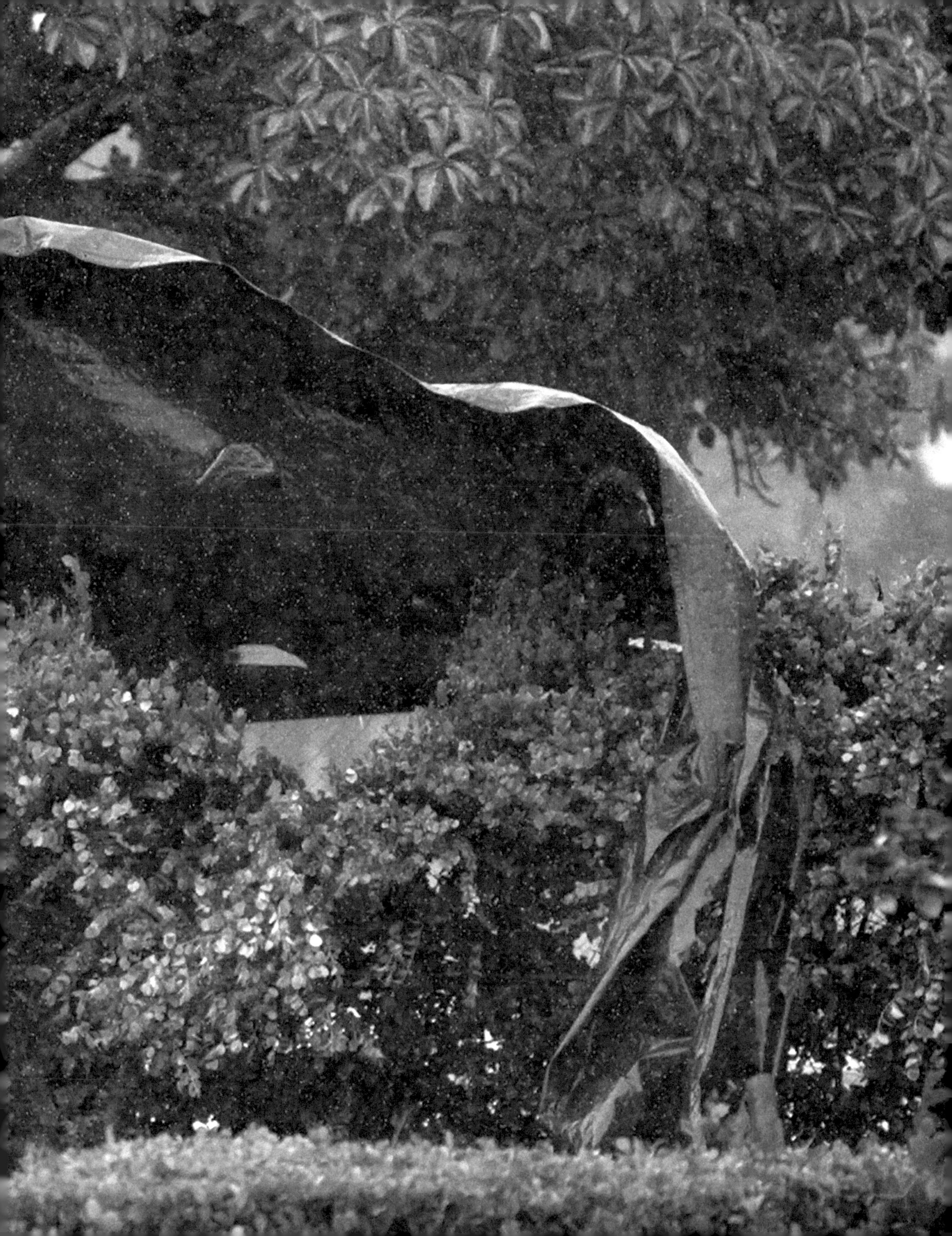

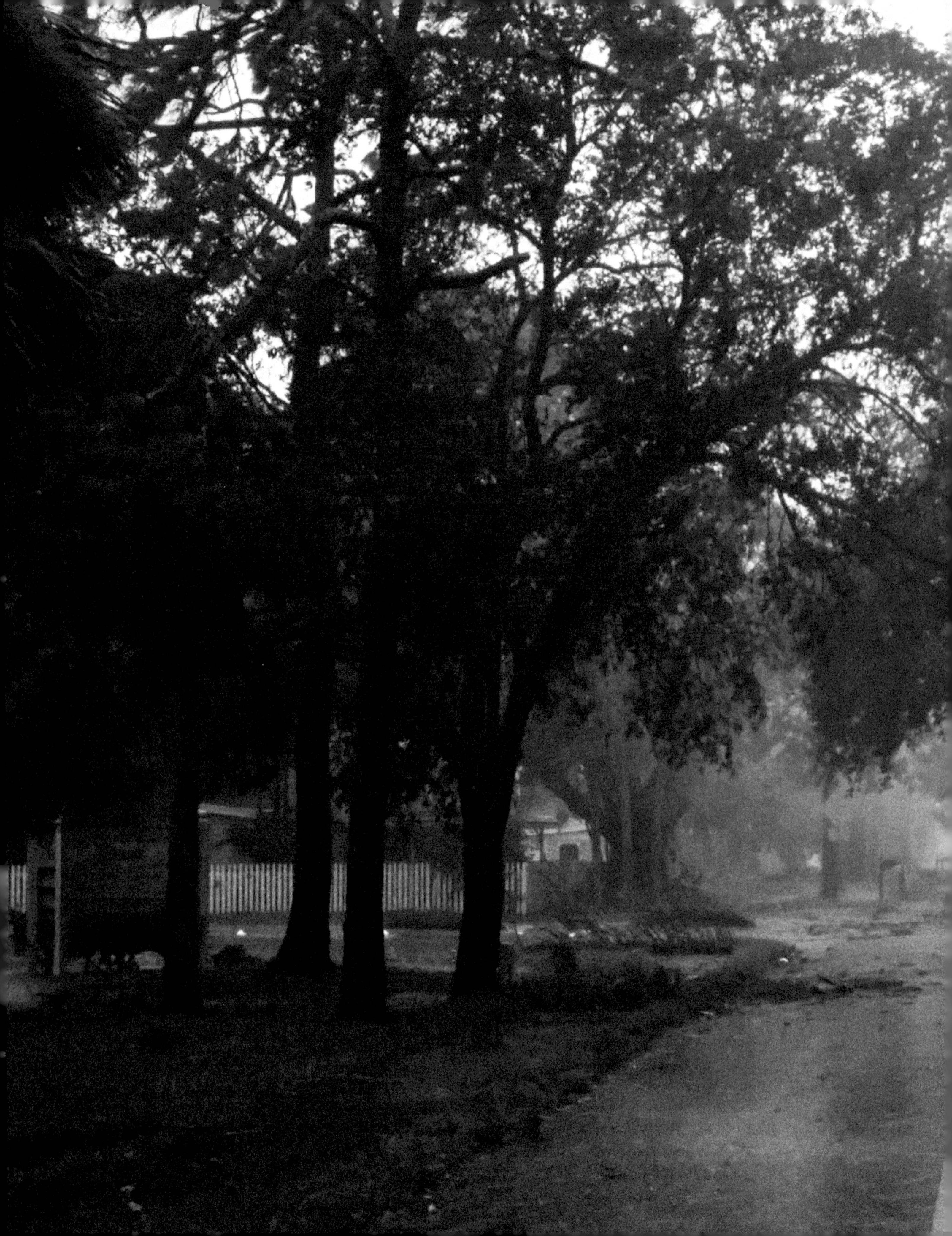

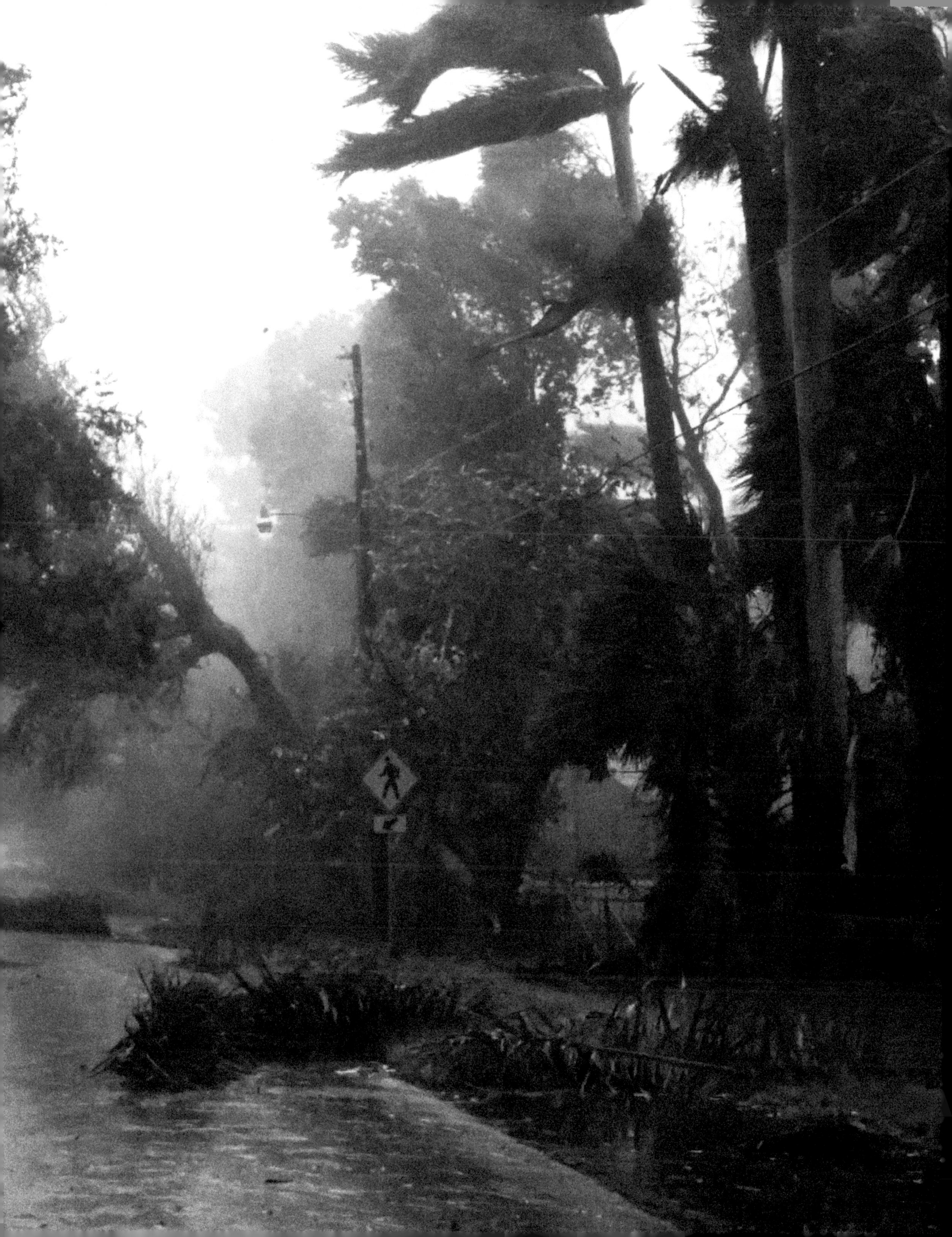

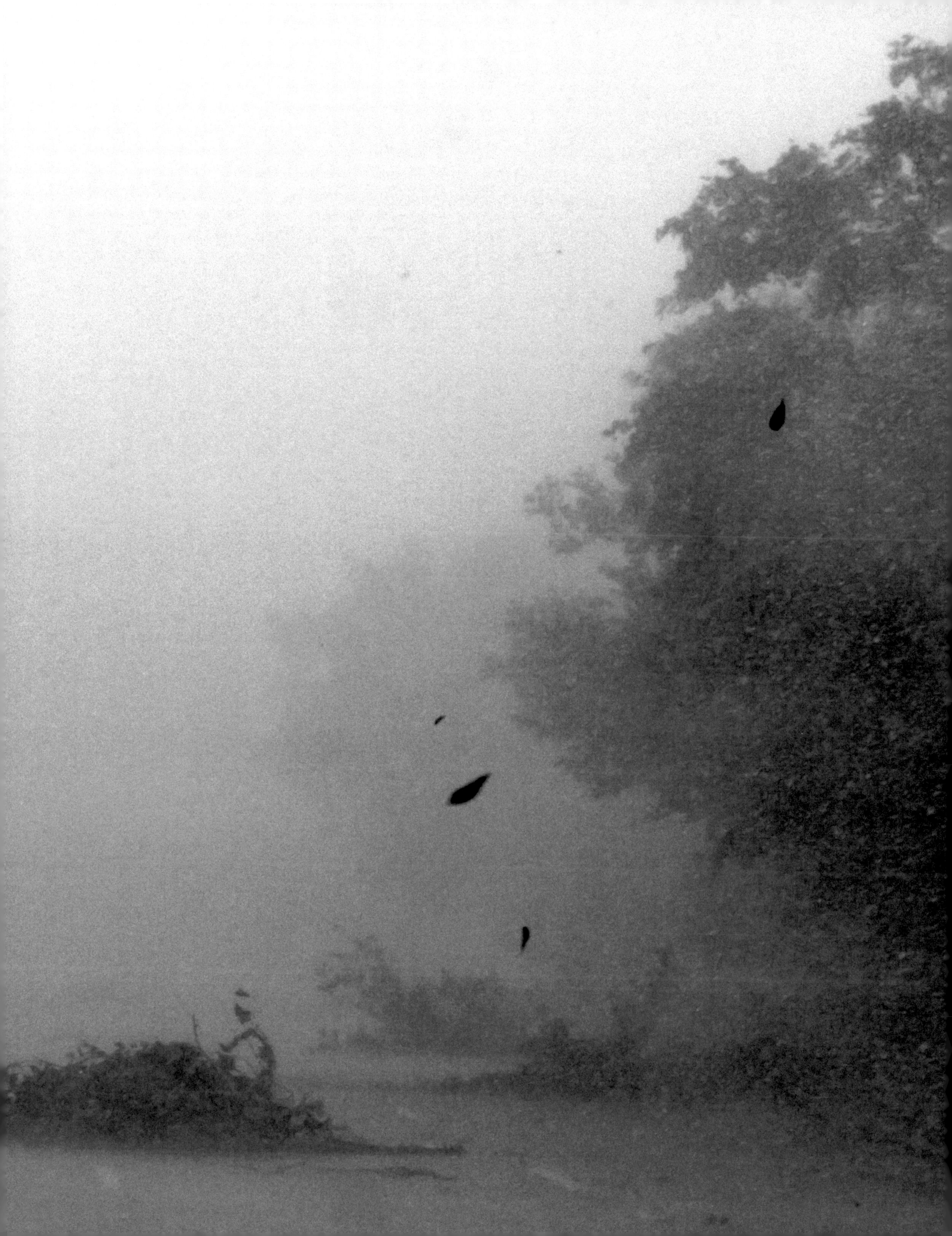

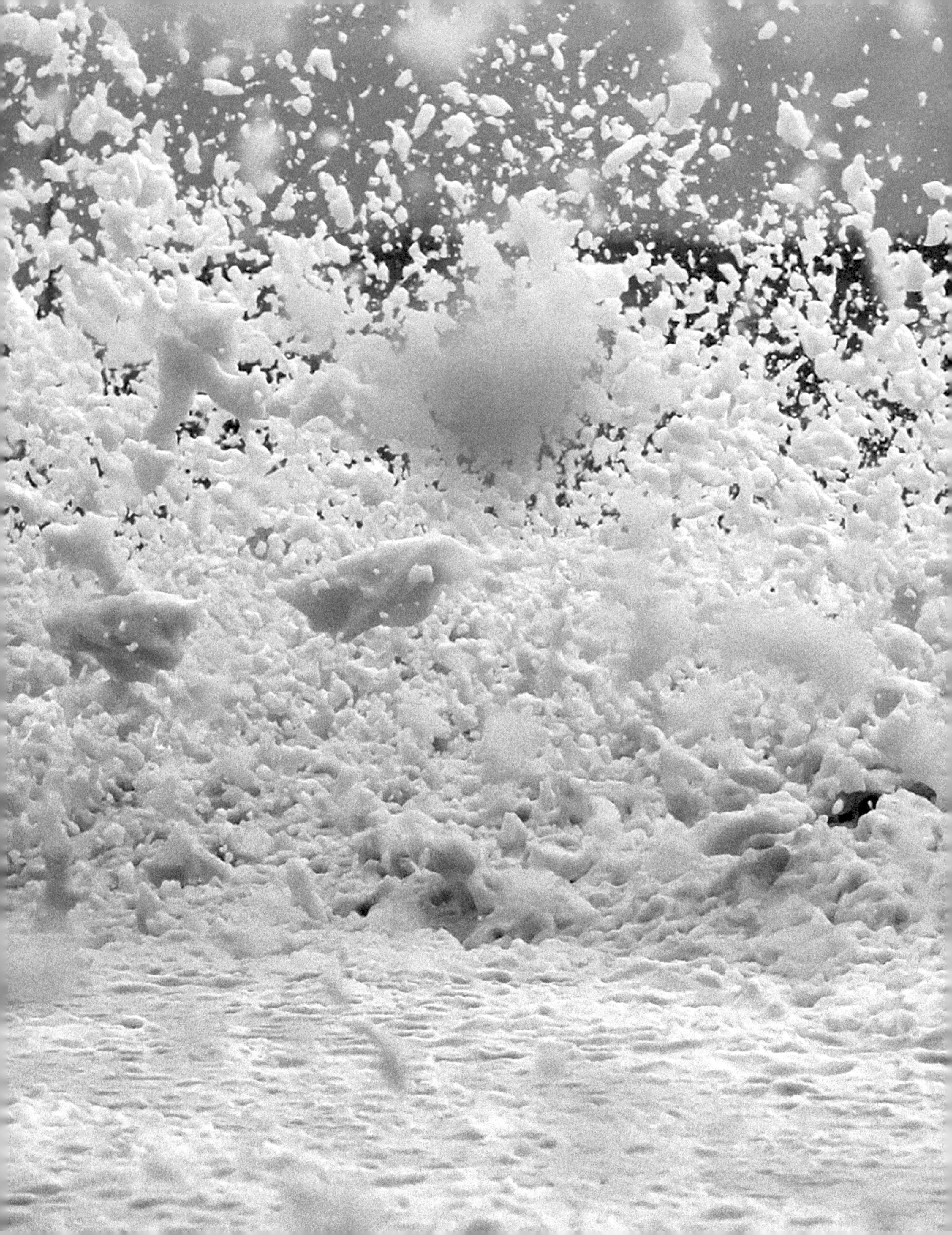

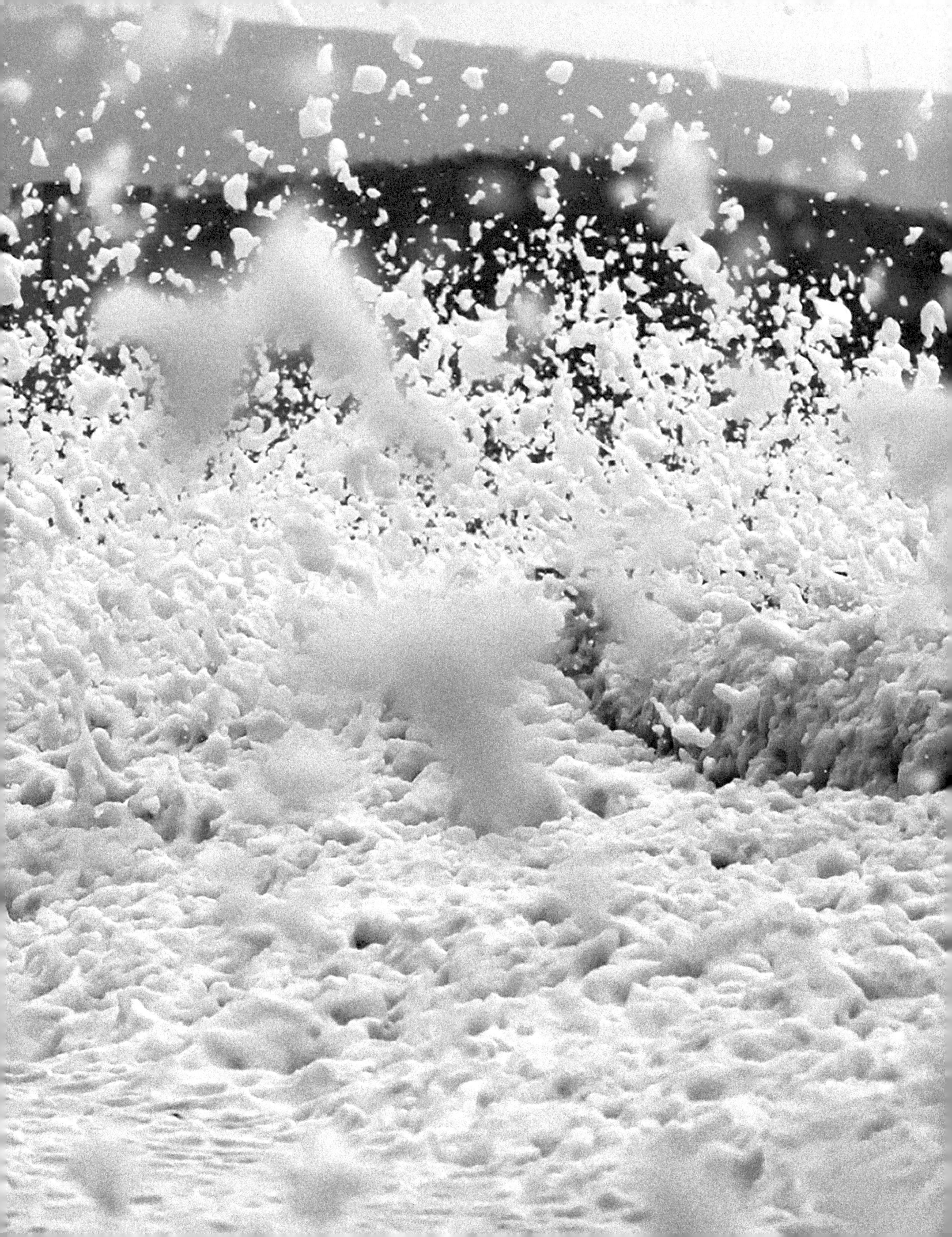

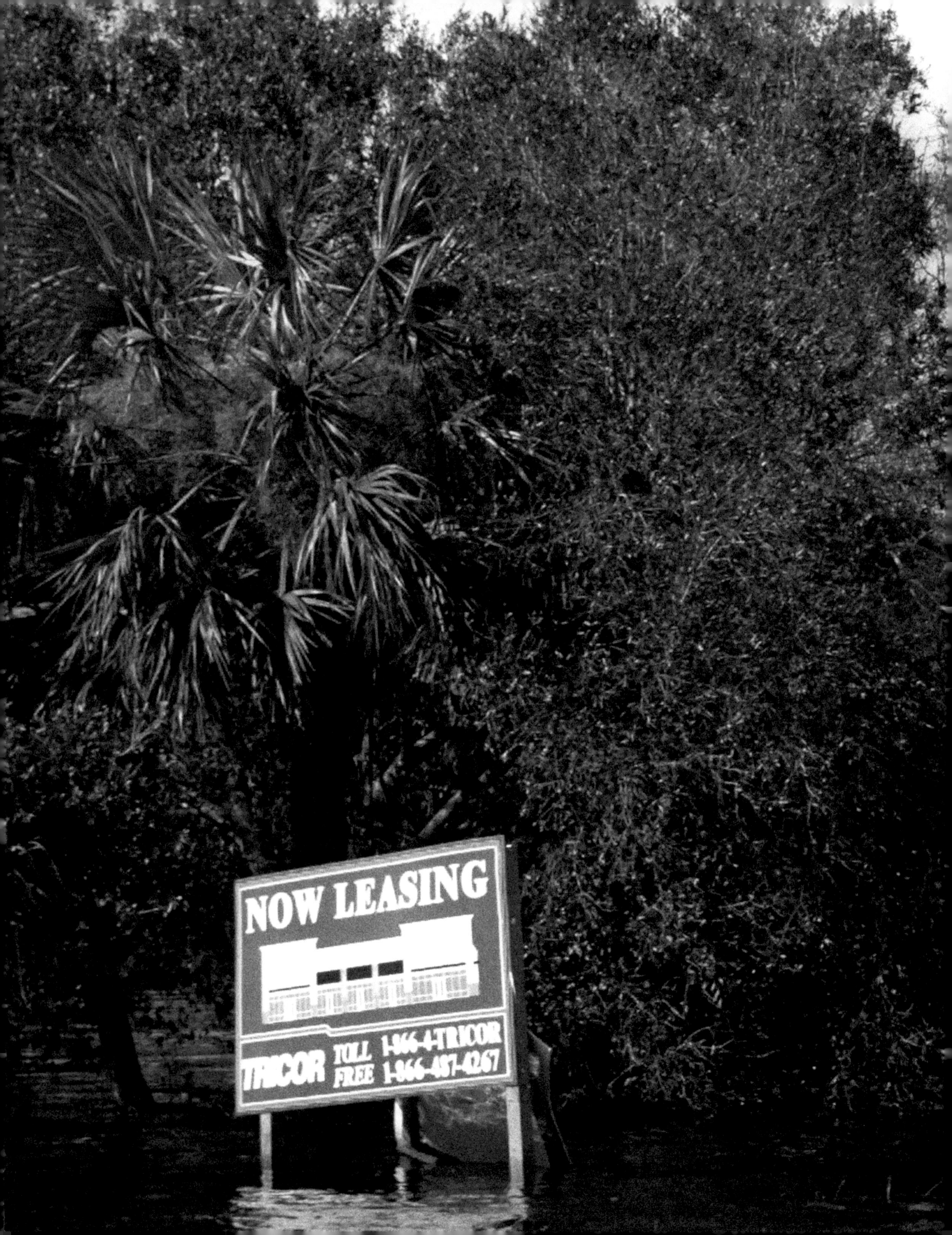
NOW LEASING
TRICOR
TOLL FREE
1-866-4-TRICOR
1-866-487-4267

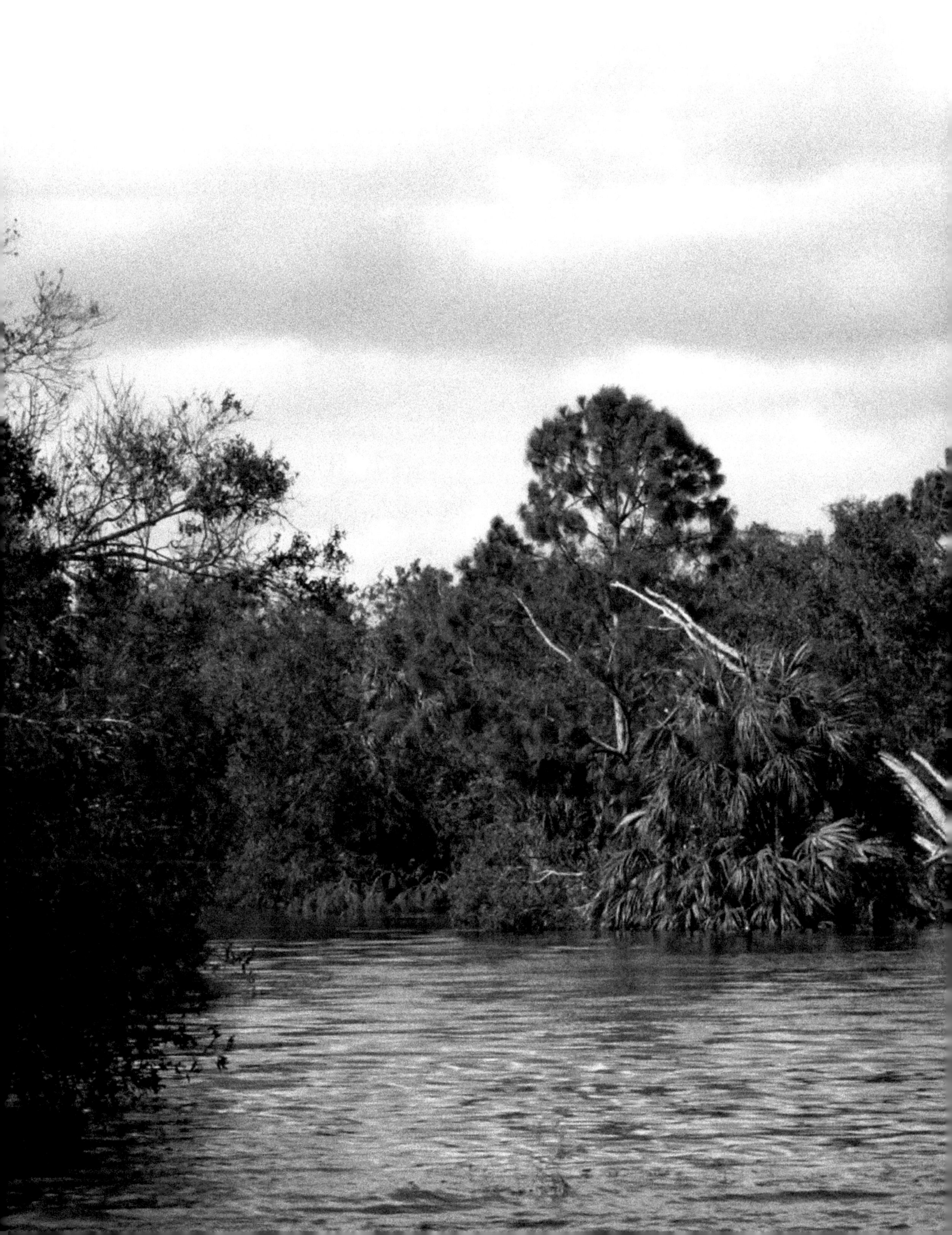

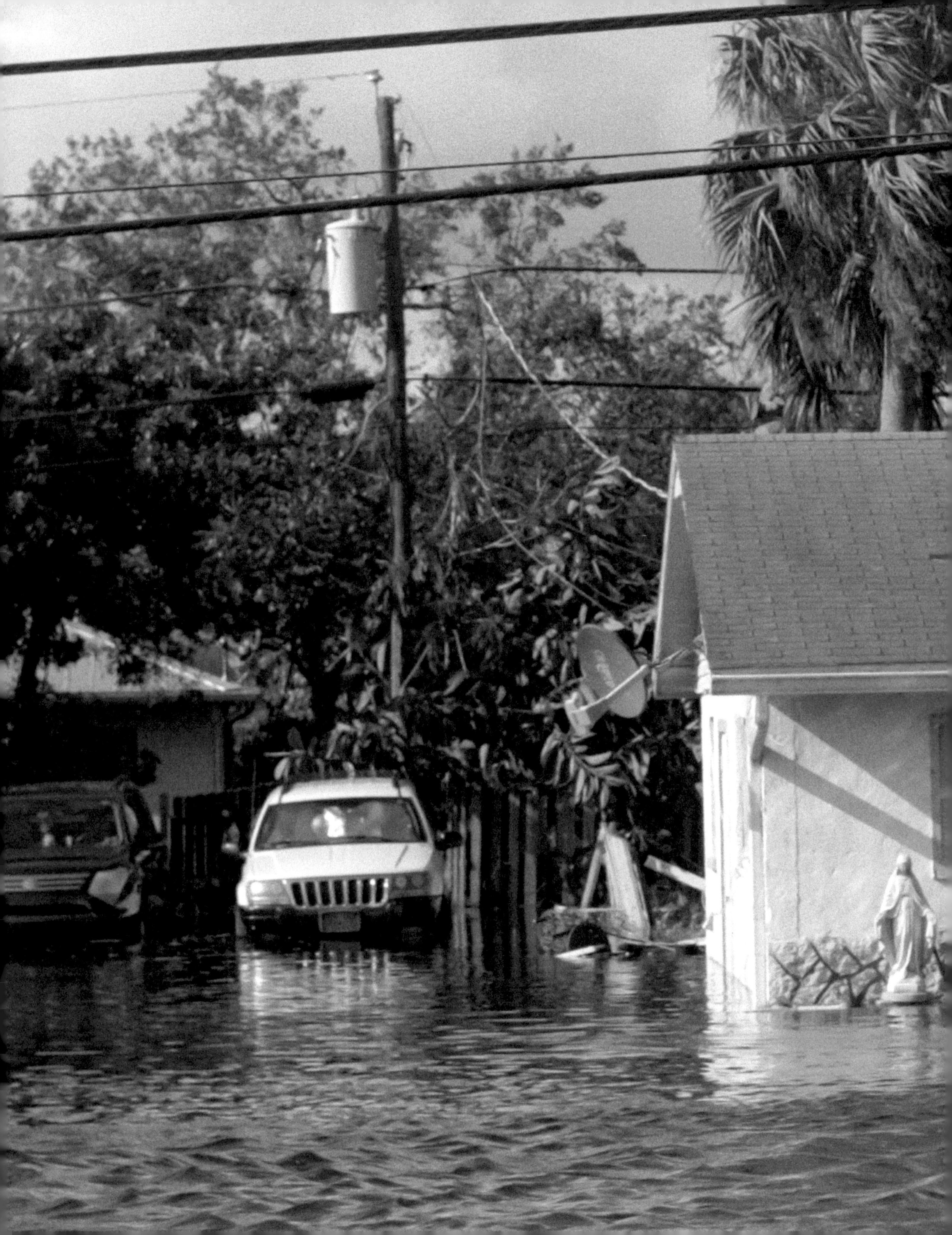

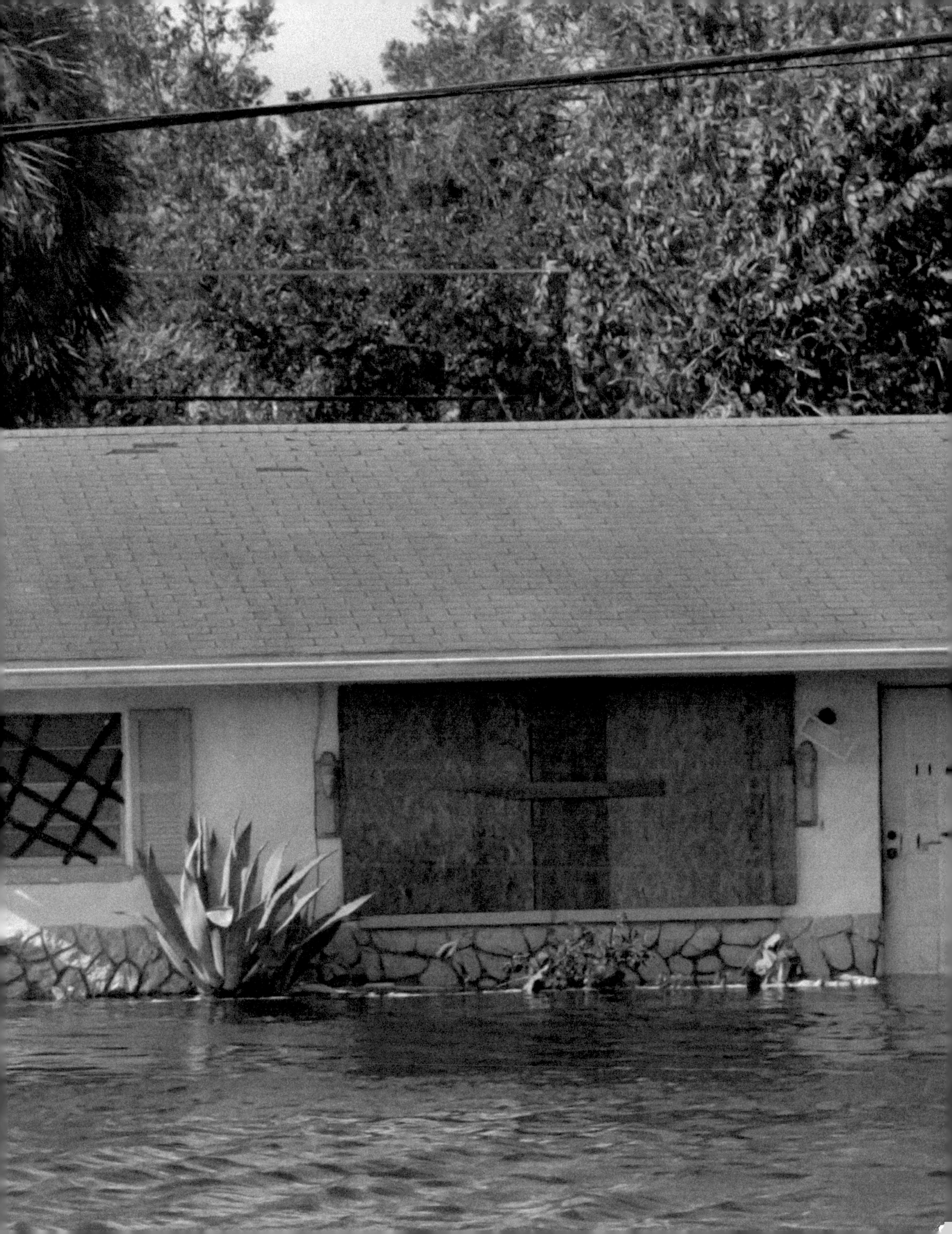

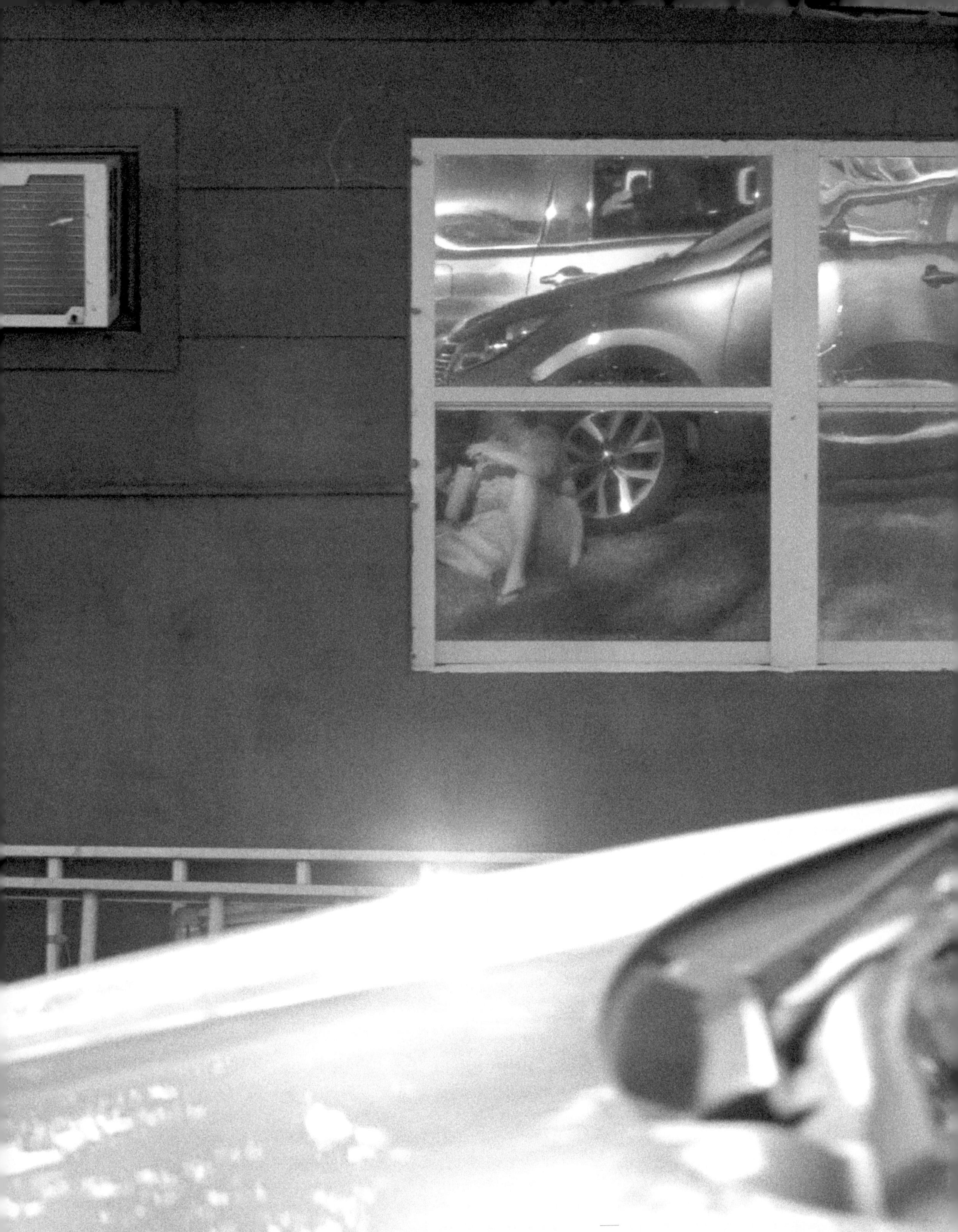

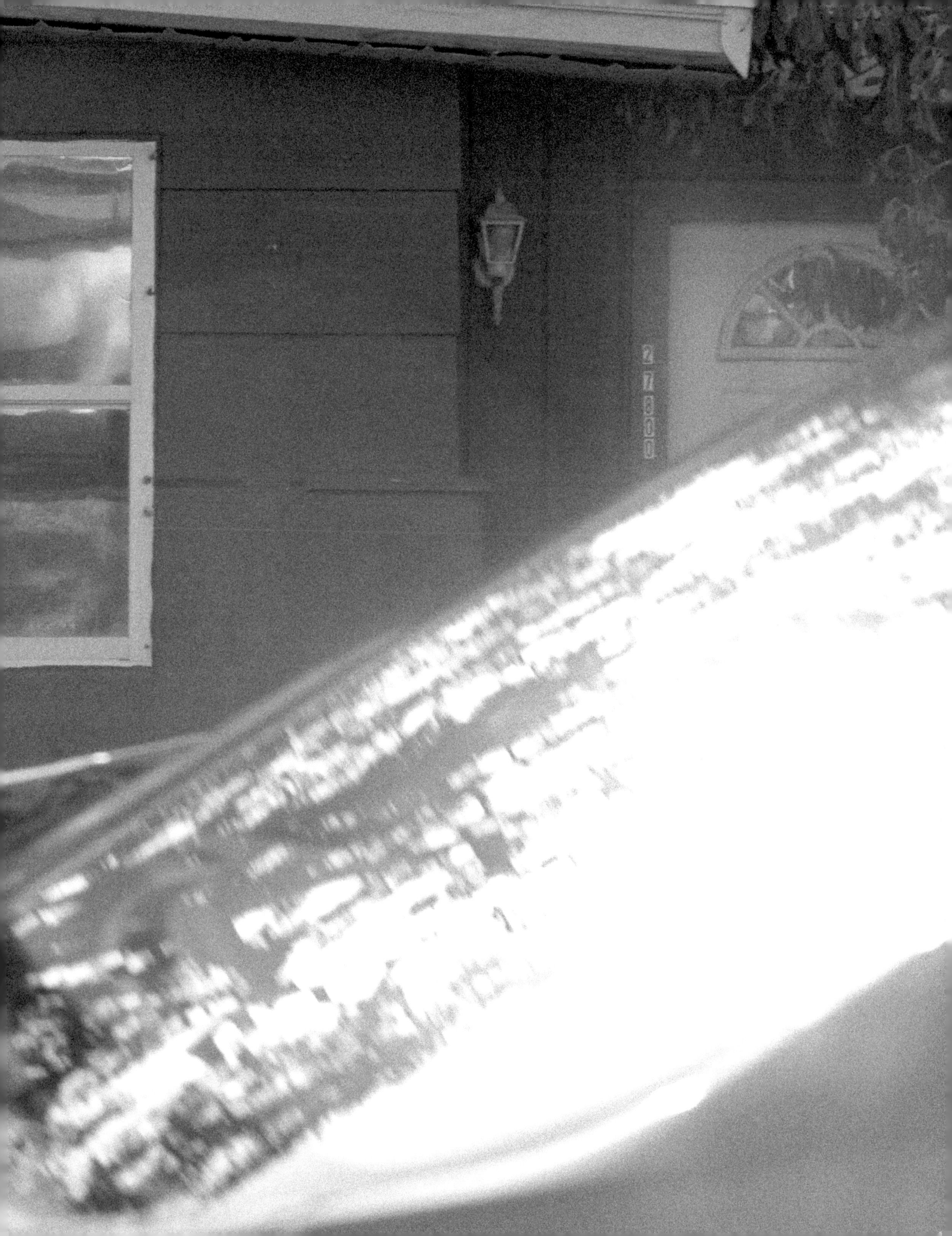

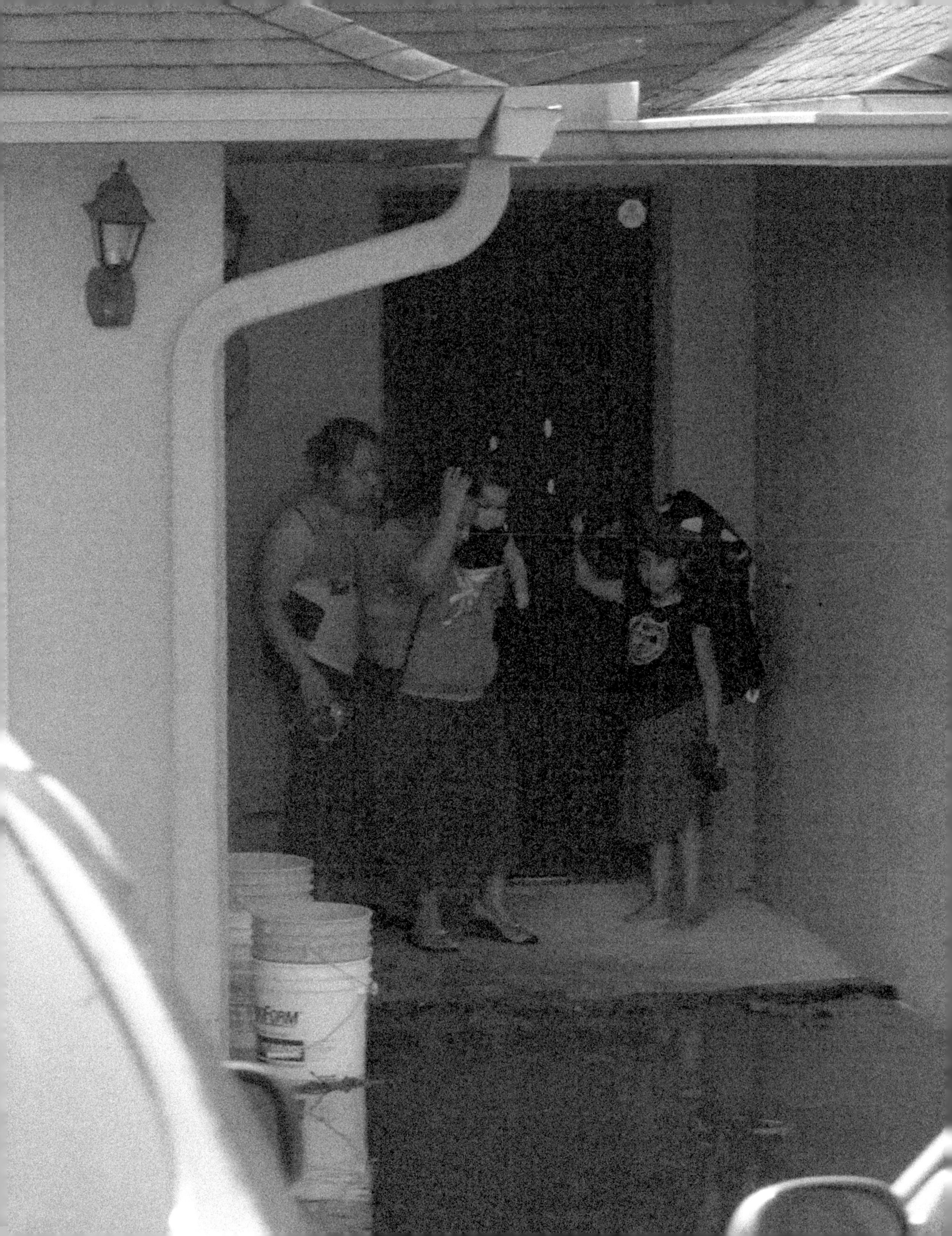

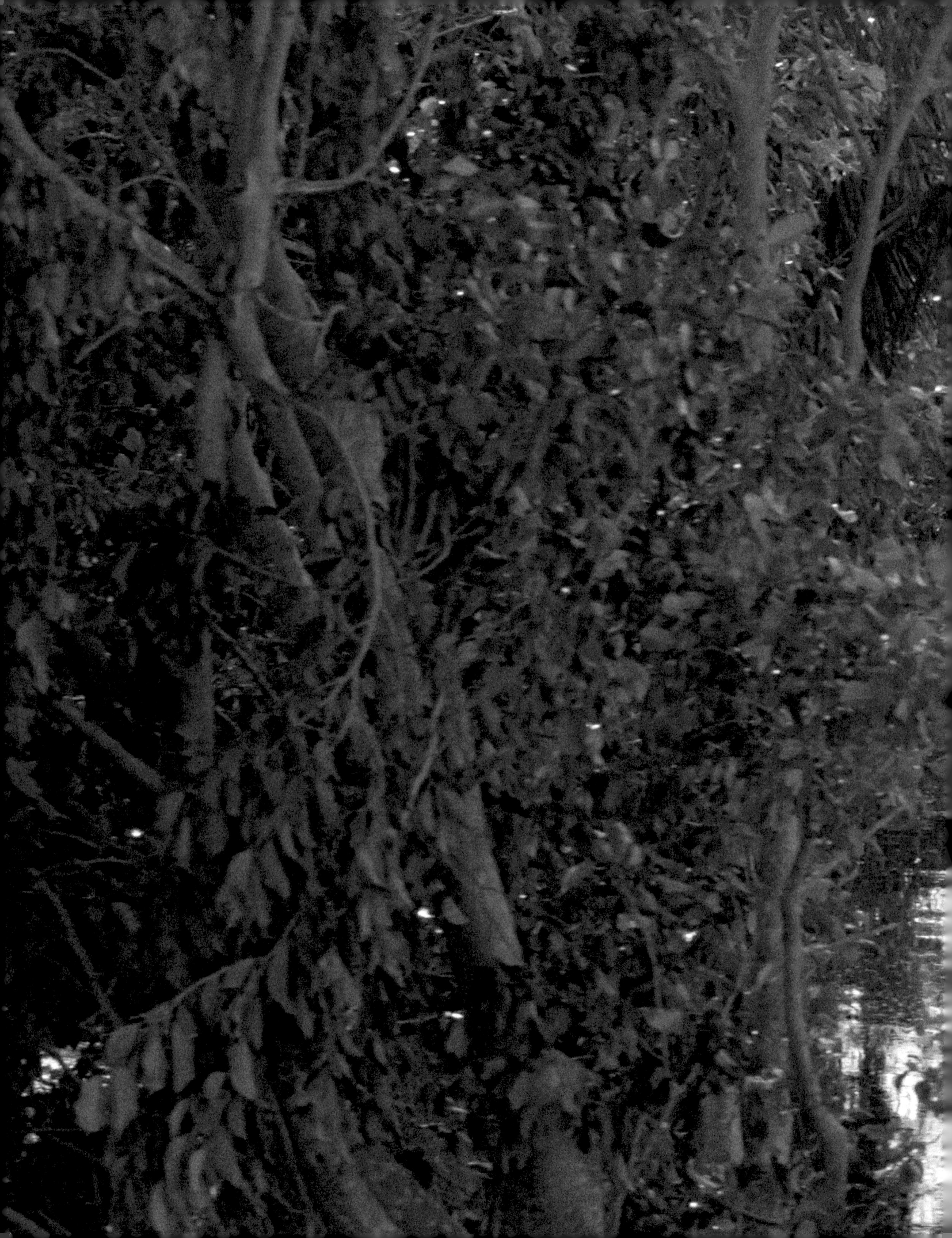

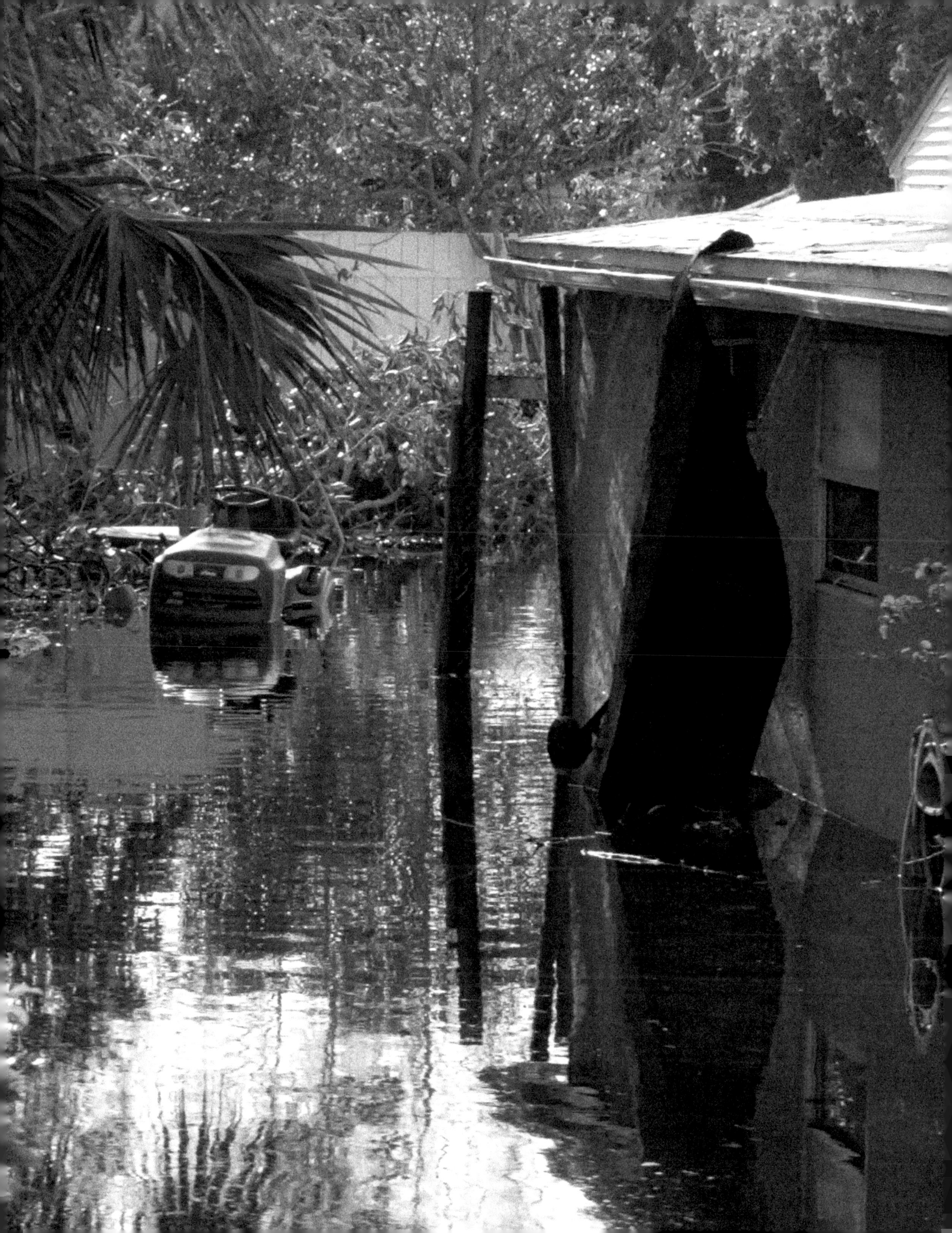

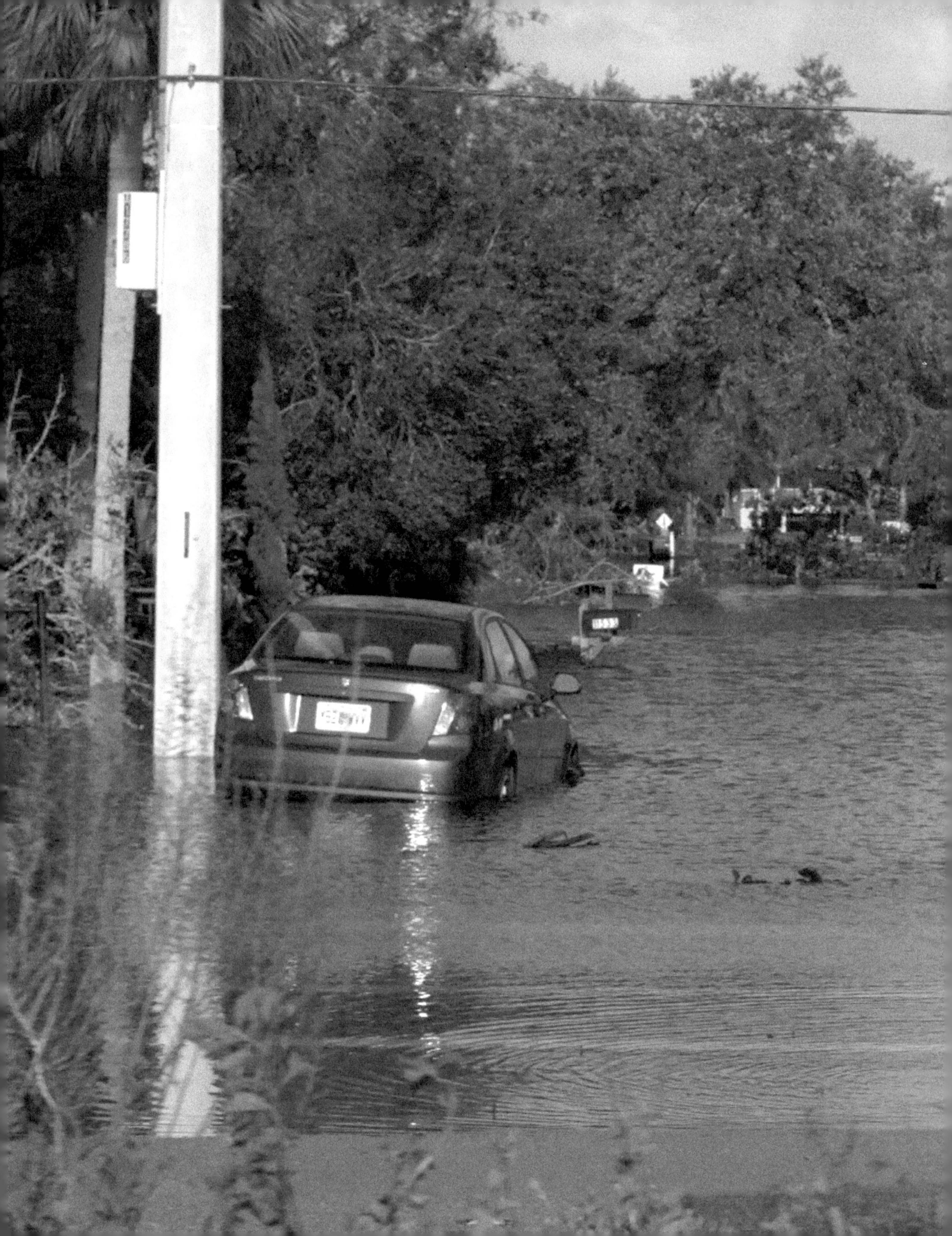

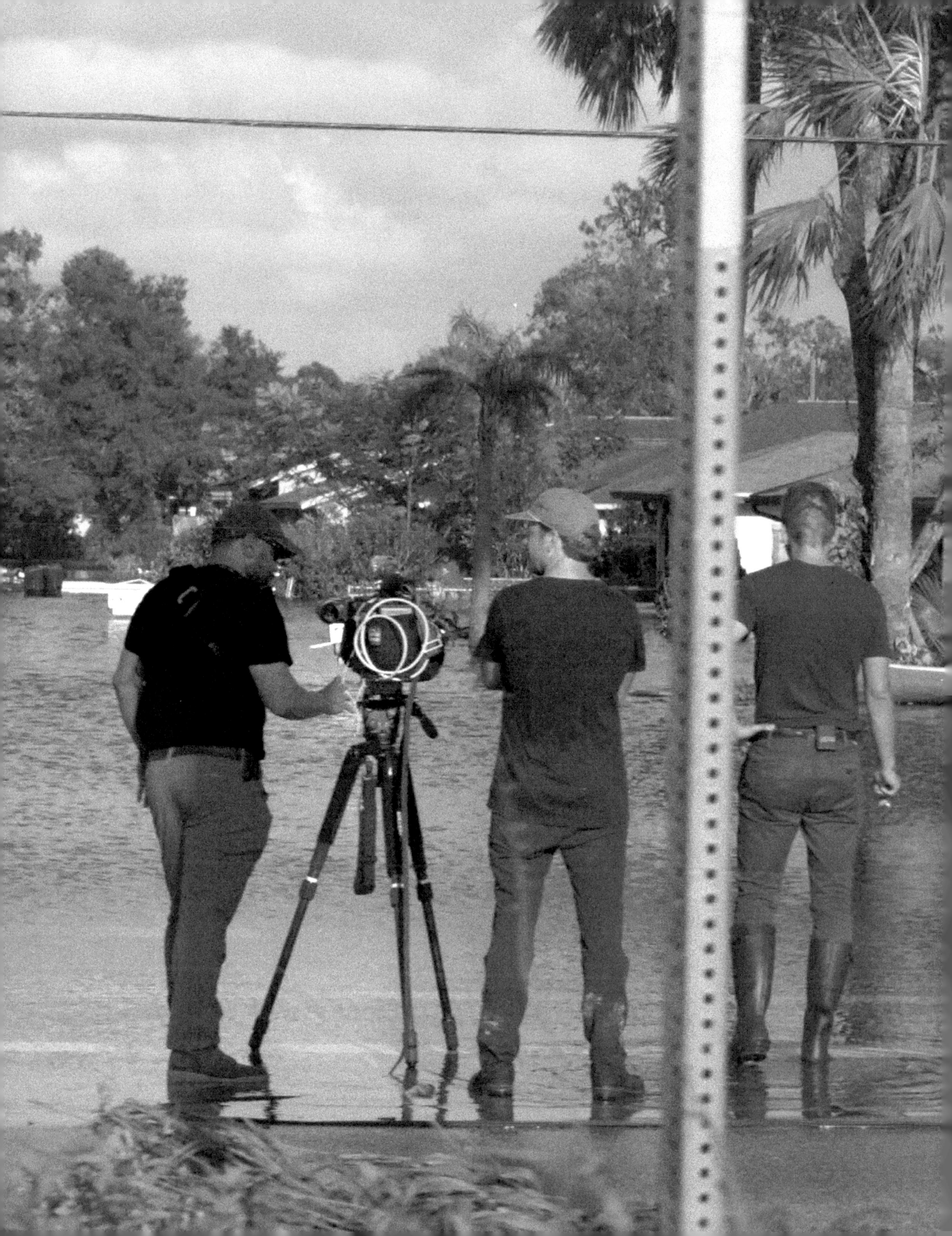

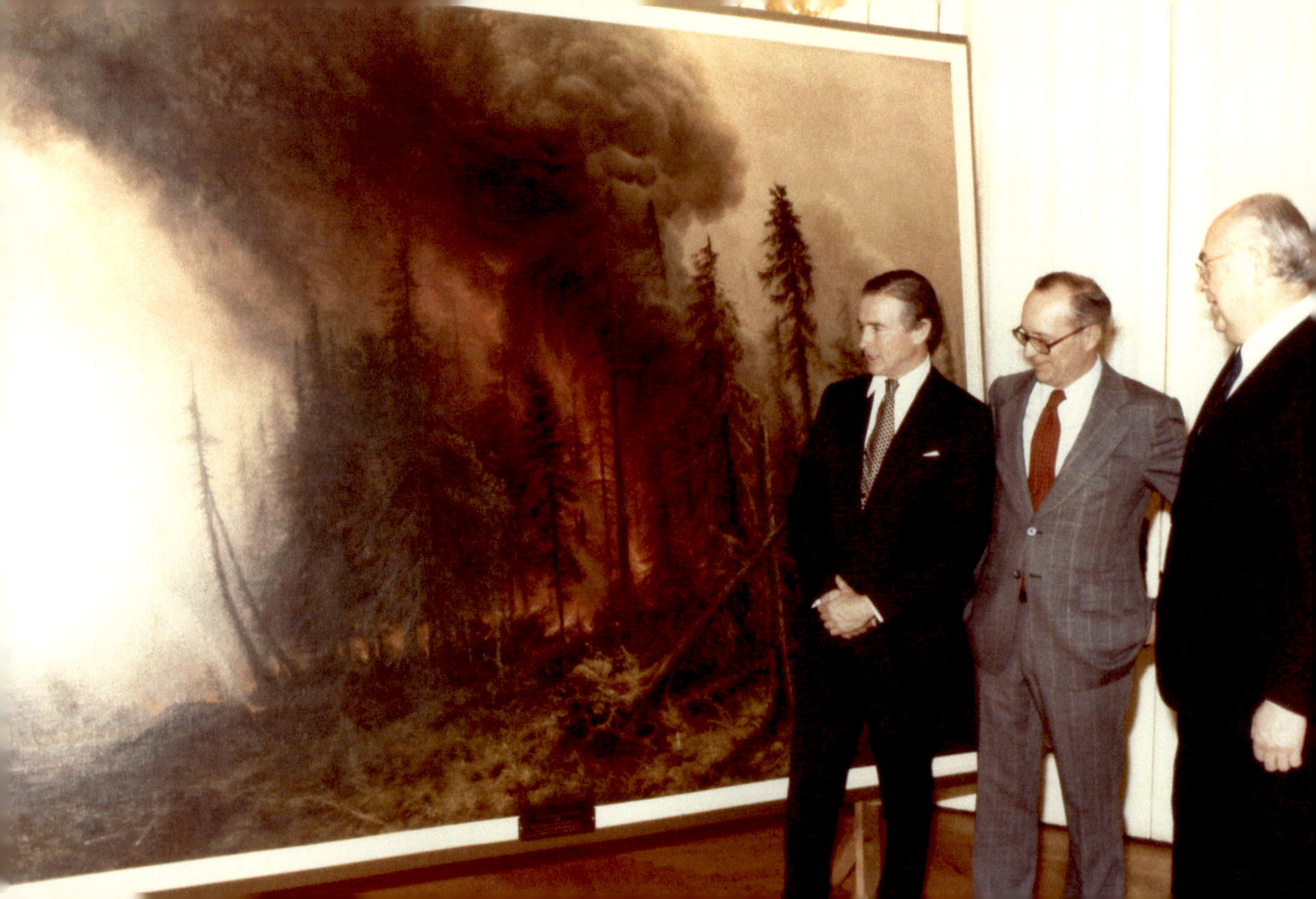

The Irrelevant Lamb

Jürgen Trittin in Conversation with
Julius von Bismarck

Julius von Bismarck: Thank you for coming here today and taking the time to talk to me. Many people in my social environment are political in various ways, but you are the first actual politician to come to my studio. I wanted to speak to you about my visual research on natural disasters due to the importance of images of natural catastrophes in your political work.

Historically art has always played a significant role in constructing nature. The images that come to mind when we think about nature are derived from paintings or, nowadays, influenced by video and photography, which still have their roots in those precise landscape paintings. The visual meaning of nature is influenced by art.

You are on the other end of the same sphere: You deal with realpolitik. You have influenced how our society deals with its environment on a legislative level.

One thing that my artistic research and your political work have in common is a very inspiring misconception, which leads to my first question: What is the difference between environment and nature? How should we distinguish between environmental conservation and nature conservation?

Jürgen Trittin: The environment is what surrounds us. Nature is ultimately an idea that is always related to the suggestion that it developed without human influence. And that's where the questions begin: Does nature even exist in the Anthropocene, which some people claim to have discovered? Or is nature not instead a product of human influence and thus a cultural entity? We normally contrast culture and nature, but the Nazis and rightwing extremists have put it the other way around. They have so to speak declared nature to be culture.[1]

I think this is the question that has to be asked today. It begins with small things. There are several national parks in Germany, but there is only a small bit of primeval forest where pastoralism never actually took place. It's on the island of Vilm near Rügen. All the others are commercial forests, more or less in a near-natural state. But they did not come into being without the influence of humans, which is apparent from the fact that there are so many oak trees on land where beech trees would normally grow. This goes back to the time of pastoralism, when pigs were driven into the forest. But what we think of as natural is actually just implied by the word "nature." In fact, if there were no people in Germany, instead of the mixture of pastureland and forest that seems so natural to us, we would have almost only beech forests in low mountain ranges, with succession plants where the beech trees have died out. But people still aren't aware of the really big issues such as how greenhouse gases are changing the planet's climate. People simply regard human beings as a part of nature that has emancipated itself from nature and appropriated it at the same time. This is problematic, and I've often had that discussion with people who have decided to be vegan for ethical reasons.

JvB: Yes, ethical reasons . . . Many people think they're hurting nature if they kill an animal. I think this romantic idea of nature is part of what got us into this situation in the first place. Our idea of nature needs to change. It's not about killing the animal, but there still may be good reasons to be vegan.

JT: Yes, and I deeply respect the choice to be vegan. But it is a human decision, one that people make based on their culture, their convictions. If I were to define nature conservation as the preservation of natural diversity as we know it—which isn't nature as we know it—then I wouldn't be able to manage without keeping a minimum of livestock, which would result in a different ethical outcome. The same is true of the pictures that from time to time appear in the tabloids of lambs that have been attacked by wolves. Well, wolves have to feed themselves too, but the ethical difference between whether a wolf attacked a lamb or whether people eat that lamb at Easter to celebrate the end of Lent is irrelevant to the lamb.

JvB: Exactly—I love that lamb-wolf situation. What worries me is that new emerging pseudoreligious way of dealing with nature that is transfiguring the whole construct of nature—that is, competing with scientific ways of describing our environment.

Coming back to my question about natural versus environmental disasters: To what extent is there a difference between natural and environmental catastrophes? What interests me here is nature as a perpetrator of violence. To what extent can this force of nature be used as a force in politics or even be exploited? Is it already actually a political force?

JT: Environmental catastrophes can even exceed natural catastrophes resulting from human activities. And that is the well-known story of the tanker that capsizes. There are effects of the large-scale contamination that can be traced back to Chernobyl. These are all environmental catastrophes that dramatically altered nature as well as peoples' lives. Chernobyl took the lives of two thousand individuals, which is more than many hurricanes.

JvB: But the biodiversity there is now greater than before. It was more catastrophic for humans if you consider the extent that human lives were affected while biodiversity has increased around Chernobyl.[2] *Natural scientists still disagree on how to categorize this catastrophe.*

JT: The biodiversity in that region has become greater because a decisive factor disappeared: use by humans. But for that we had to pay a price which was much too high. Another example: since the reunification of Germany, a lot of military training grounds, where Russian and American tanks used to drive around, have been closed, with a very good outcome for biodiversity. Opening these areas, partly for nature conservation purposes but also for nature-related tourism, has put pressure on biodiversity. When you try to describe this in a neutral way, you have to admit: seen in terms of biodiversity, the worst thing that can actually happen is not tourism, but agriculture.

This might now seem harsh for farmers, but from the perspective of biodiversity it is accurate. Natural catastrophes can occur again and again. Forest fires, for instance, come about in nature on a regular basis, and they are responsible for certain turnovers and also contribute to biodiversity in natural forests. They are not only caused by human beings as a result of negligent or willful actions, handling of fire, or real-estate speculation. Fire has always had an impact on nature. Political discussions are now turning from the natural catastrophes we are confronted with—not that a chemical plant has dumped chemicals into the water or that a chemical plant is on fire, or something like Chernobyl—to something that always existed in the past. The question then arises of whether human activities have contributed to the frequency and seriousness of such events. That is the discussion about climate change. The differences between an environmental catastrophe and a natural catastrophe suddenly begin to blur.

JvB: In the case of Fukushima, a tsunami, a natural catastrophe that cannot be blamed on human beings, triggered an environmental catastrophe. This incident had an enormous influence on realpolitik even though the disaster's source was geological.

JT: Exactly. It had an impact on German politics at least. In my perception it certainly ensured the phasing out of nuclear energy. It led to changes in other countries as well. It was only in Germany that it led to the reinstatement of the law that I had introduced in 2001, which was partially annulled by the CDU/FDP government in 2010. The term was simply extended, but since the term restrictions remained, the old law has been put into effect again. That means that it wasn't only the catastrophe, but the fact that the catastrophe occurred in the wake of a bitter dispute the previous year, at a moment when attempts were being made to reverse the 2001 decision to phase it out—a phasing out of the phasing out, so to speak. The German case is particular because of that back story. Without that story, the catastrophe might possibly have had the same effect that Three Mile Island in Harrisburg, Pennsylvania, or Chernobyl had. There were heated discussions for two years, and then things simply continued as usual.

JvB: If we transfer that example to power generated from coal, what kind of disaster would be required for coal to be phased out? What kind of disaster would be needed to bring politics or society to the point that they would be ready to make the changes necessary to achieve, for example, the 1.5-goal?

JT: When they are suffering, people are forced to make a compromise to do something about it, and the damage is then remedied a bit. The rivers have become cleaner, and the hole in ozone layer is closing. That has been the classic mechanism. However, it doesn't work for the climate crisis. There are various reasons for this. One is the emission of carbon dioxide into the atmosphere, which cannot simply be reversed. The second is what climate science calls tipping points: once they have gotten started, they are self-reinforcing processes. In the face of climate change, it's basically important to react—experience has taught us this—before such mechanisms emerge. And that's what makes things so incredibly difficult. That's why arguments such as "switching from coal to renewable energies creates jobs and also has economic advantages for particular regions" are actually superfluous from the perspective of climate protection. But how to set in motion a learning process, a process of change, in a society that can't wait until the tipping point has been reached—that is the question that needs to be asked today. Regarding the taiga and the amounts of carbon dioxide contained in the ground, essentially permafrost that is beginning to thaw, releasing carbon emissions—have we already exceeded the tipping point in this process? There are other researchers examining the glaciers in Greenland who say that melting processes are already going on today—processes that certainly don't always occur above ground, but also under the ice, meaning that corresponding canals are forming under the ice—to such an extent that you have to seriously wonder if this process can still be halted or only mitigated.

If the temperature were to increase by 2 or 2.6 degrees Celsius, which is the most likely scenario if we continue with business as usual, the ice in Greenland would not melt overnight but over a longer period of time. As a result, the sea level would rise seven meters, which would turn the Lüneburg Heath into the Lüneburg Sea.

JvB: That is exactly what I mean. These tipping points might not be visible, but their effect is immense. I examined something that is very visible: last year's forest fire. I don't know whether you remember when suddenly there was a fire in Sweden. It was the first fire that season, and Europeans were upset about it. Poland and Germany and many other countries sent fire brigades. When I then finally arrived at the fire's source—it was in a military training area—I had to fight my way through until I met a high-ranking fire fighter who let me accompany him. He explained to me, while on the way to set a counter fire, that he didn't really understand why people were so upset. On a few trees he showed me the marks of a fire fifty years ago and one hundred years ago. He said that fire is totally normal, that we only extinguish them so that people do not get upset. It's a natural process. In the European media it was presented as if it were the first time that Sweden experienced such a wildfire, and as if it were completely out of control.

JT: And people first become aware of them when there are being reported on and/or because people are injured or lose their homes. There were certainly fires in California with fatalities in the past, but now that Thomas Gottschalk's house has burned down it is all over the media.

JvB: I have the impression that such pictures play a very important role in the political arena.

JT: Yes, and that's why the pictures that people saw of Chernobyl and the pictures of Harrisburg—few people from my generation remember that—didn't suffice. Pictures inherently mobilize. But other social factors were needed, something to supplement the pictures, to translate impulse into action. I think that the picture of the destroyed reactors was necessary, that practically iconic picture of Chernobyl, or that famous television camera footage of Fukushima, which actually had nothing to do with the real problem. It was an explosion. Nevertheless, what stuck in people's minds was that an atomic power plant had exploded. This iconography was of central and crucial significance. But horror and avoidance always have two effects on the human psyche. One is acting preventatively, and the other is suppressing them and fatalism. Both responses are inherent in us.

JvB: Absolutely. That emotional reaction to images is also an important factor for the next topic that I find relevant. In your book you write that a lot of people being active in green parties have an "emotional, romanticized, aesthetic, quasireligious relationship to nature."[3] I've observed a similar development not just among Green Party voters. The significance of the Christian religion is dwindling, and churches are somehow losing power. Also the number of people who vote for the Green party, but also deal with nature spiritually, and sometimes behave in an almost religious way toward nature. This is not just an awkward subcultural group, it includes people with influence and a certain societal elite.

They are people who perhaps would have gone to church in the past, but now search for meaning somewhere else, who also feel bad in their relation to nature. I think that this is a transferal of Christian original sin to their feelings about nature. In that perception human beings are per se something evil in comparison to nature, because wherever human beings are, nature is suffering. Do you think that this mystification continues? Will this nature fiction become a big pseudo religion? Or is it only a minor side effect?

JT: Well, it does exist, but I doubt that it will spread. It also exists in day-to-day life. Romanticizing nature is not something that's somehow specific to people who vote for the Green party. The German forest is an ideological myth. The German forest is a plantation that consistently lacks species diversity, to be extremely precise. But the fact that people think that nature is pure, and that we and our problems are rather problematic, is problematic in itself. What we experience as nature today has indeed already been manipulated by us in many ways. That's why I said before that this separation between what nature is and what we consider natural denies the other aspect: that people naturally have an influence on reality. That's why people use the term "Anthropocene." But we shouldn't fool ourselves. Human beings are also part of nature—they grew out of it. Perhaps people have emancipated themselves a bit. But they can't emancipate themselves from specific things.

JvB: And now we've come back to that separation of nature and environment again. What I am trying to get at is what will our feeling about nature be in ten or twenty years? What will nature mean to us? Will the term "nature" still exist, or will everyone by then understand that this separation no longer exists?

JT: I think it will still exist. I think instead that we are attracted to such a tendency. The more that nature is designed by human beings, the more it is fetishized as natural. It's paradoxical.

For example, there are initiatives that criticize wind turbines because so many insects die because of them. But many insects are eaten by birds. Wind turbines are also killing birds, although the number is markedly lower than the amount killed by cars. This shows how nature, or a specific aspect of nature, is instrumentalized for conflicts of interest between different social groups.

JvB: Exactly. That's why I think that natural catastrophes play a big role. I think that something will happen in the next twenty years. The environment will change intensively. And I think that positions such as those that Trump is now taking are the last instance that such a position can even exist. I imagine that there will be a coexistence of various green strategies in the future. And the political dispute will then be more about HOW we want to help the environment or HOW we can repair it.

JT: That's the optimistic variant. I have optimistically observed that people merely fight about the means, even if the objective is the same. Now there is suddenly a boom in aggressive, anti-ecological awareness, which is not only found in the Midwest of the United States.

I don't know what will happen. One side wants to get to the root of the problem and promote renewable energies, while the other wants to regulate things by making climate engineering manageable and using carbon capture and storage.

For example, when you see the accumulation of microplastics in the food chain due to the extreme pollution from plastic—these are actually problems that could be solved. I'm not being pessimistic and prophesizing that a big catastrophe is on its way. Humankind has often found solutions to such things in the end.

JvB: If in ten years we are still fighting about the same political topics as we are today, it would actually be the best case because that would mean that everything has so far still held up relatively well, something that is actually out of the question if you consider the report of the Intergovernmental Panel on Climate Change (IPCC). In ten years, twenty years, there will already be a massively perceptible climate change.

JT: It's already perceptible today. If you compare what the IPCC experts were saying when I was Minister of the Environment with the reality today, with what it predicted for today, the panel would be forced to recognize that their prognosis was extremely cautious and gave a rosier view of the situation. They may have a reputation of being doomsayers, but if you compare the old reports with the current reality, they were too optimistic.

There's an interplay between society and nature. And, for nature, it incidentally doesn't matter whether humankind survives. That has always been true. Human beings are one of many species. If we go extinct, there will be others. It is human beings with their knowledge and abilities who are faced with the question of whether we will manage to preserve a planet that is livable for human beings. I firmly believe that the frequency of catastrophes will increase and that natural catastrophes will again and again call the existence of humankind into question if we do not act now.

Jürgen Trittin and Julius von Bismarck met in April 2019 in Julius von Bismarck's studio.

---

1 During the Nazi regime, landscape was seen as a culture-shaping element that inevitably resulted in interaction between the land and its inhabitants. This basic idea resulted in both ideologically charged landscape projects in occupied territories and attempts to preserve local nature. Although it contains elements of contemporary environmental conservation, the Nazi concept of landscape was often motivated by economic interests and served to legitimize ideological goals. Under Jürgen Trittin as Federal Environmental Minister, the Federal Ministry of Environment, Nature Conservation, and Nuclear Safety encouraged Germans to reflect on the perception of nature and nature conservation in the Nazi era and their significance for the current political situation. For more information see Joachim Radkau and Frank Uekötter, eds., *Naturschutz und Nationalsozialismus* (Frankfurt am Main, 2003), which includes a contribution by Jürgen Trittin.

2 The nature around Chernobyl, which since the reactor catastrophe in 1986 has for the most part been free from human influences, is a unique area for research. There is an ongoing debate among scientists about how to evaluate the consequences of the accident. On one side of the debate researchers are intensively investigating the consequences of radioactive radiation on the environment and constantly publishing scientific studies on the genetic changes and deteriorated health observed in animals as a result of the nuclear catastrophe. On the opposite side researchers are examining the enormous increase in local biodiversity. Due to the absence of human intervention nature has been able to regenerate itself, and far from being disastrous, the state of nature is better than before the beyond-design-basis accident. See T. G. Deryabina, S. V. Kuchmel, L. L. Nagorskaya, T. G. Hinton, J. C. Beasley, A. Lerebours, and J. T. Smith, "Long-Term Census Data Reveal Abundant Wildlife Populations at Chernobyl," *Current Biology Magazine*, October 5, 2015, R824–26, https://www.cell.com/action/showPdf?pii=S0960-9822%2815%2900988-4.

3 Jürgen Trittin, *Stillstand Made in Germany* (Munich, 2014), 113.

Die Luft muss man sich wegdenken
(One Must Think Away the Air)

2017
Steel wire, 800 × 1100 cm

Flowing lines of bent steel flow through the exhibition space, its chassis glinting in the light. Suspended from the ceiling, *Die Luft muss sich wegdenken* floats at the height of a human figure, tracing a topography of peaks and troughs through its precise curves. This interplay of bent and welded steel rods forms the image of a wave that was 3D-scanned from the Irish coastline during the 2017 hurricane Ophelia, the worst storm to make landfall there in fifty years. Digitally remodeled, the ephemeral disturbance of the waters was converted, at scale, to curving radii and then pressed into steel with a wire-bending machine—a computer-controlled device normally used for industrial mass production. While attempting to describe the ocean's volatile surface, whipped up by the wind, the scanning process proves incapable of fully capturing its dynamism. These errors and blind spots mechanically recorded in the sculptural description.

ONE MUST THINK AWAY THE AIR

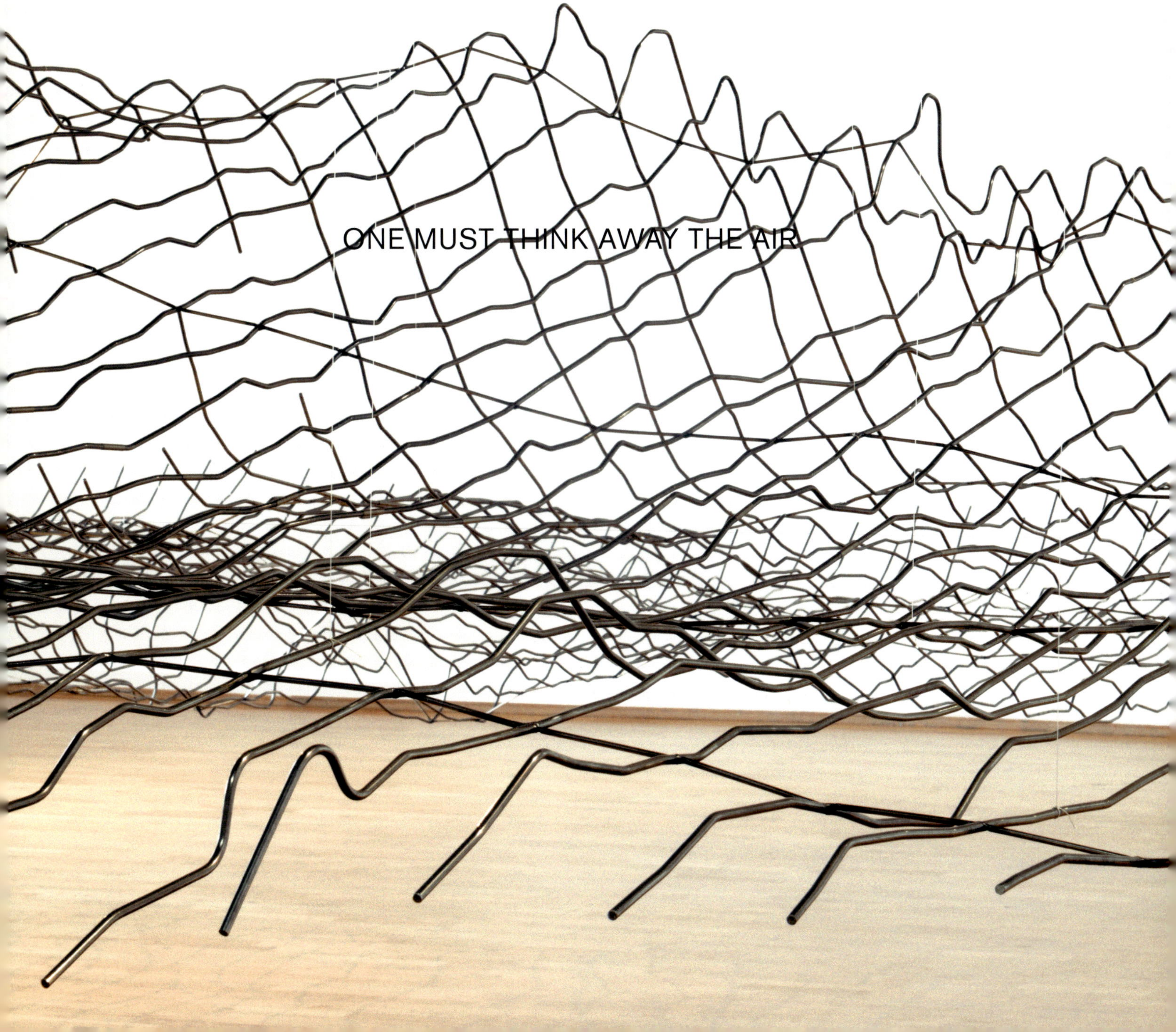

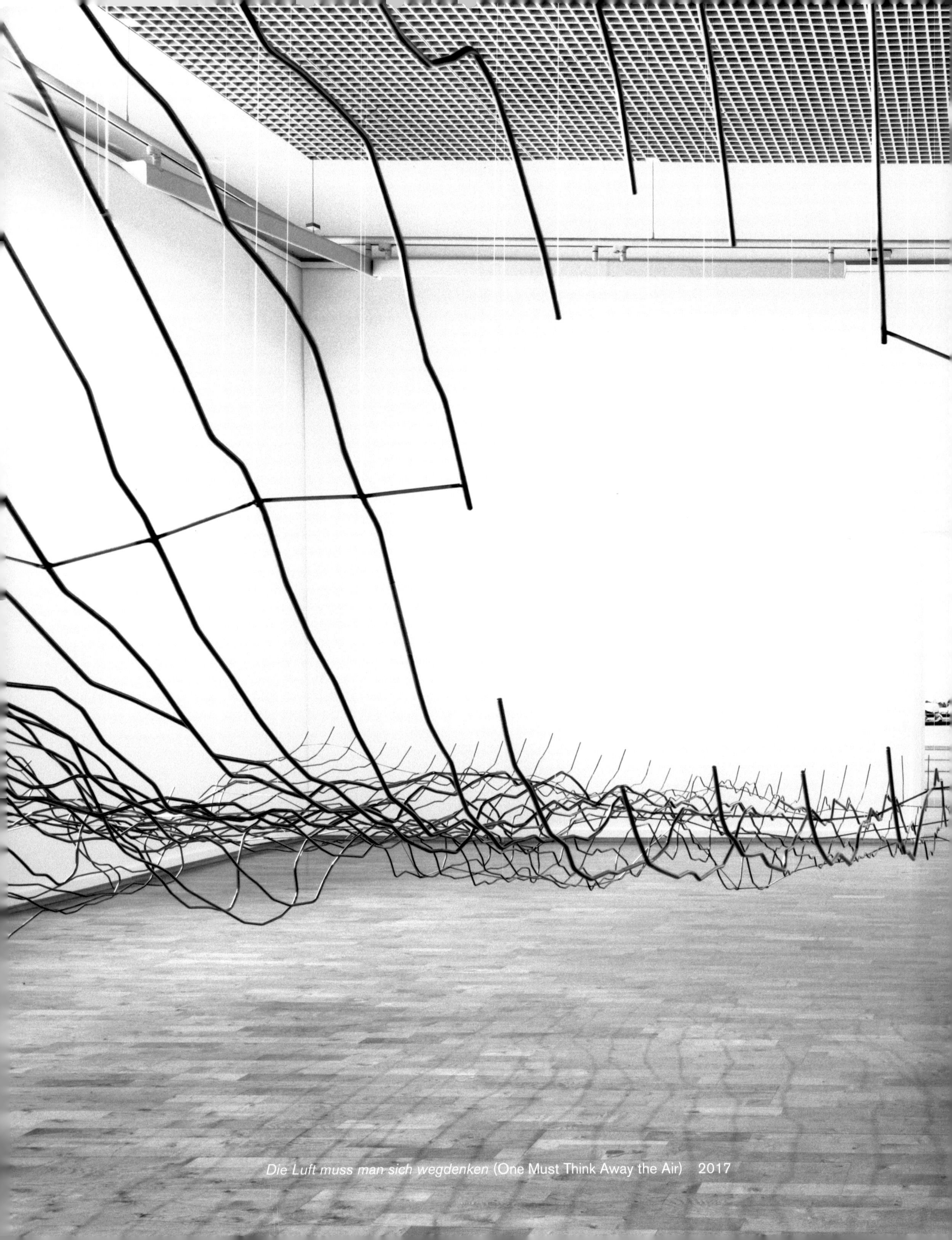

Die Luft muss man sich wegdenken (One Must Think Away the Air) 2017

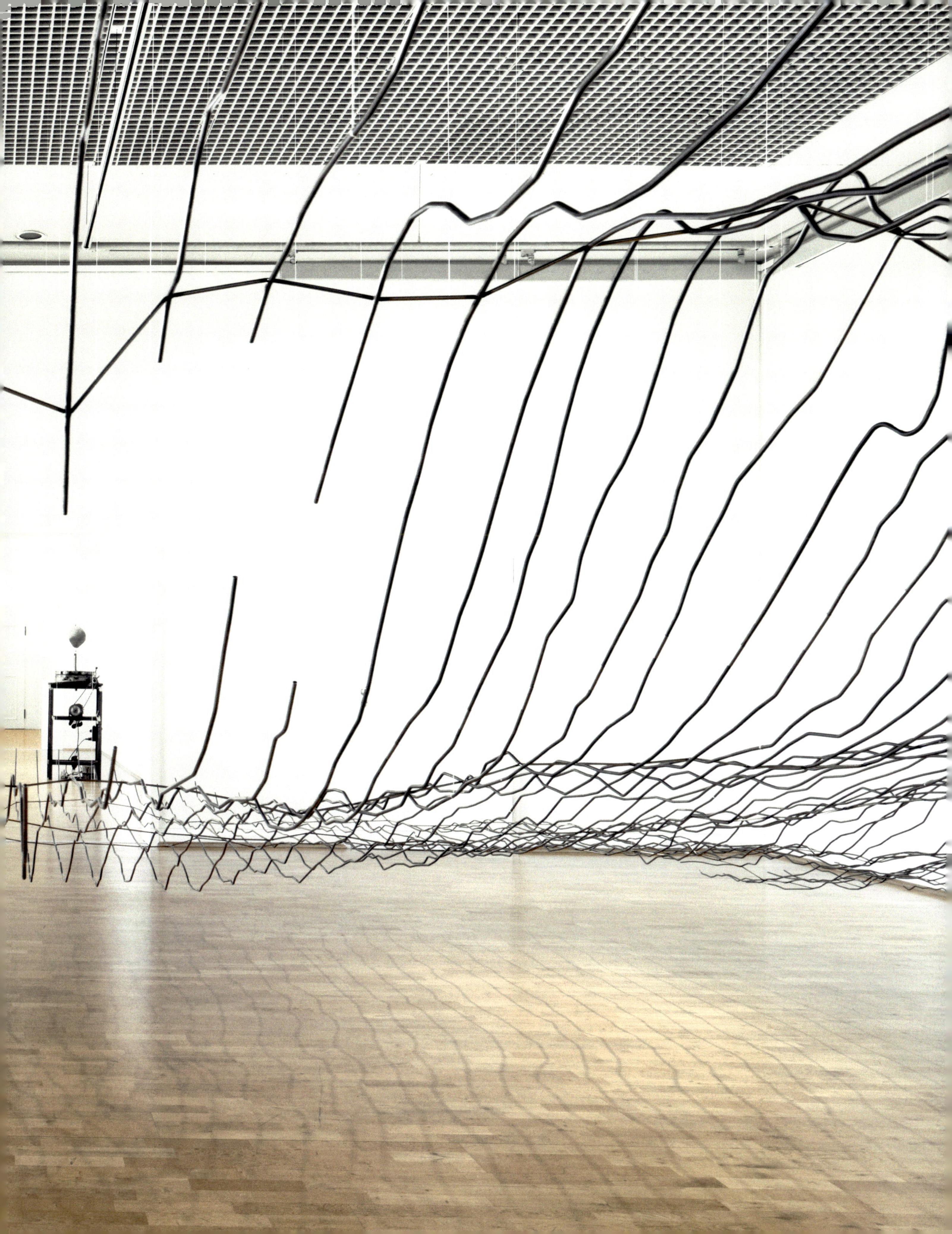

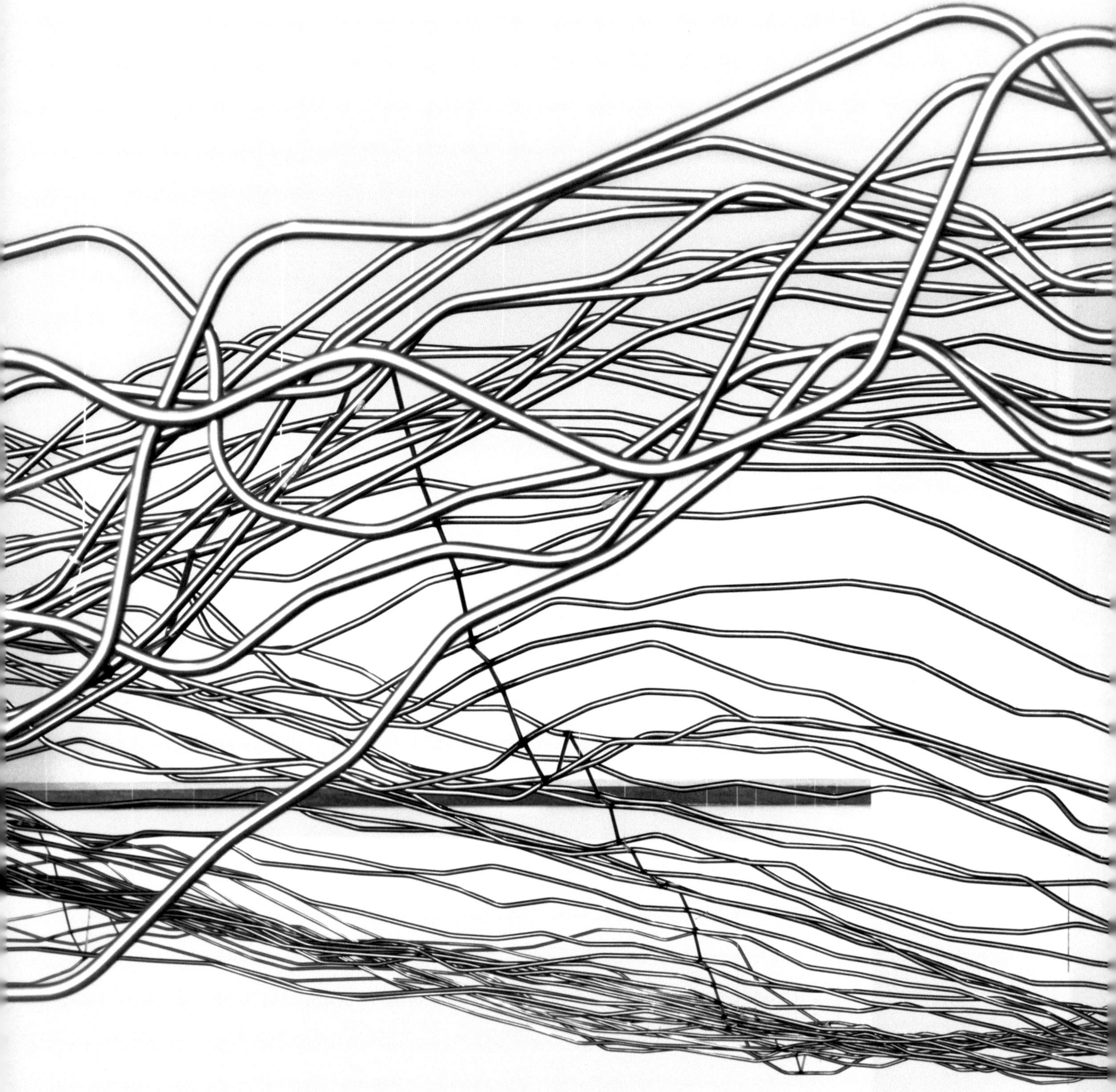

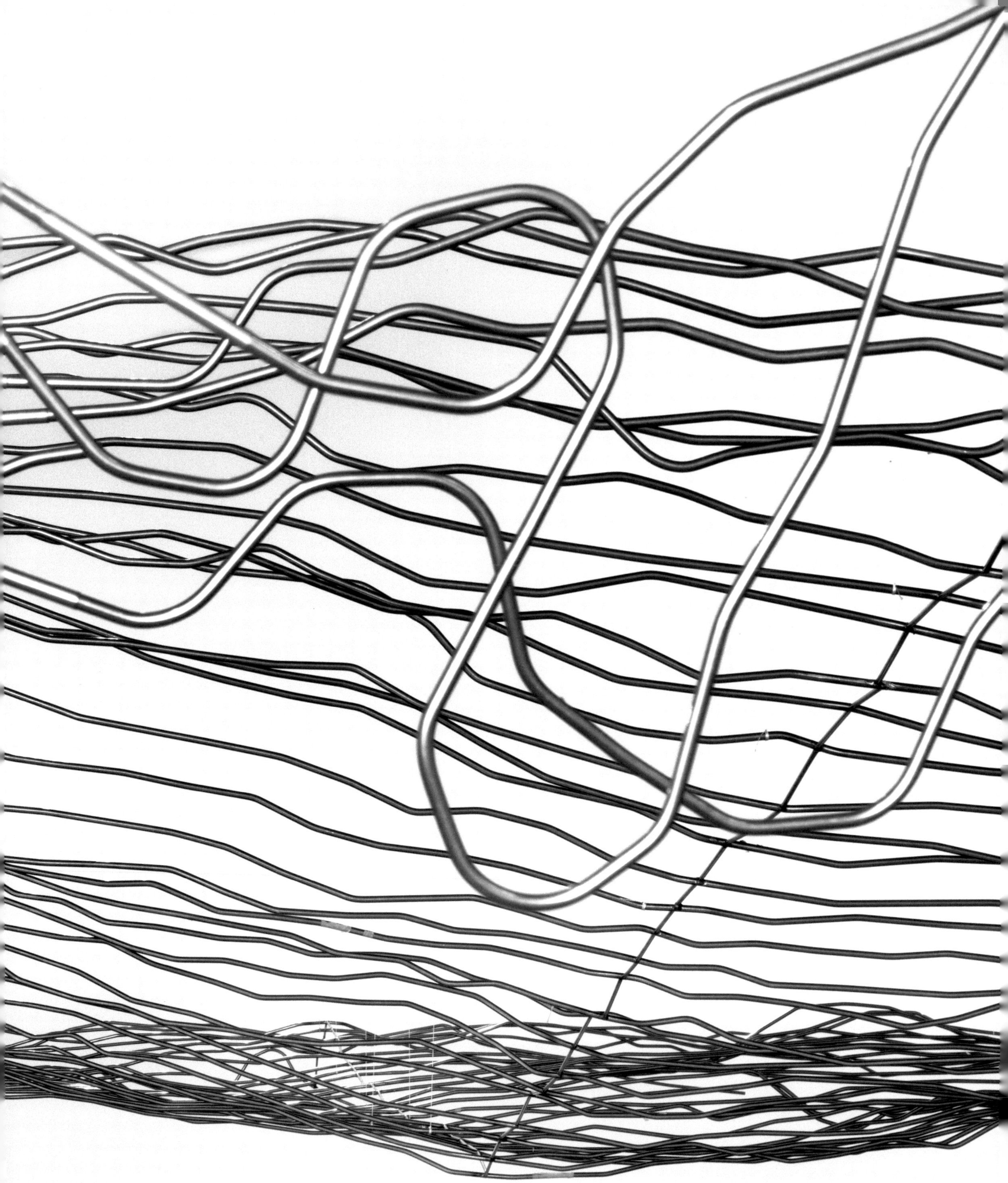

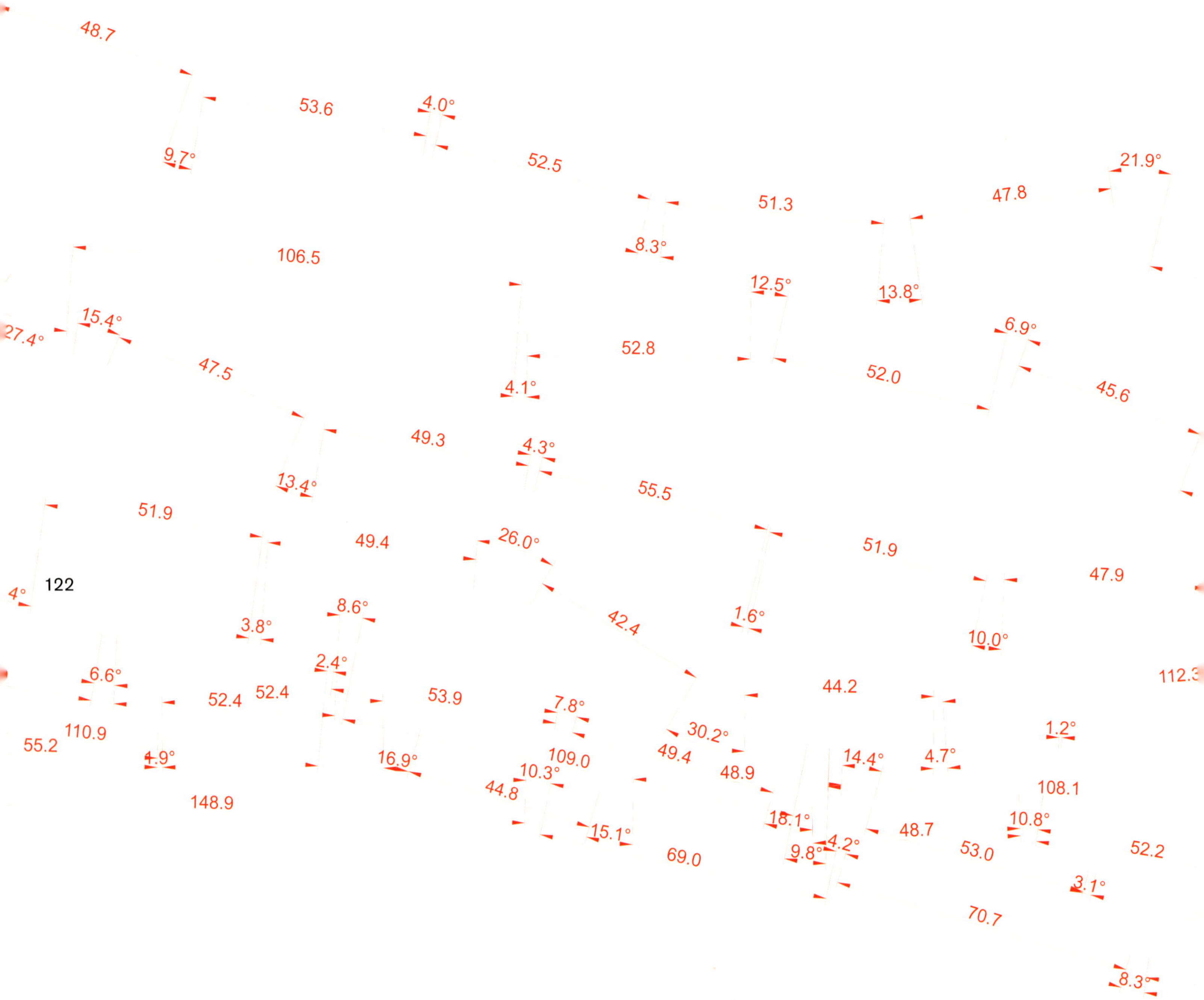

48.7
53.6
4.0°
9.7°
52.5
21.9°
47.8
51.3
8.3°
106.5
12.5°
13.8°
15.4°
27.4°
6.9°
52.8
47.5
52.0
4.1°
45.6
49.3
4.3°
13.4°
55.5
51.9
49.4
26.0°
51.9
47.9
4°
8.6°
3.8°
42.4
1.6°
10.0°
2.4°
6.6°
112.3
44.2
52.4
52.4
53.9
7.8°
30.2°
1.2°
55.2
110.9
4.9°
16.9°
109.0
49.4
14.4°
4.7°
48.9
10.3°
148.9
44.8
108.1
18.1°
10.8°
15.1°
48.7
4.2°
9.8°
53.0
69.0
52.2
3.1°
70.7
8.3°

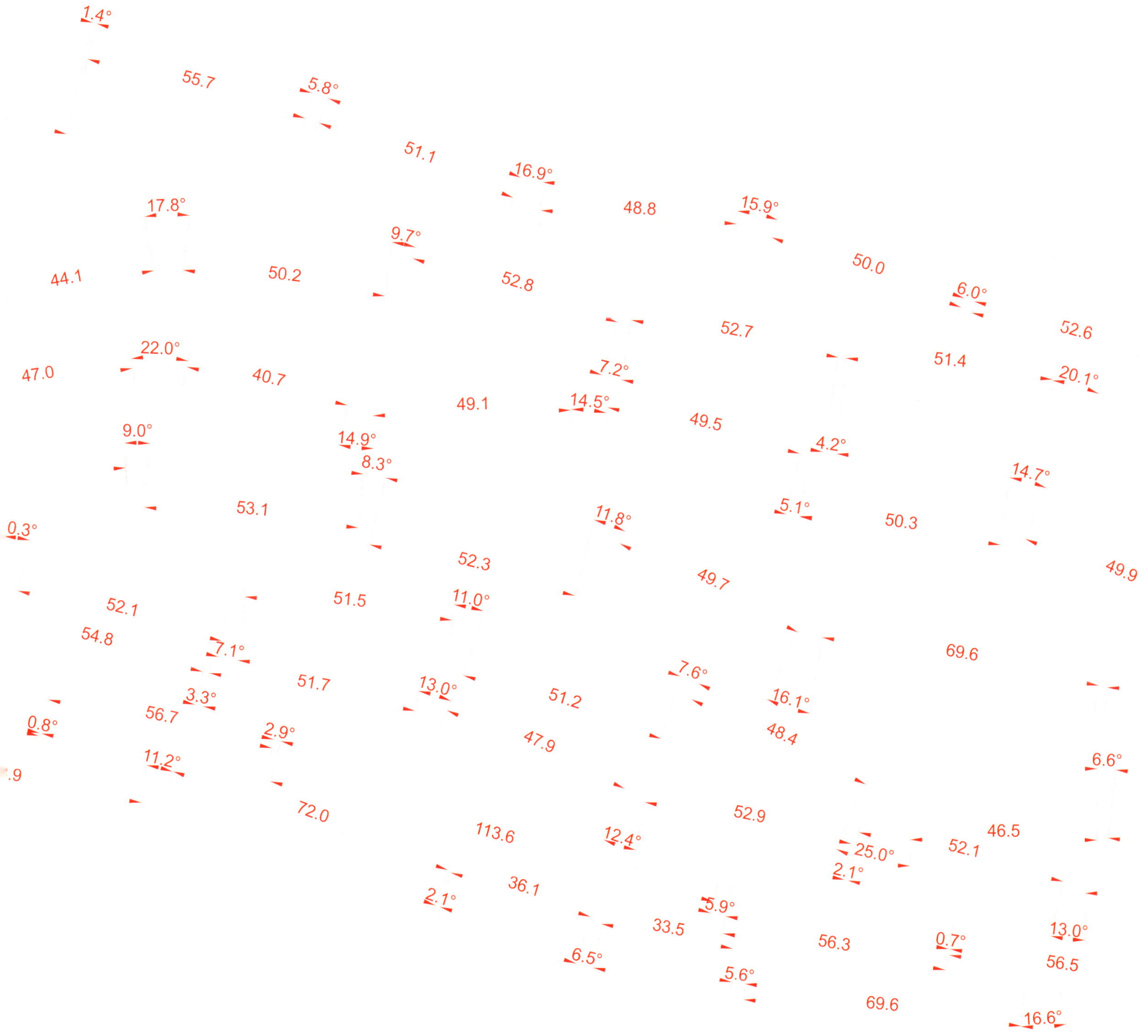
1.4°
55.7
5.8°
51.1
16.9°
48.8
15.9°
17.8°
9.7°
44.1
50.2
52.8
50.0
6.0°
52.7
52.6
22.0°
47.0
40.7
7.2°
51.4
20.1°
49.1
14.5°
49.5
9.0°
14.9°
8.3°
4.2°
14.7°
53.1
0.3°
11.8°
5.1°
50.3
52.3
49.7
49.9
52.1
51.5
11.0°
54.8
7.1°
69.6
51.7
13.0°
51.2
7.6°
16.1°
3.3°
56.7
0.8°
2.9°
47.9
48.4
11.2°
6.6°
.9
72.0
52.9
113.6
12.4°
25.0°
46.5
52.1
2.1°
36.1
2.1°
5.9°
33.5
56.3
0.7°
13.0°
6.5°
5.6°
56.5
69.6
16.6°

Die Mimik der Tethys
(The Expressions of Tethys)

2019
High-sea buoy, motors, cable winches, site-specific installation

Silently, a high-sea buoy, its corroded metal surface covered with traces of shells and seaweed, glides overhead through the museum atrium. The massive object appears to fly through the air weightlessly, moving along three dimensions. In perpetual motion, it registers the movements of its normal location at the SEM-REV test site, off the French coast in the Atlantic Ocean. Sometimes calm and gentle, at others given to sudden and wide-ranging motion, its varying behavior has a hypnotic effect. High-sea buoys are interchanged for maintenance reasons on a regular basis. During one such an exchange, the artist placed an accelerometer on a buoy being installed at sea. Continuously transmitting movement data via satellite to its relocated double, suspended in the exhibition space, the information guides eight electric motors and cable winches, the latter precisely reproducing the former's movements. Inspired by the figure of Tethys—a sea goddess in Greek mythology, the daughter of the sky (Ouranos) and the earth (Gaia)—*Die Mimik der Tethys* functions as a barometer of nature's moods as expressed by the constantly changing surface of the ocean. The steel object's irregular rise and fall conjures the sea's presence in the museum. Its ocean referent is not the romanticized one that commonly features seafaring tales but another, registering the sea of data in which we are all immersed today.

THE EXPRESSIONS OF TETHYS

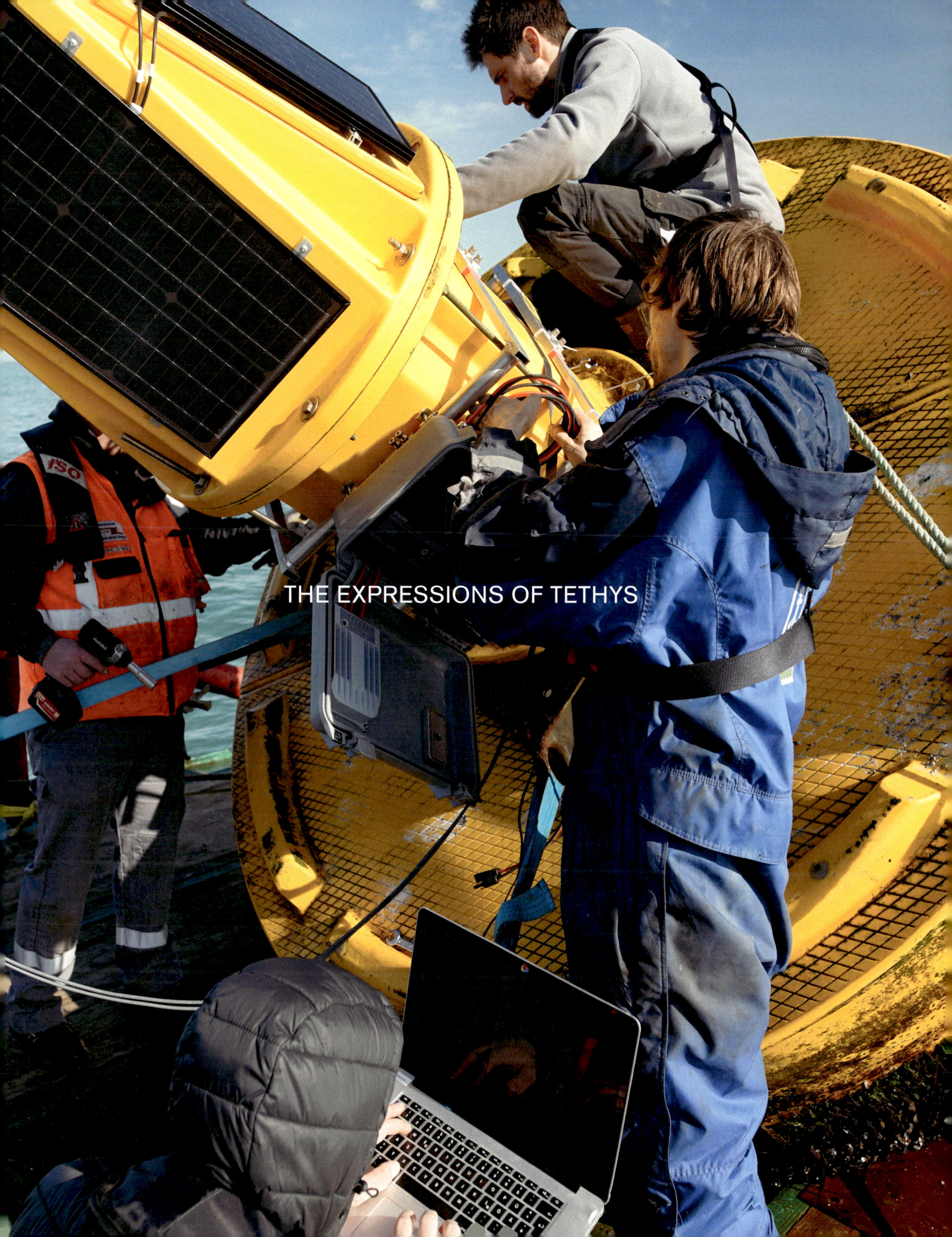

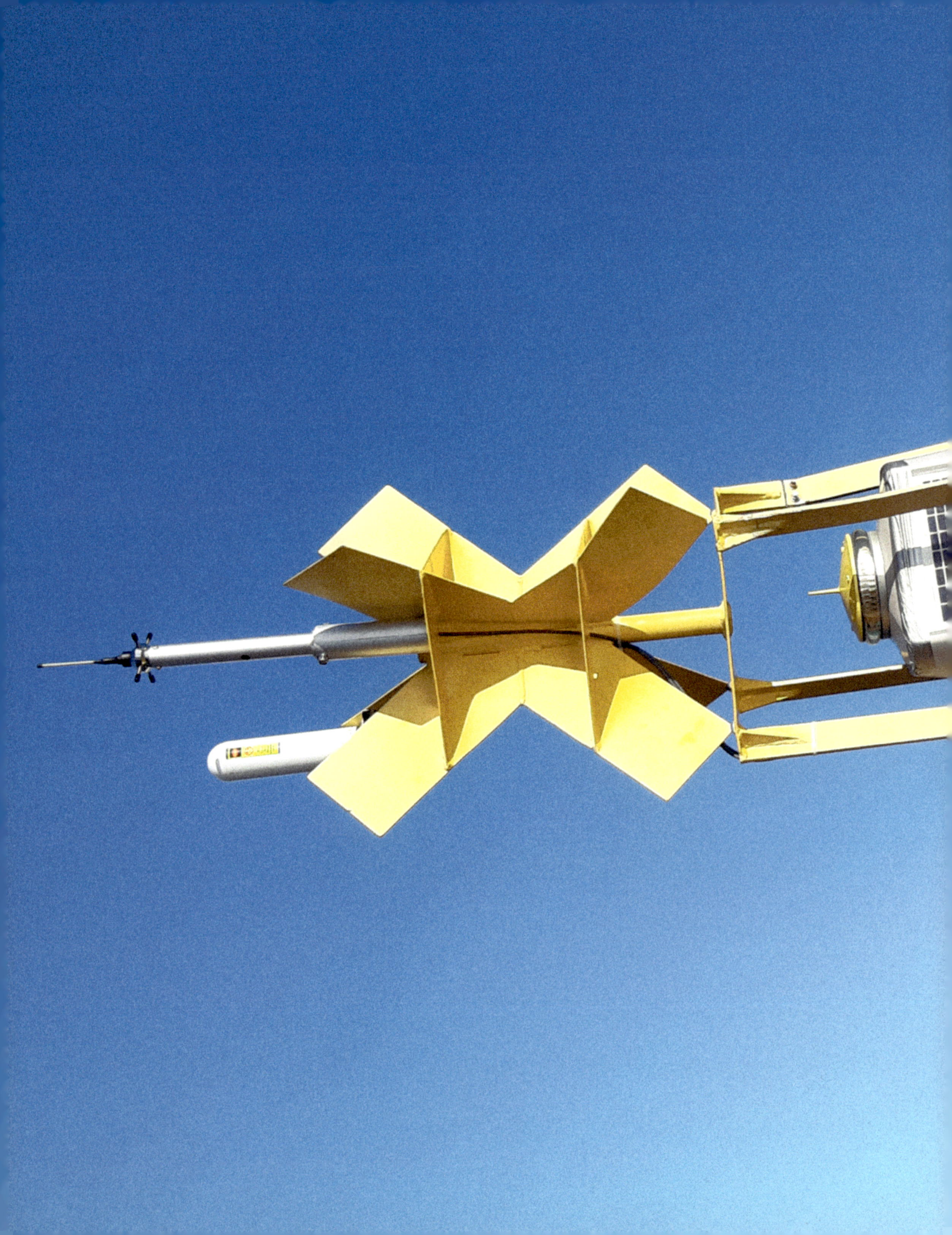

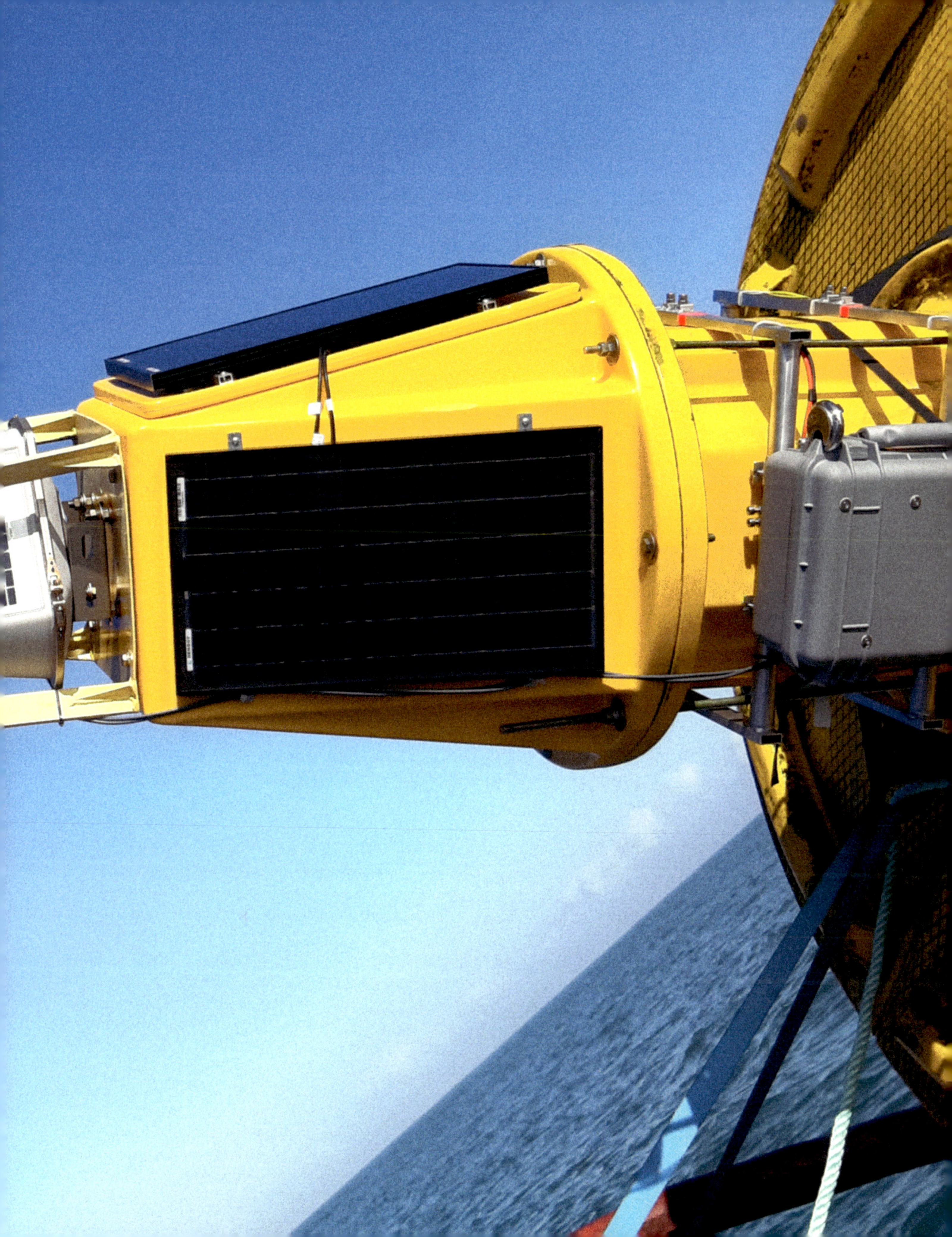

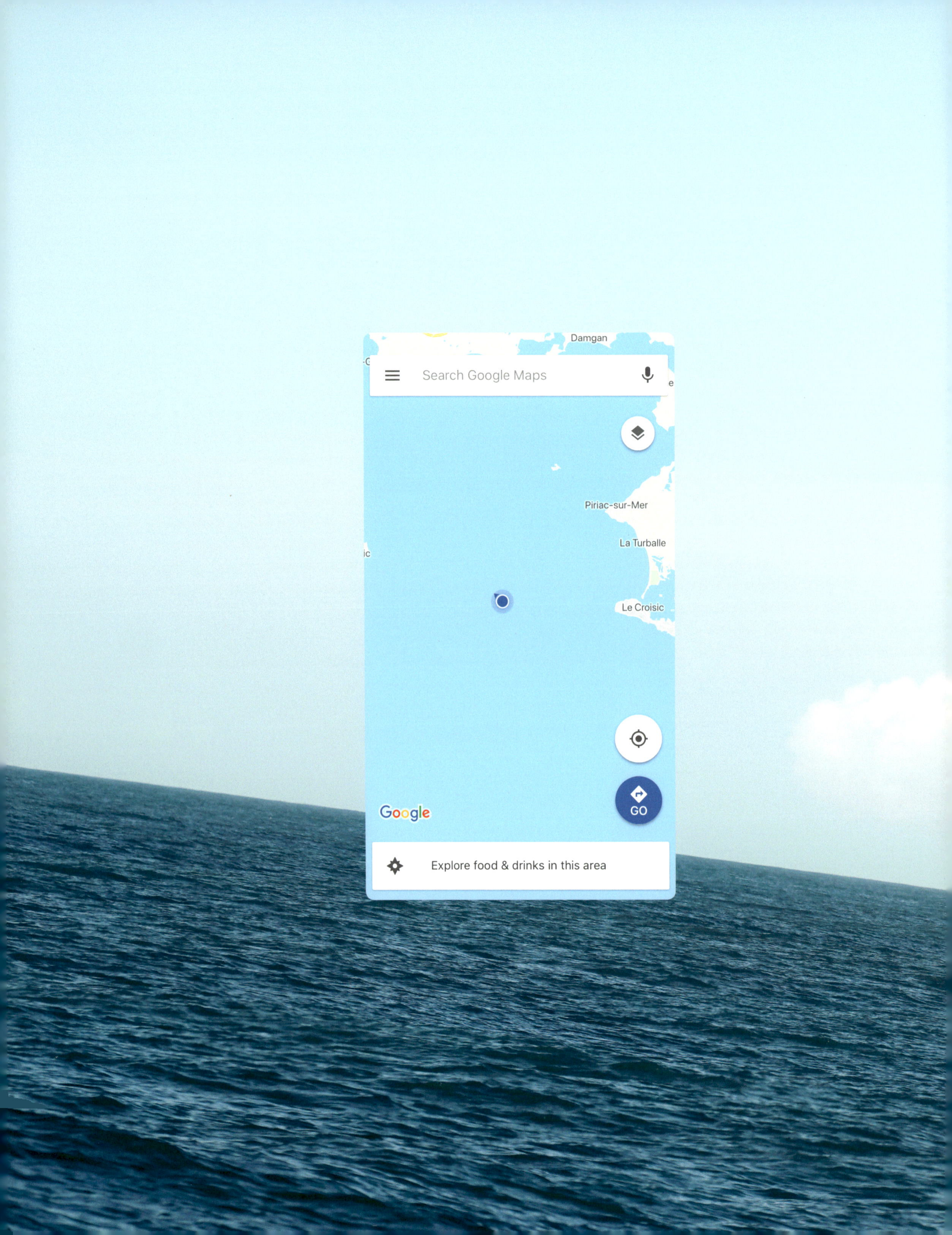
Damgan
Search Google Maps
Piriac-sur-Mer
La Turballe
Le Croisic
Google
GO
Explore food & drinks in this area

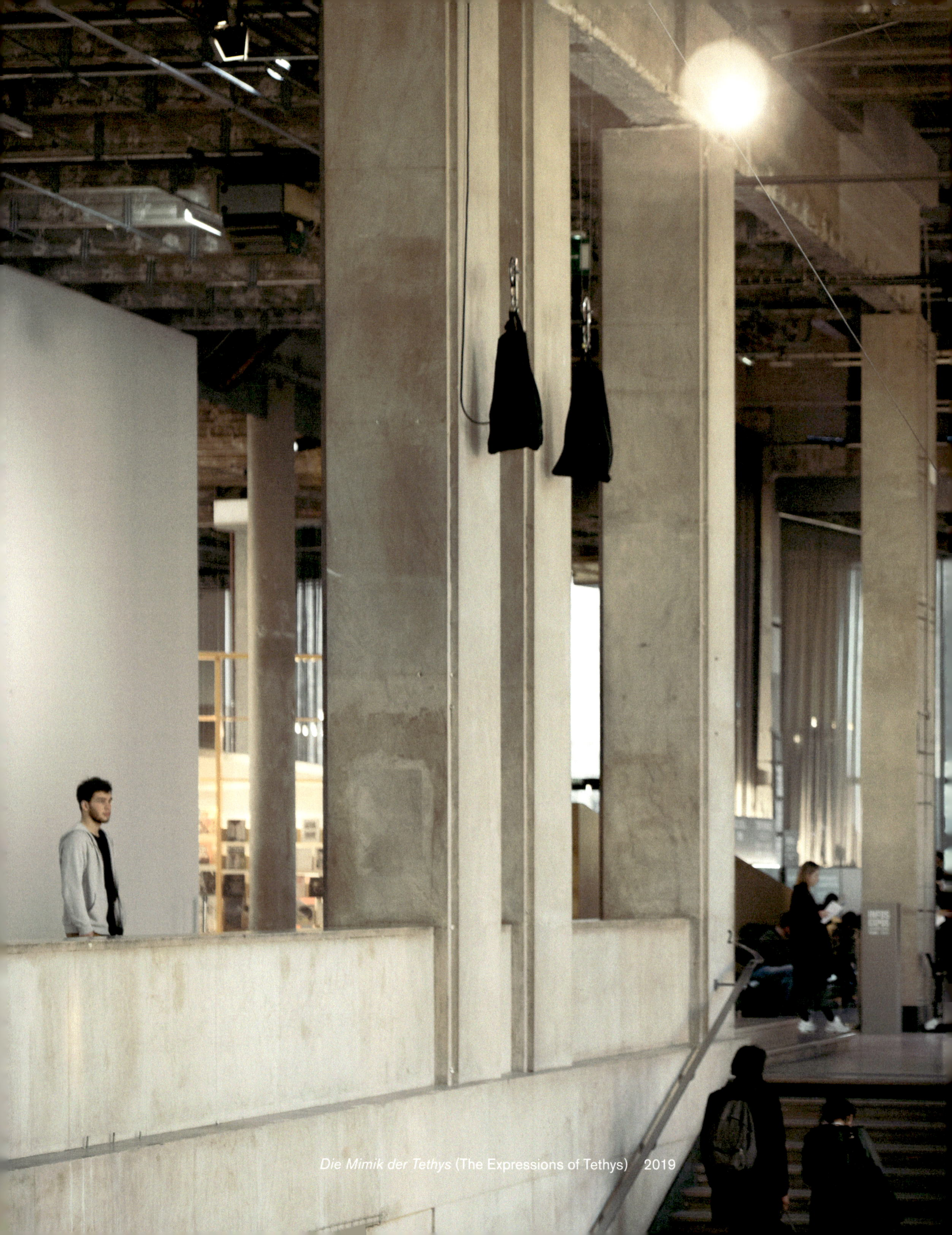

Die Mimik der Tethys (The Expressions of Tethys) 2019

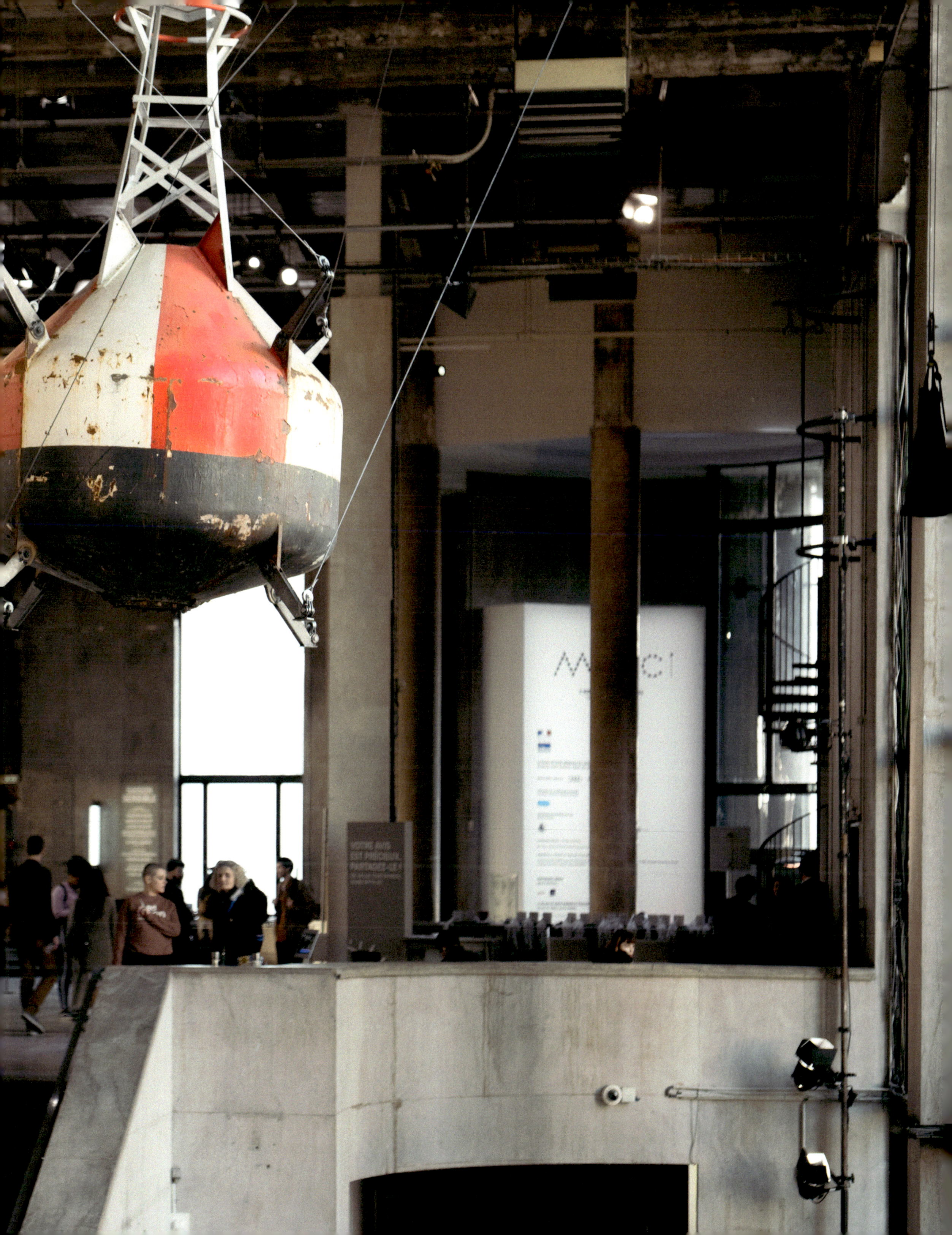

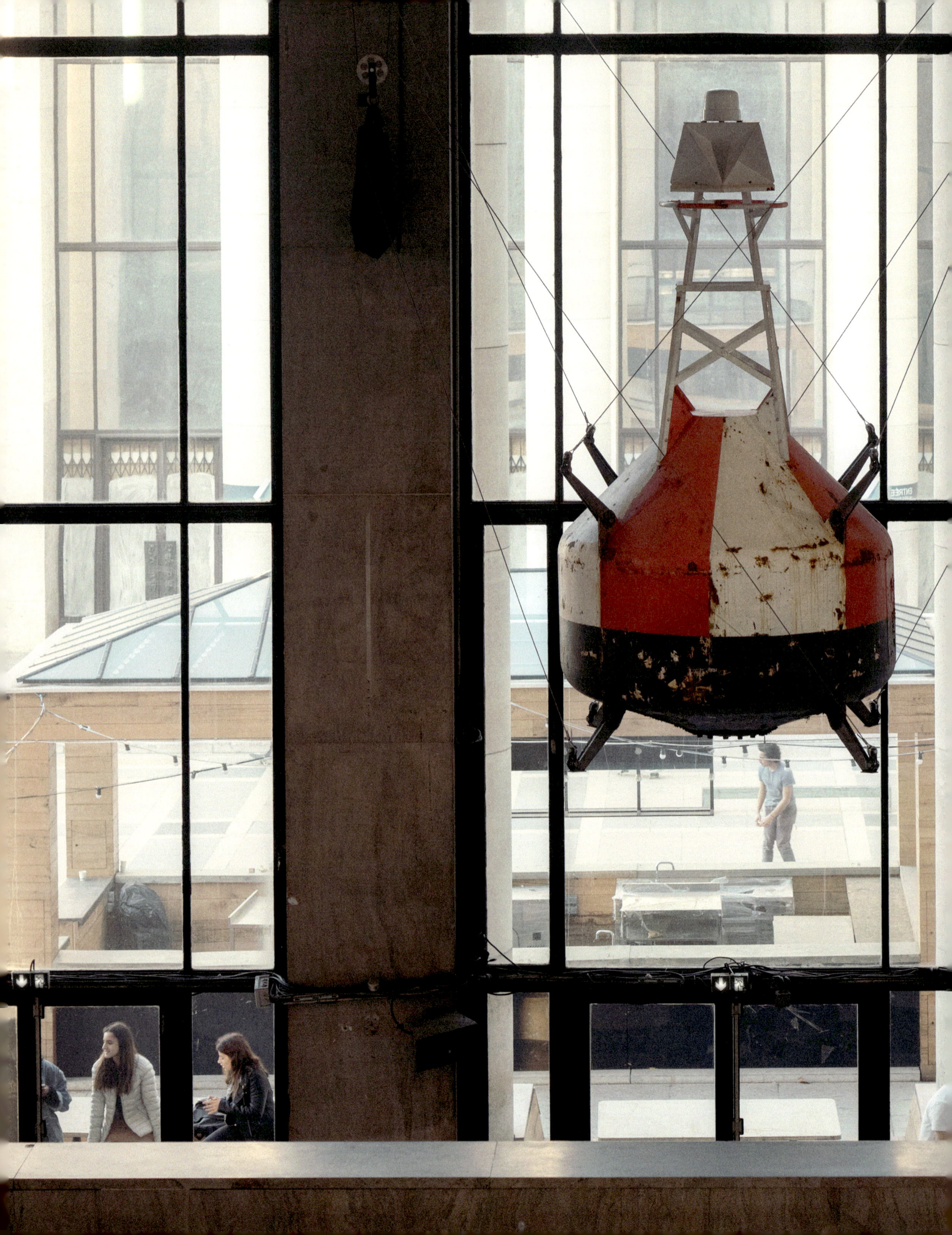

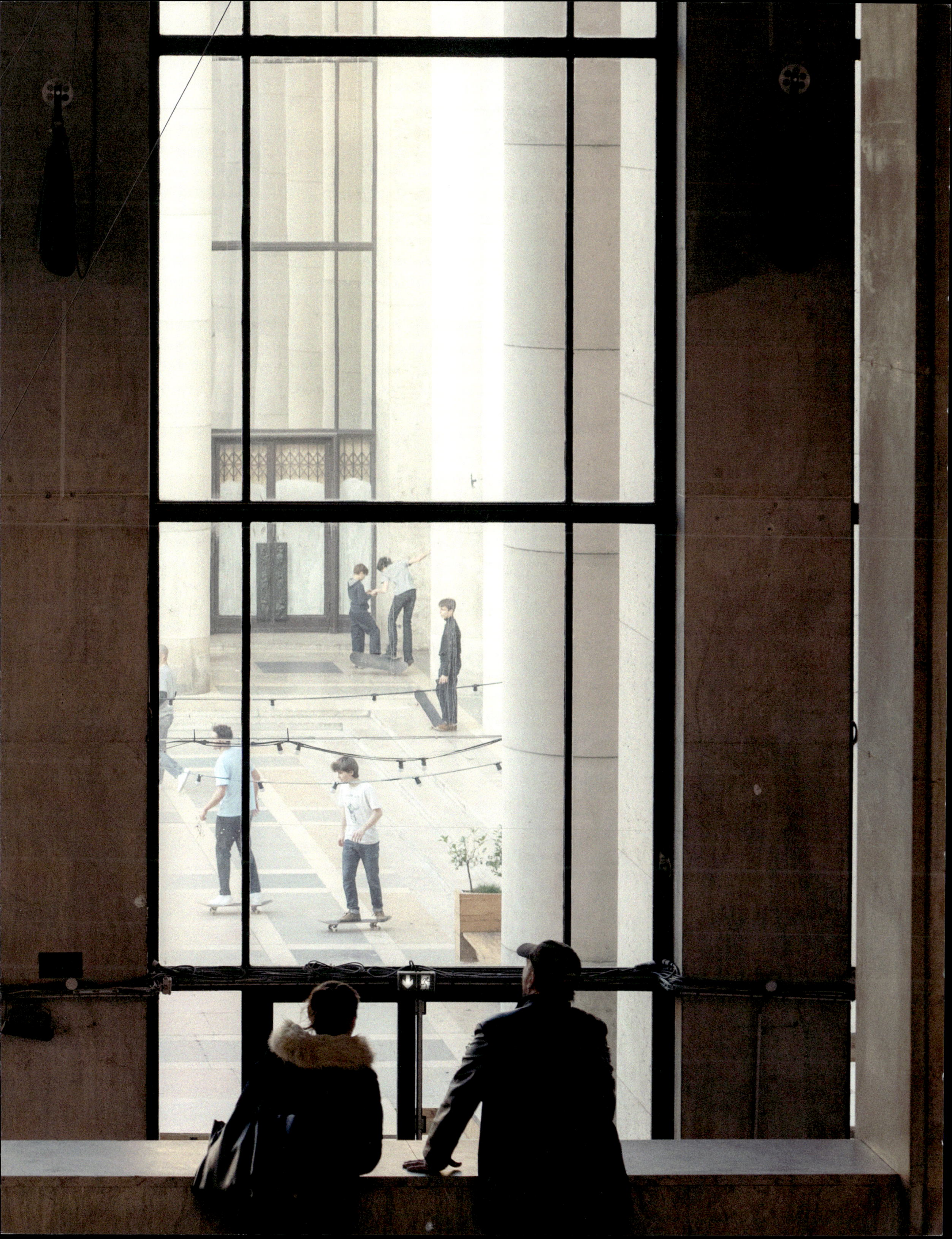

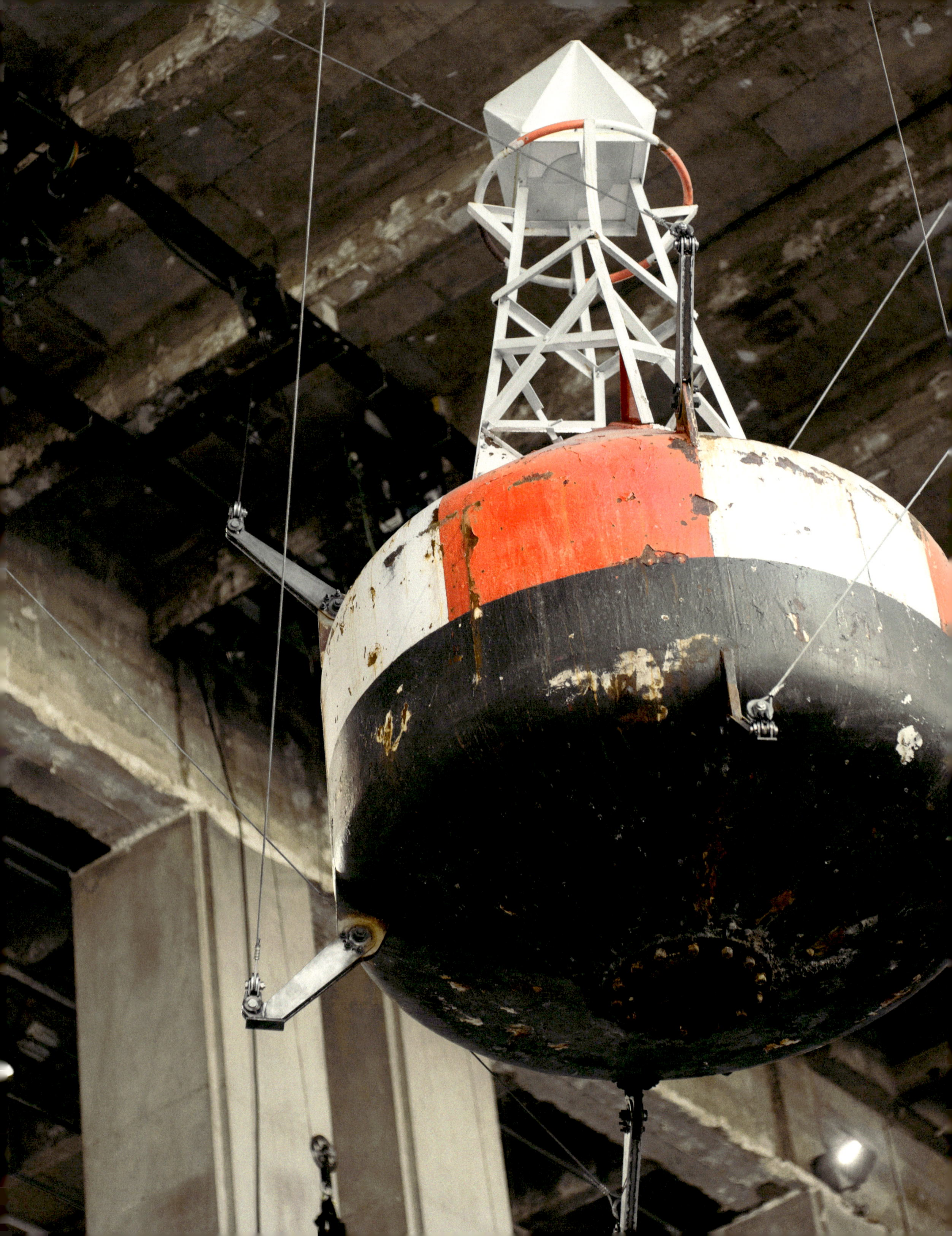

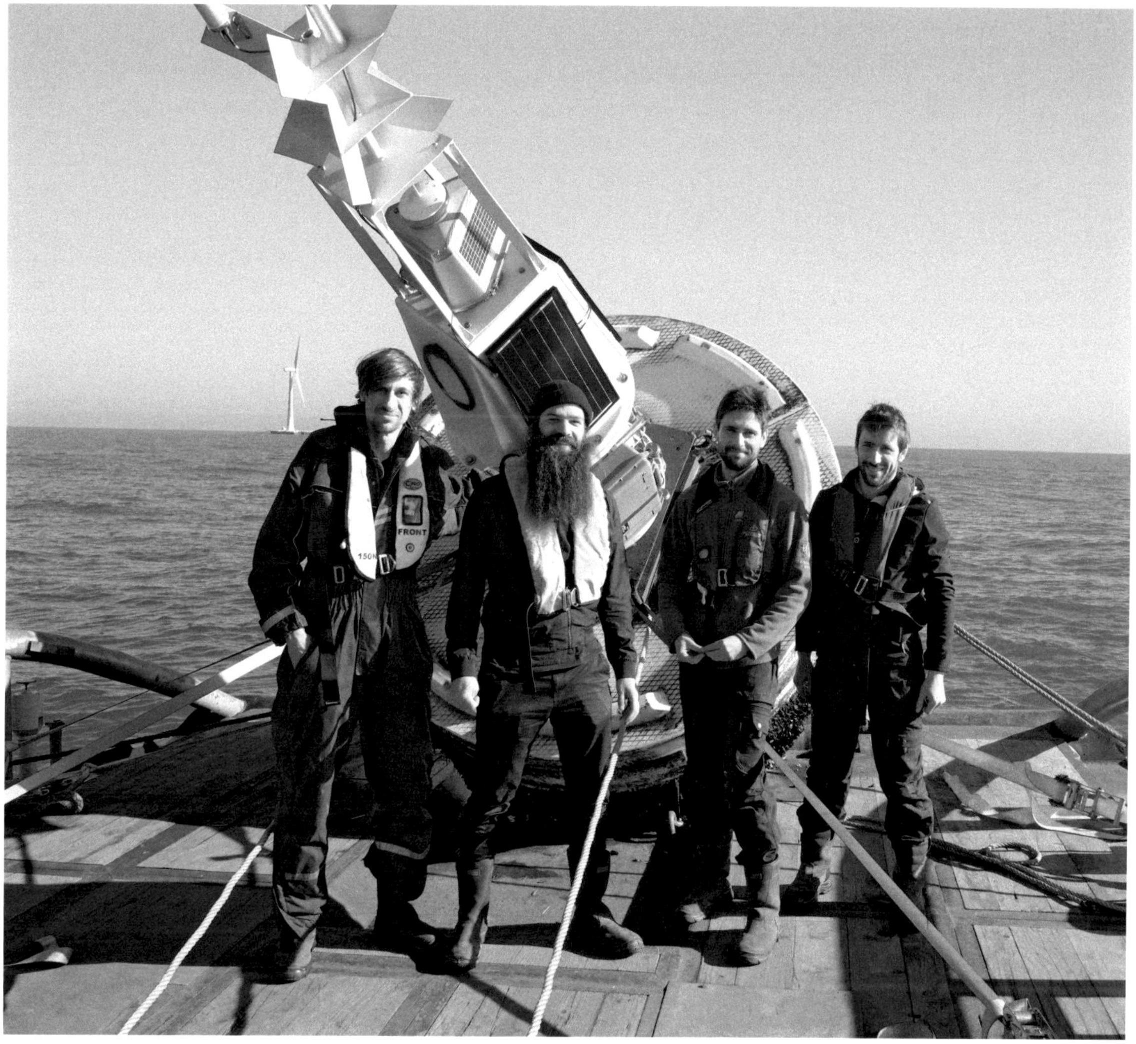

Atlantic Ocean, Biscaya 2019

Fire with Fire

2018–19
(Work in progress)

In continuation of his works on natural disasters, Julius von Bismarck turned his attention to wildfires in 2018, which saw one of the most destructive fire seasons on record worldwide. Building on research in progress, the artist visited Sweden, Germany, and California to film and photograph wildfires and their management. In order to gain access to restricted areas, he was supported by Swedish firefighters and the California Department of Forestry and Fire Protection. The photographs and film stills in this book are part of ongoing visual research on the phenomenon of fire that is a work in progress.

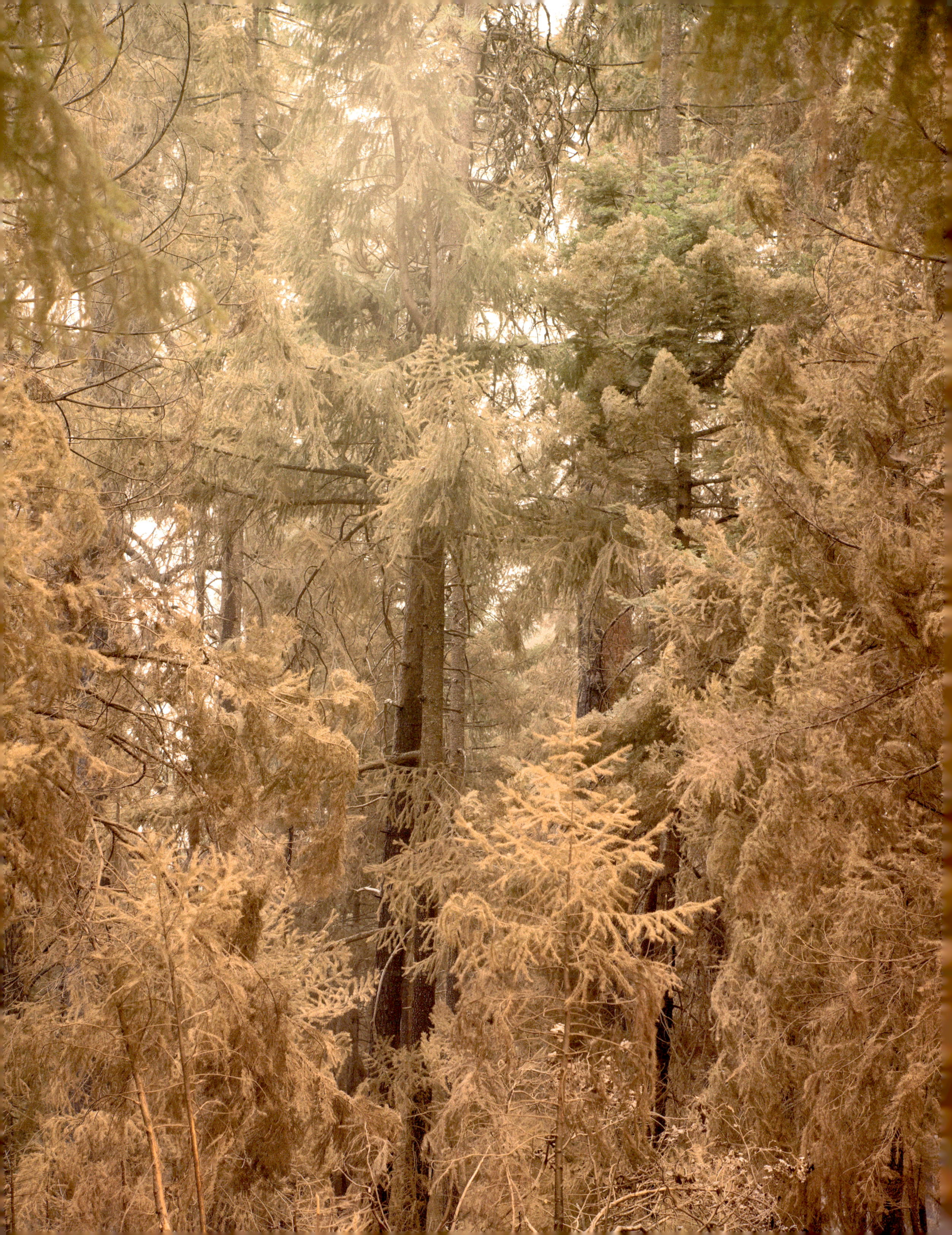

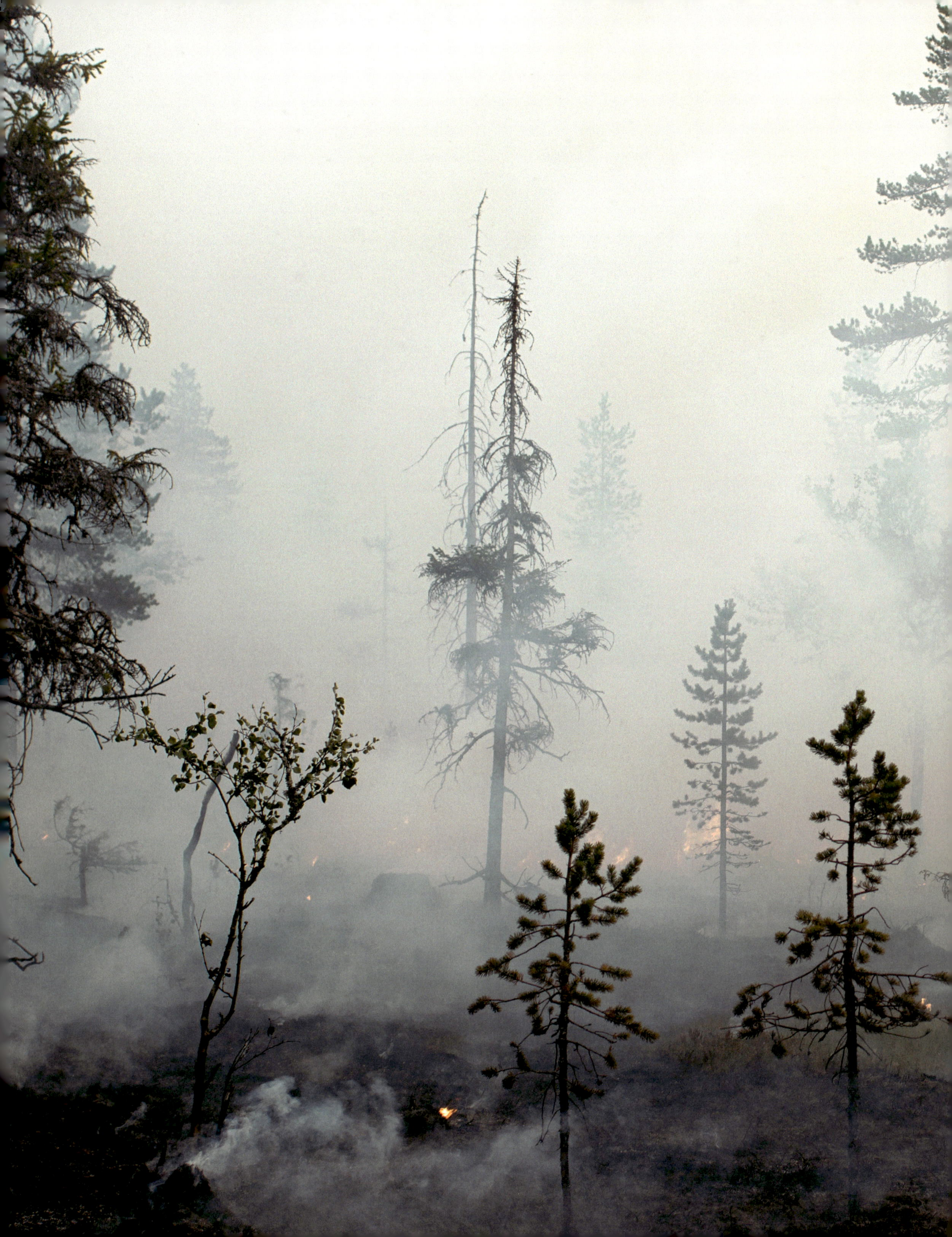

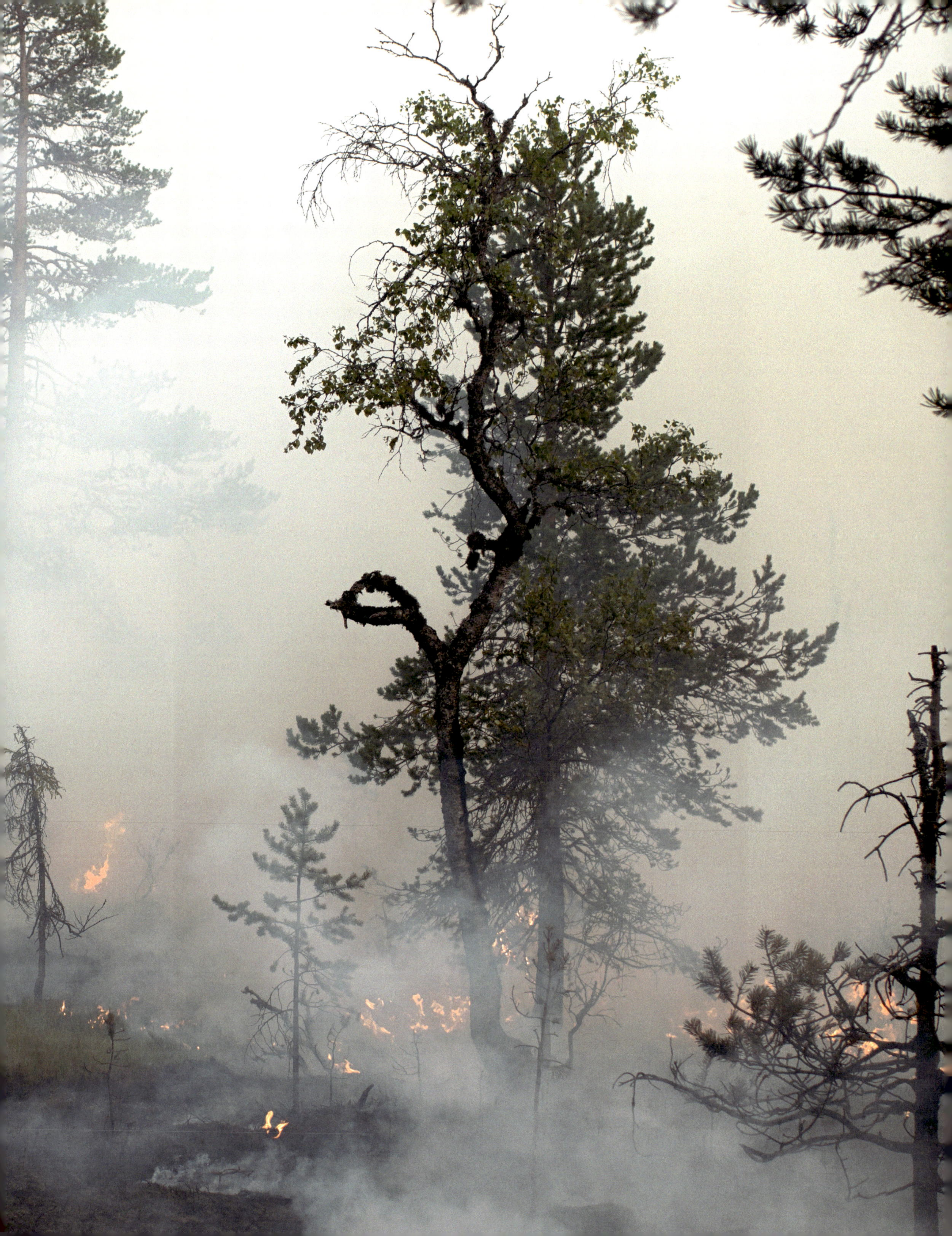

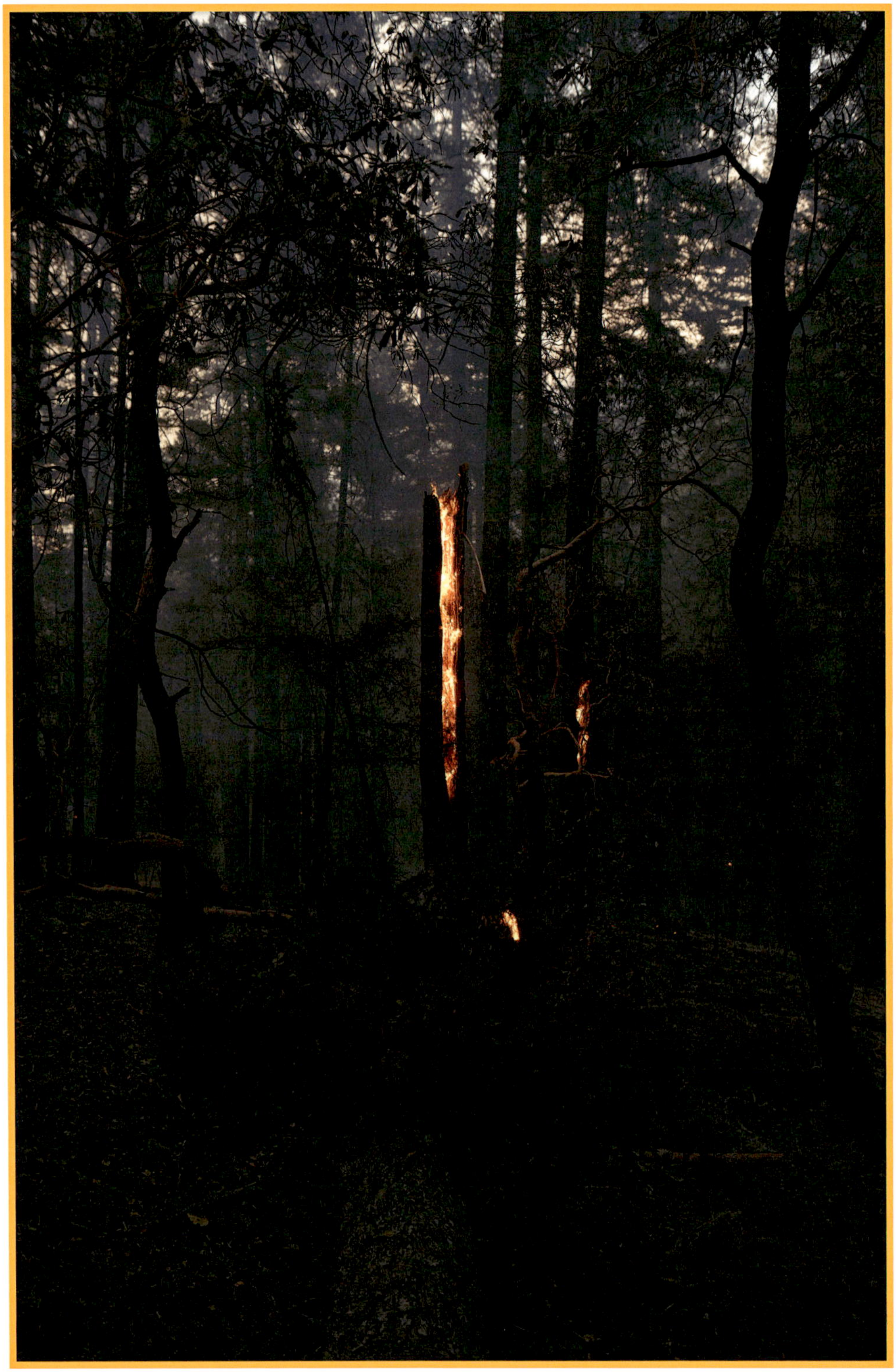

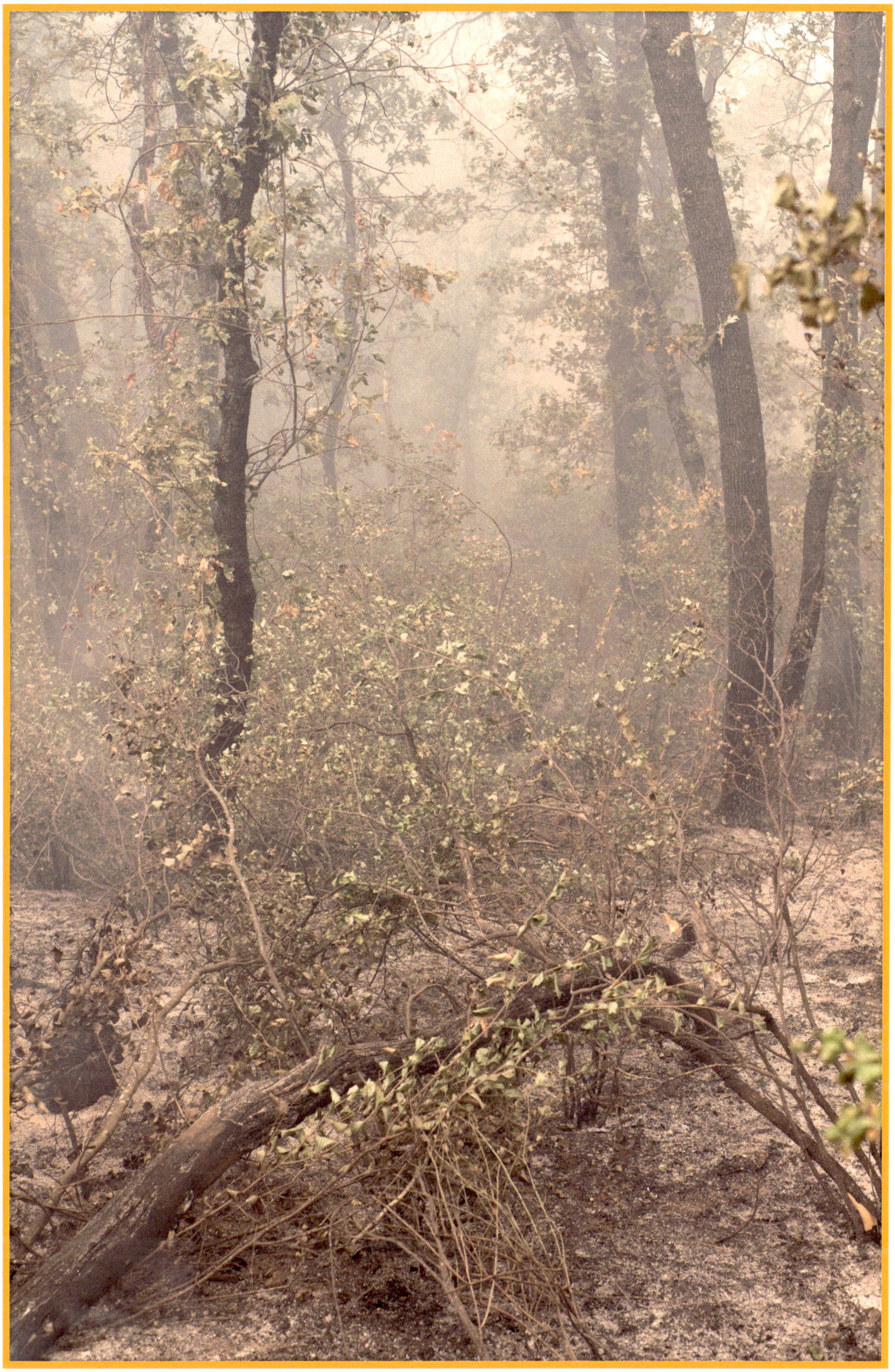

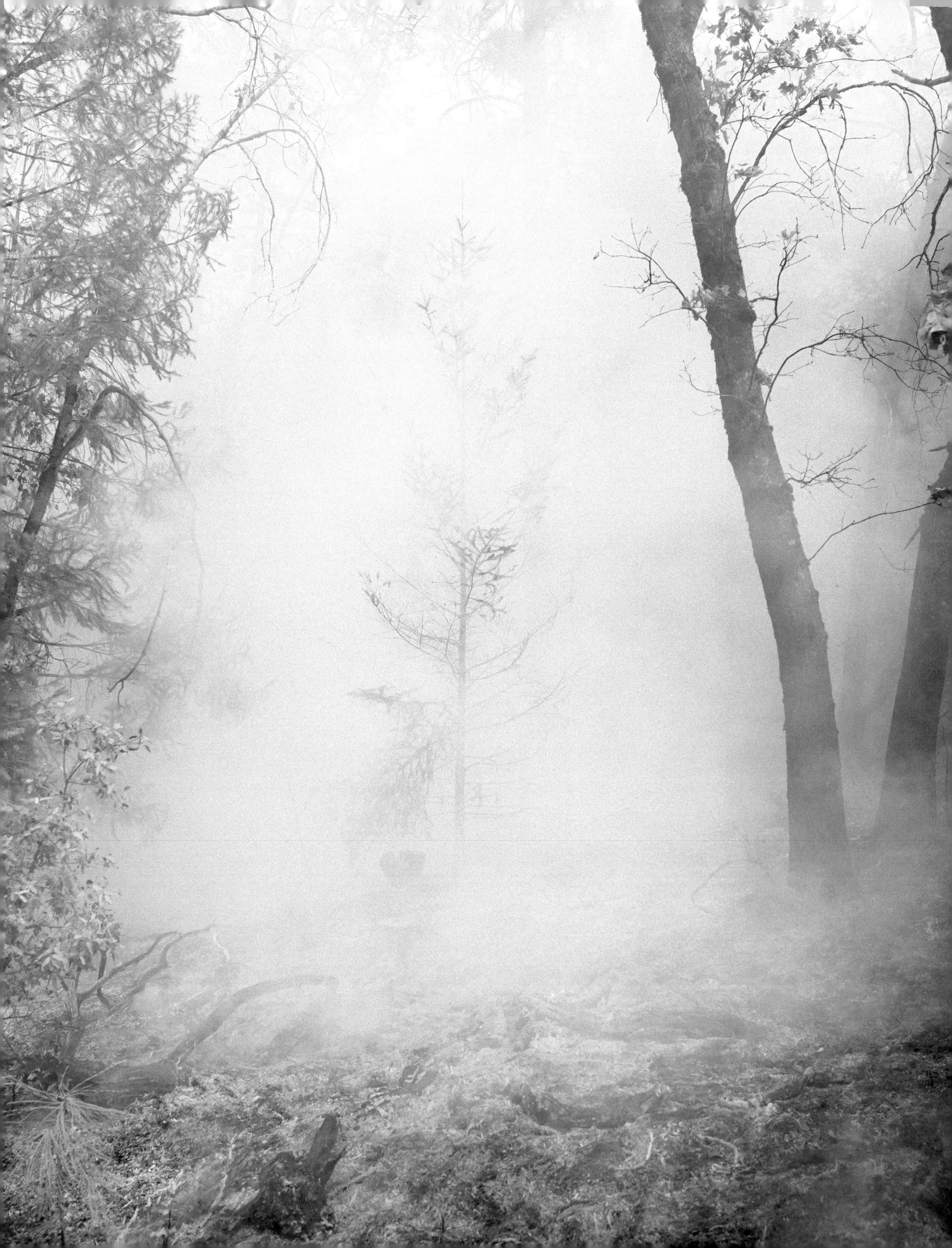

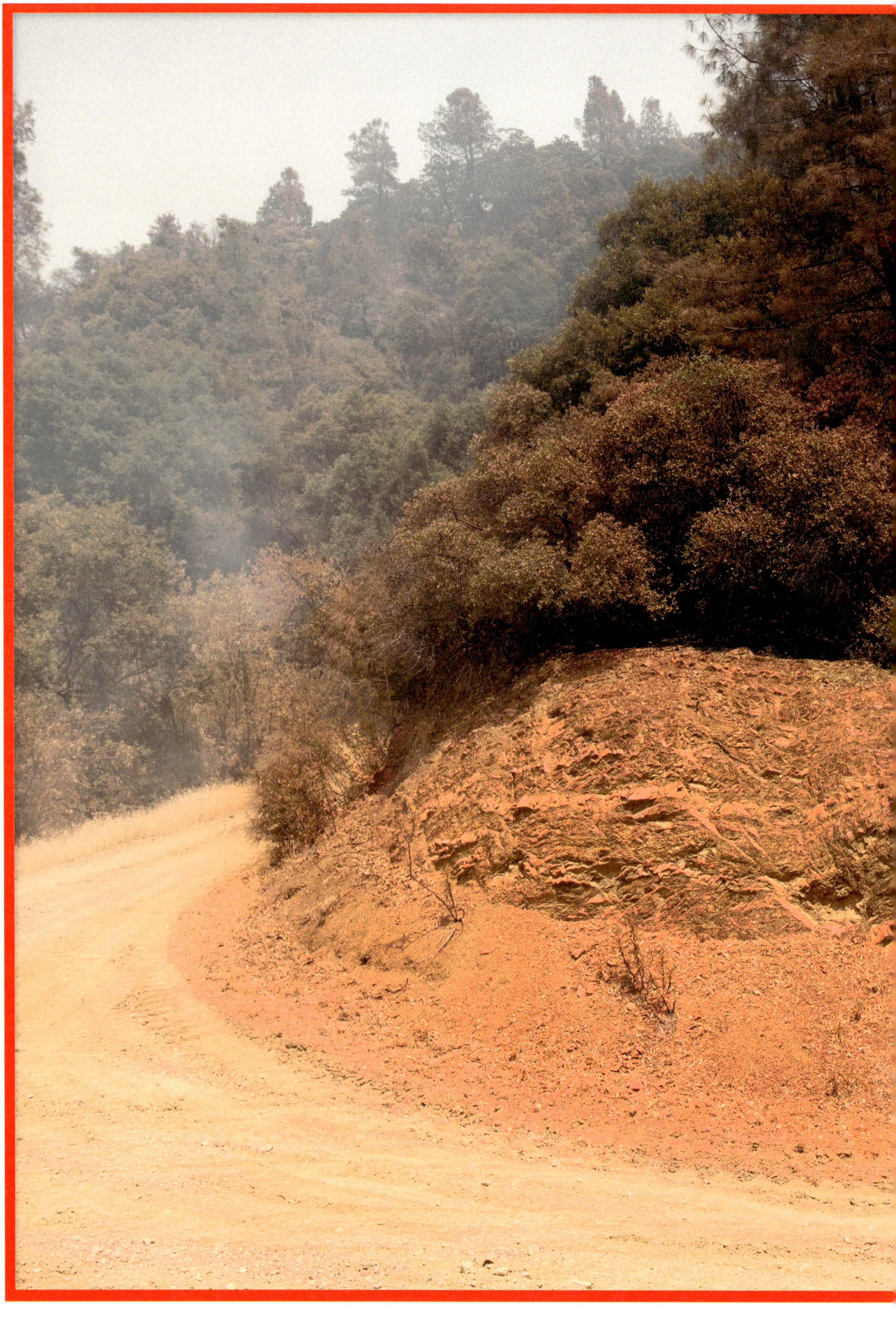

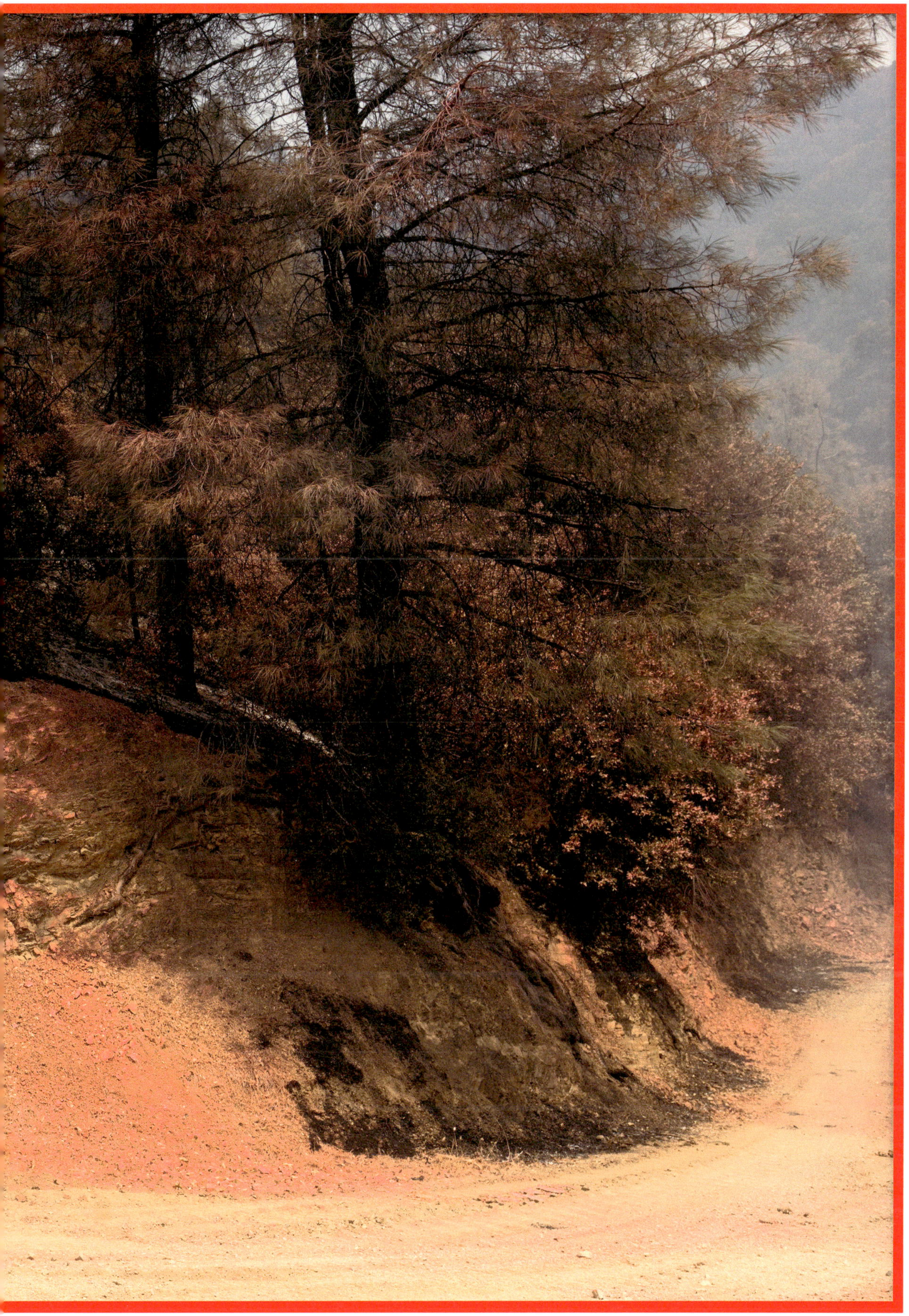

Reflections on the Pyrocene

Stephen Pyne in Conversation
with Dehlia Hannah

Dehlia Hannah: As former firefighter and historian based in a school of life sciences, you have a very different perspective on fire than most people—one born of practical experience as well as an interdisciplinary understanding of fire ecology. How are people's perceptions shaped by direct encounters with fire?

Stephen Pyne: If you're looking at people engaged with fire, don't just limit it to firefighters, because there is a whole category of firelighters, who are people trying to restore it. That is also part of our managed relation to fire. We burn for ecological effects and to make the land more habitable, not just to prevent wildfires. Florida, for example, burns more than two million acres a year. But controlling bad fires is a powerful reason. We substitute our fires, a kind of tame fire, for wildfires, just as we'd rather have dogs than wolves. We would domesticate dangerous or useless species and make them helpful. We did the same with fire, and it may be that fire is our first domestication. Even in our language, we have to kindle it, we tend it. The language is very similar to raising children. You have to take care of it all the time, you can't let it go out, you can't let it go wild. There is a whole social relationship with fire that we don't have with other natural elements. We're attracted to light, warmth . . .

DH: Speaking of lighting fires, recently there seems to have been a rise in the size and frequency of wildfires, often in locations that we are not used to seeing burn; above the Arctic Circle, for example. Some of them are directly caused by human activity, such as burning peatlands and virgin jungle to make way for oil palm plantations and cattle ranches, and even petty arson. In others cases it's indirect . . . What's driving the apparent increase in wildfires?

SP: I would characterize the fire scene—locally and globally—as one with too much bad fire, too little good fire, and too much combustion overall. Bad fire gets most of the attention, but the absence of good fire is an equally pervasive disturber; and behind each is the combustion regime of a fossil-fuel civilization.

In preindustrial societies there were occasional outbreaks of bad fire, when society broke down and was no longer able to control fire on the landscape in the way they wanted. In many areas, when it was away from settlements, fire burned untrammeled. We only very recently began to substitute fossil fuels for living fuels—we quit burning living landscapes and started burning lithic ones. That has caused a huge imbalance, not only in the presence of fire, but how we relate to it.

It is not just that we are burning fossil fuels but that this has shaped how we live on the landscape; it has shaped our transportation systems, how we cultivate food, how we use the land, whether we create parks and reserves. All of this creates whole other sets of conditions for fire to burn in, and for the two realms of fire to clash. In the recent California fires, for example, how many of the blowups have been the result of power lines failing in high winds? Not all those power lines carry electricity from power plants burning fossil fuels, but most do. The violent intersection of the two realms of fire is a particularly visible expression of how these two realms can clash, but the underlying tension is everywhere in industrial societies.

We have tried to take fire out of the landscape, and in the process we have created whole new opportunities for free-burning fire. We are not farming or grazing the land outside these communities because we live off an industrial service economy rather than a rural economy. When the natural or quasi-natural landscape does not get the fire it needs, this makes communities vulnerable. We cannot substitute for open fire in landscapes in the way we can in our houses and factories. We do not want open flames anymore; we have tried to project that same logic of technological replacement into living landscapes, and it has been a disaster. It is not like replacing a candle with a lightbulb, or a hearth fire, which was used for cooking, heating, and illumination, with an electric stove. There are lots of reasons to make that substitution—we do not have to constantly scrounge for fuel, we do not have to tend it all the time and deal with indoor pollution from smoke, the illumination is better, and so on. But when we project that experience out into the living landscape, we get all kinds of strange effects. We are left with what people call the fire paradox: the more people try to remove fire from fire-prone and fire-adapted landscapes, the worse the fires get. It is partly a matter of fuel, partly a matter of climate, and partly how an industrial society lives on the landscape.

DH: It suggests that fire is diagnostic of our intrarelationship with our living environs; of how sustainable it might be in the long term. There's something archaic about that idea, as though fires are like lightning bolts thrown down in judgement from the gods. Can we still think of fires as omens, of a sort?

SP: Pyromancy lives, in a way. Since it integrates its surroundings, fire is a great index of what is going on. So if you have bad fires it is because the environment in which fire is burning is out of whack.

People keep wanting to know: what is fire? Fire is a shape shifter. It synthesizes its surroundings; it takes its character from its context. There is no fire in the way you can pick up a rock or have a bag of air. What you have with fire are the ingredients that make the reaction.

If you look at some of the pictures coming out of Paradise, California, the trees came out fine. It is the houses that burned down to concrete. Most of the burned forest was right next to a structure—so the structural fire caused the damage to the trees. Well, the trees are adapted to fire, they can even survive a high-intensity fire in ways that the urban-built landscape cannot.

Cities and countryside used to burn in similar ways, not least since they were made of similar materials. We broke that cycle and have gotten accustomed to the idea that cities do not burn anymore, but this is sort of like saying we have solved measles, or smallpox, or polio, so we don't need to vaccinate anymore. In some ways, having cities burn is like having an old plague come back, because we quit thinking about it and taking appropriate steps to prevent bad fires.

But we should think also about cultural landscapes, like European heathlands, for example. If you eliminate fire, the heaths cannot survive. They need some kind of routine disturbance; fire and grazing were part of what created them, and that is what they need to continue. Weirdly, some of the best heaths in northern Europe are on active or former military sites, often for artillery training. Of course, too much blasting and burning can ruin a place; but so can too little. It is not just natural landscapes but cultural landscapes that need the right fire regime.

DH: So is this another aspect of the transformation of wastelands into wilderness areas? As we see in places like the North Korean demilitarized zone and exclusion zones created after nuclear accidents, places where people prohibited from living and visiting become wildlife reserves by default. Do they also become hospitable to fire?

SP: The DMZ is regularly burned. In the spring strong, dry cold fronts pass through and carry winds from the north. So if you light up on the north side, the winds will carry it across the DMZ, and there have been several episodes where those fires have escaped and burned cultural sites. South Korea has restored its environment at great expense, and fire suppression has been part of that strategy. But they should be thinking about how to reintroduce fire, because if they don't, then they will be subjected to wildfire.

There are many similar examples: the Canary Islands were basically rocks a century ago. With great effort they have been rebuilt, reforested, and promoted as an ecotourism site. And now, La Gomera, Tenerife, and a quarter of Gran Canaria have been burned by wildfires, because all this stuff is growing up, and it is a very fire-prone Mediterranean climate. Fire returned with the forest, and the first response was to suppress those fires. That is not a sustainable strategy, however. Probably they will have to reintroduce fire and other practices, even some prescribed grazing. It's a nice example of unintended consequences. The Canaries had done a good thing by bringing nature back to an area that had been pretty well stripped of it. They forgot they were also bringing fire back as well.

DH: As you pointed out, initially we're attracted to fire, which is always a source of joy and fear. It is one thing when it's "tame" and you can say, "don't touch the burning log," in the stove or the hearth. But speaking of tourist destinations like Tenerife, is it possible to imagine wildfires as part of the attraction—along with the beaches, birds, and monkeys? We go out to see volcanoes erupting, chase tornados, and lust after all sorts of dangerous phenomena. Do people do that with wildfires?

SP: There are examples of pyrotourism. In Kansas, the Flint Hills are famous for burning. They were never ploughed, remained a pastoral economy, and retained traditional spring burning. In fact, the old cattle drives would come up out of Texas, and there were actually contracts with the owners that stipulated when it would be burned, so that by the time the herds arrived there would be no threat from wildfire and fresh forage would exist for the cattle to feed on. That practice never ended, and now it has become a tourist attraction; people will even pay to be able to walk with a drip torch and assist with some of the burning. There's also a great tradition of American fire art on prairies that goes way back into the nineteenth century and continues today. So yes, there is an ecotourism for fire.

Some of America's national parks will even give some tours if there is a fire burning in an area and it is near a trail. Rangers will escort people through the site and use it as an educational opportunity and part of the recreational scene, like watching geysers or other features of nature. But there are also areas where people will come out to watch the fires, and it's like the old tradition of setting large bonfires. Most of our great seasonal ceremonies involved fire—but those were always controlled fires. It's an exotic phenomenon for people who have grown up in cities to have a sense that this potentially terribly dangerous thing is now being controlled. It's a kind of natural fireworks.

We have to be attracted to fire, or we would have been out of the gene pool a long time ago. You light a fire, and people will gather around it. Recent research has examined how much time people in aboriginal societies spend around the fire at night; that's where a lot of culture is transmitted, where stories are told, and myths are recited.

DH: Do you have a favorite story or myth about fire?

SP: All peoples have their fire myths, and in many of them it is also an origin myth; people become human when they get fire. The Promethean myth, of which there are many versions, is the same. There was nothing distinctive about us until we got fire. We got fire, and then we began cooking food, and that was the toggle switch: we got small guts and big heads. Then we went to the top of the food chain because we cooked landscapes. And now we have become a geologic force because we have begun to cook the planet. So, we've carried it too far.

These myths have been collected by James Fraser, the great folklorist, who has a whole book of them. My favorite story comes from southeast Asia and tells how people begged to their local god that they need fire to survive, and he refuses to give it to them. He says, "You won't be able to control it. It is too dangerous to you." And, in some respects, it was the same with Prometheus. Fire has to be taken by force; it is not given freely, because fire is power. Almost all of our environmental power is a fire power, when you trace all of the connections. In some respects, our acquisition of fire was our first Faustian bargain. We were willing to make it because it gave us so many advantages, and we have continued to amplify fire. We are fire creatures, we are the keystone species for fire on the planet. Many people assume that we don't want to live in places that burn, but, no: we do want to live in places that burn because it magnifies our firepower. But unfortunately, we're overdoing it now.

DH: A focus on fire has the potential to cast current debates about the Anthropocene in a new light. You propose that we have recently entered a new era that would be better called the Pyrocene. Have we overcooked the planet so much that we've entered a new era? What is the Pyrocene?

SP: I invented "Pyrocene" to convey the sense in which fire, largely in the hands of humanity, has shaped the Earth in recent times.

The past 2.6 million years have veered between cold and warm, between glacial epochs and interglacials. The most recent interglacial has increasingly reflected the effects of anthropogenic burning.

The age of humans is an age of fire. Fire is the great enabler of humanity's presence: it is what we do that no other creature does. It is the mark of our ecological agency. Our environmental power is in great measure a firepower.

The process quickened when people started burning lithic landscapes as well as living ones and changed the dynamics of planetary fire. For most of humanity's existence our burning was limited by the amount of fuel available and by the ecological constraints within which the burning happened. But fossil fuels are virtually unbounded, and their combustion occurs without regard to old boundaries. They can burn day and night, winter and summer, through drought or deluge. Their limitation lies not in sources of combustibles but in the sinks available to absorb the resulting effluent.

Our burning has unhinged Earth's climate, even interrupted the Milankovitch cycles that set the compounding rhythms of ice advance and retreat. Climate history is becoming a subset of fire history. Paradoxically, our combustion power may spare us the forecast return of the ice. But if unchecked, fire will destroy as ruthlessly as ice.

In recent years Anthropocene has emerged as shorthand for the age of humans. I would use it not as an epoch within the Holocene but to characterize the Holocene overall. The warming started by nature; thanks to humanity it has not ended. Since we speak of ice ages, it seemed appropriate to call the present epoch a fire age. The Holocene is an Anthropocene. The Anthropocene is a Pyrocene.

DH: That's interesting. It has been proposed that the Anthropocene began with the advent of agriculture, rather than industrialization or nuclear fallout, but I have never heard it suggested that it began with fire. Maybe the Pyrocene is a better characterization of the environmental shifts that have happened in the last few centuries, and a useful concept, because it calls attention to the political and technological infrastructure that's required to extract and burn the lithosphere. Everything looks different when fire is in the picture. Speaking of which, is there an artwork that embodies the logic or the visual quality of fire for you?

SP: There is one painting that I have always loved. In many ways it is an archetypal painting; you see it reproduced over and over again. You can buy copies on eBay . . . They are all based on a painting by the Russian artist Alexei Denisov-Uralsky that won a silver medal at the World's Fair in Saint Louis in 1904. It was reproduced in color for newspapers, then used as a fire-prevention poster. It occurs in a boreal forest, and at the focus there is a little bit of fire on the ground, hidden by the forest, and then a swirl of flames spiraling up through the canopy. The artist became obsessed by fire, and for years tried to capture its essence. The painting's history has been mired in scandal, and for decades the original has been missing . . . allegedly it has recently been found in the basement of a museum in Tomsk.

Forest Fire (*Lesnoi pozhar*, 1897), by Alexei Kuzmich Denisov-Uralsky, is now held in the Perm State Arts Gallery. After its exhibition in 1904, the painting changed hands and was copied many times before being acquired by the Anheuser-Busch family and hanging for many years in the Anheuser-Busch Brewery in Saint Louis, Missouri. It was returned to the Soviet Union in 1979 in advance of the scheduled Olympic Games, through the American National Endowment for the Arts. The photograph on the cover of *Talking to Thunder,* taken by Robert Williams, depicts (from left to right) Missouri senator James Symington, head of the NEA Joseph Duffy, and Soviet ambassador Anatoly Dobrynin looking at this iconic image of wildfire.

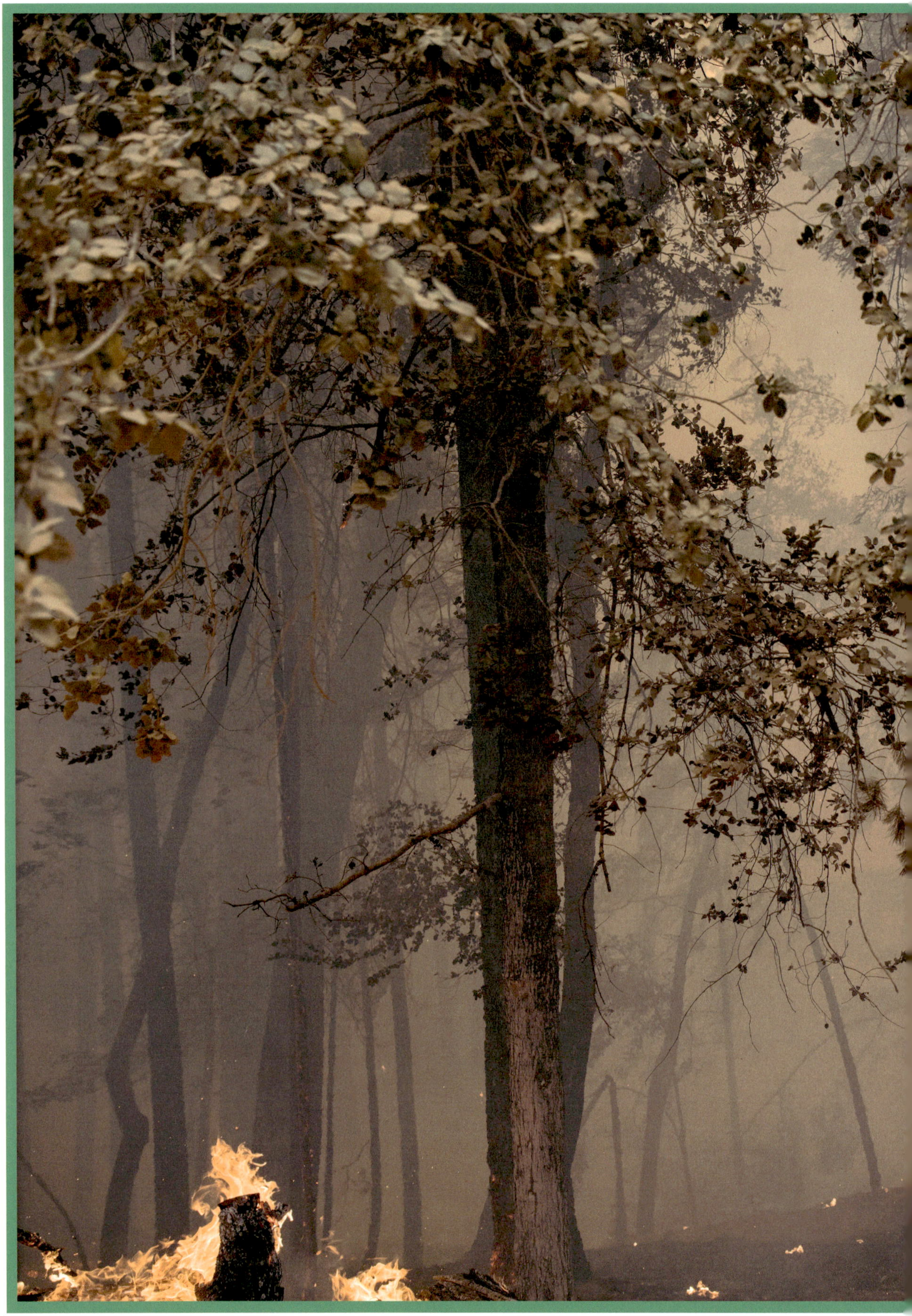

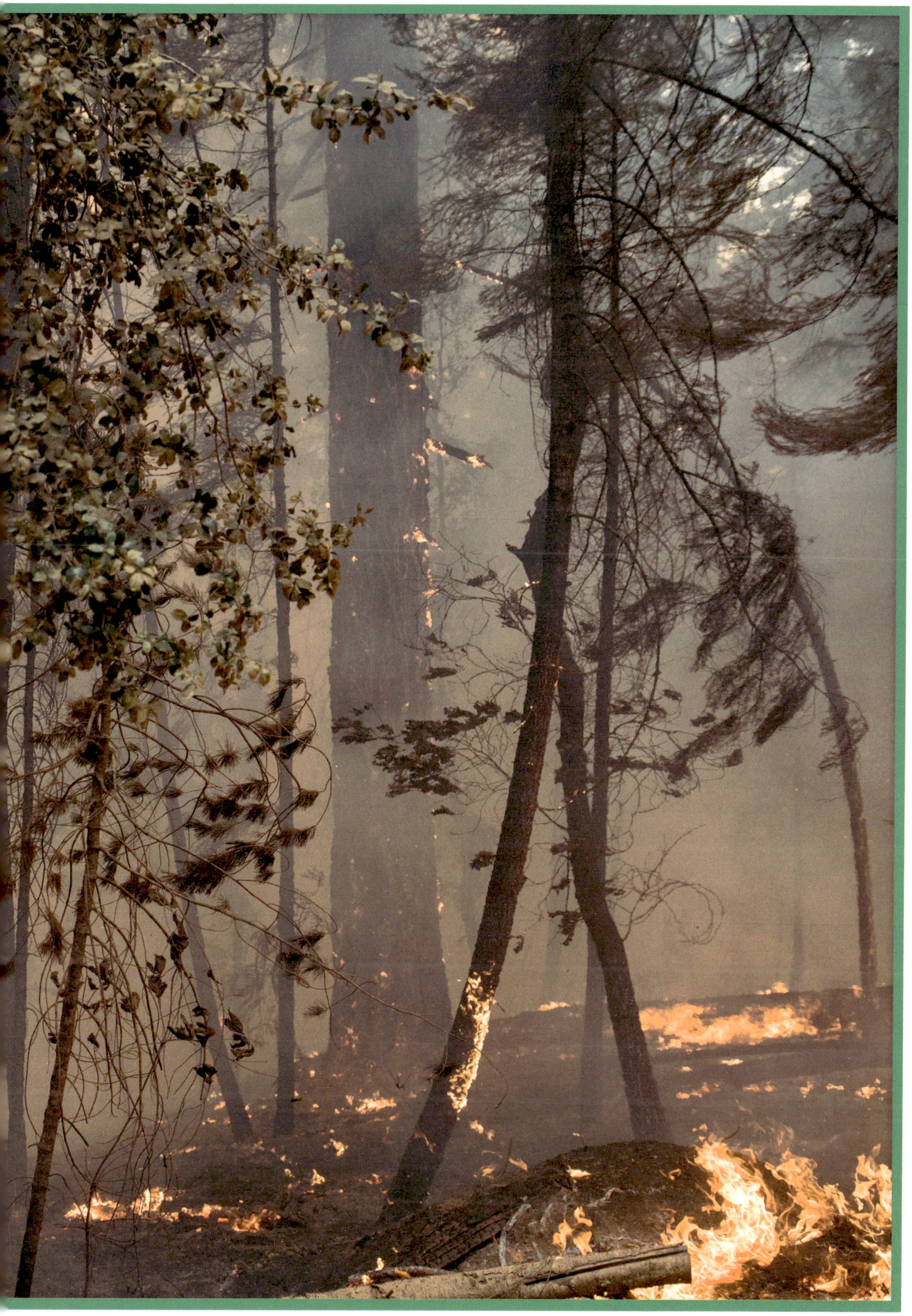

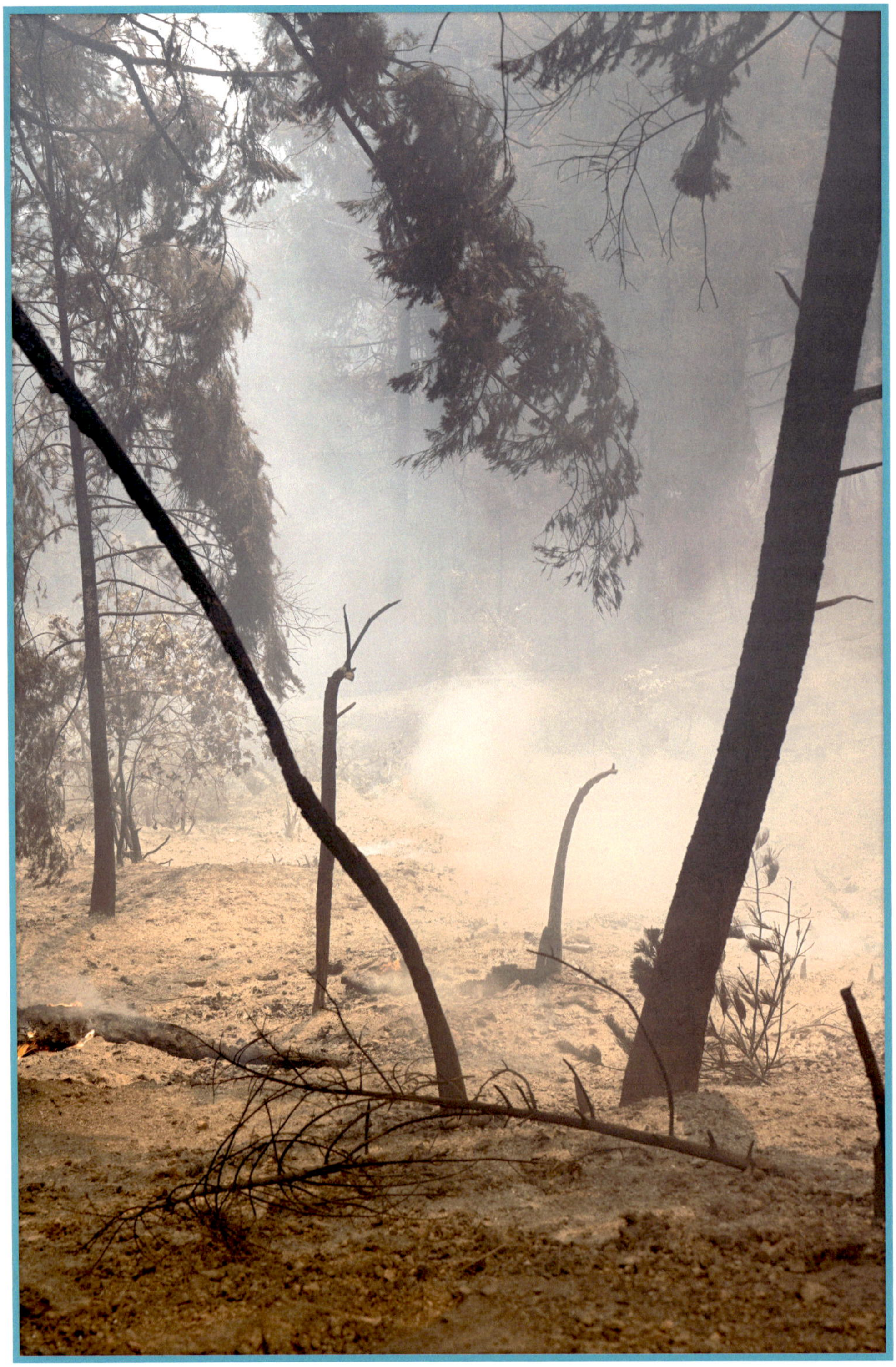

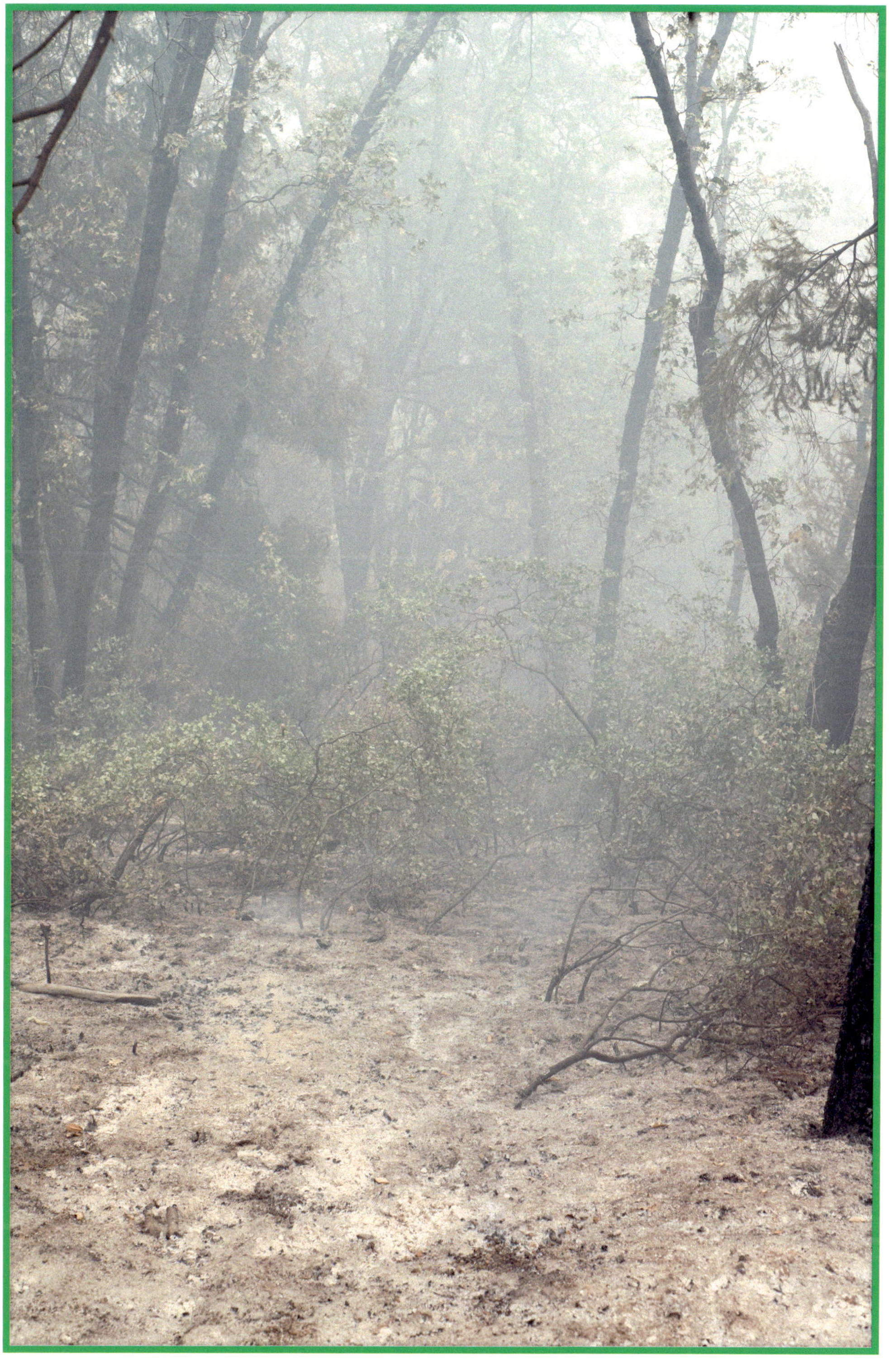

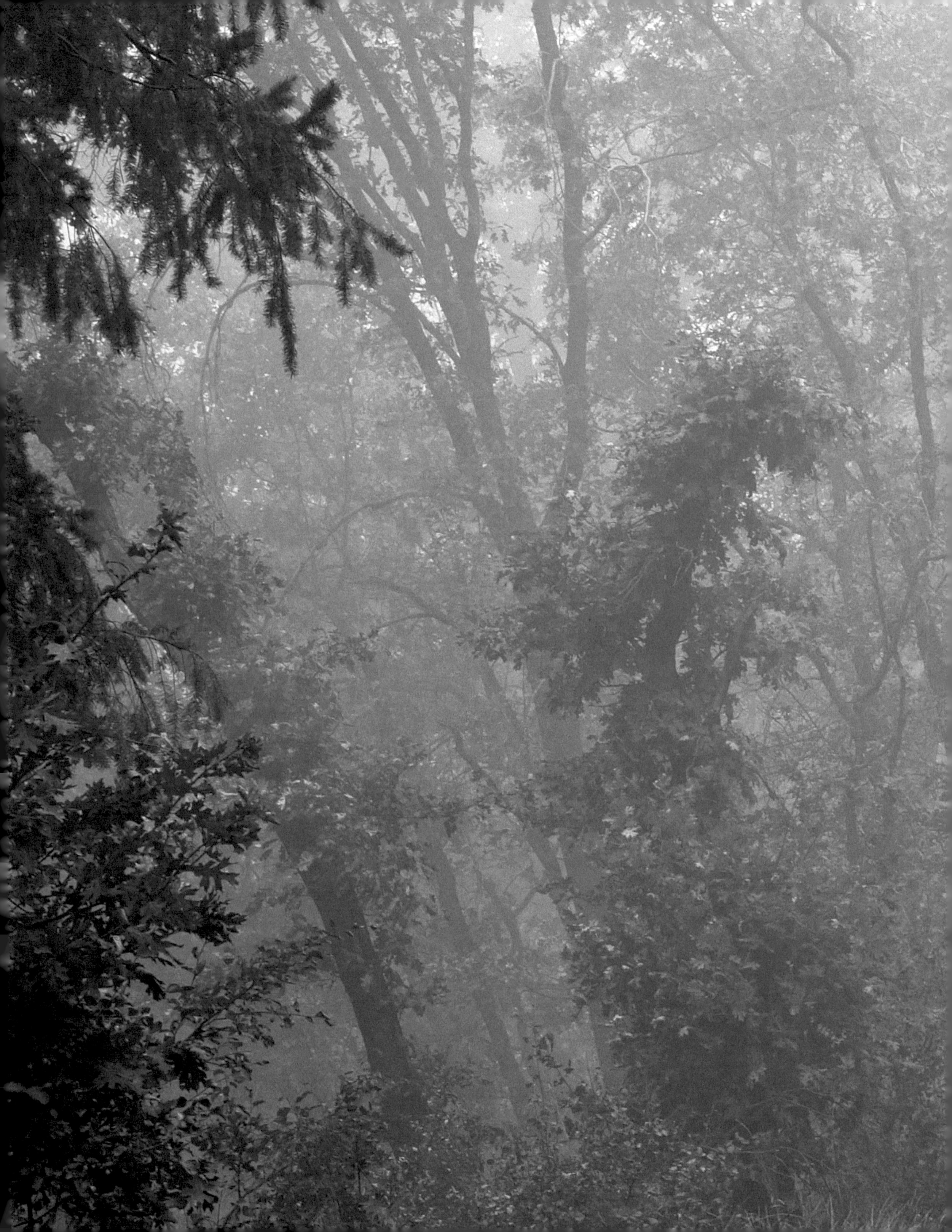

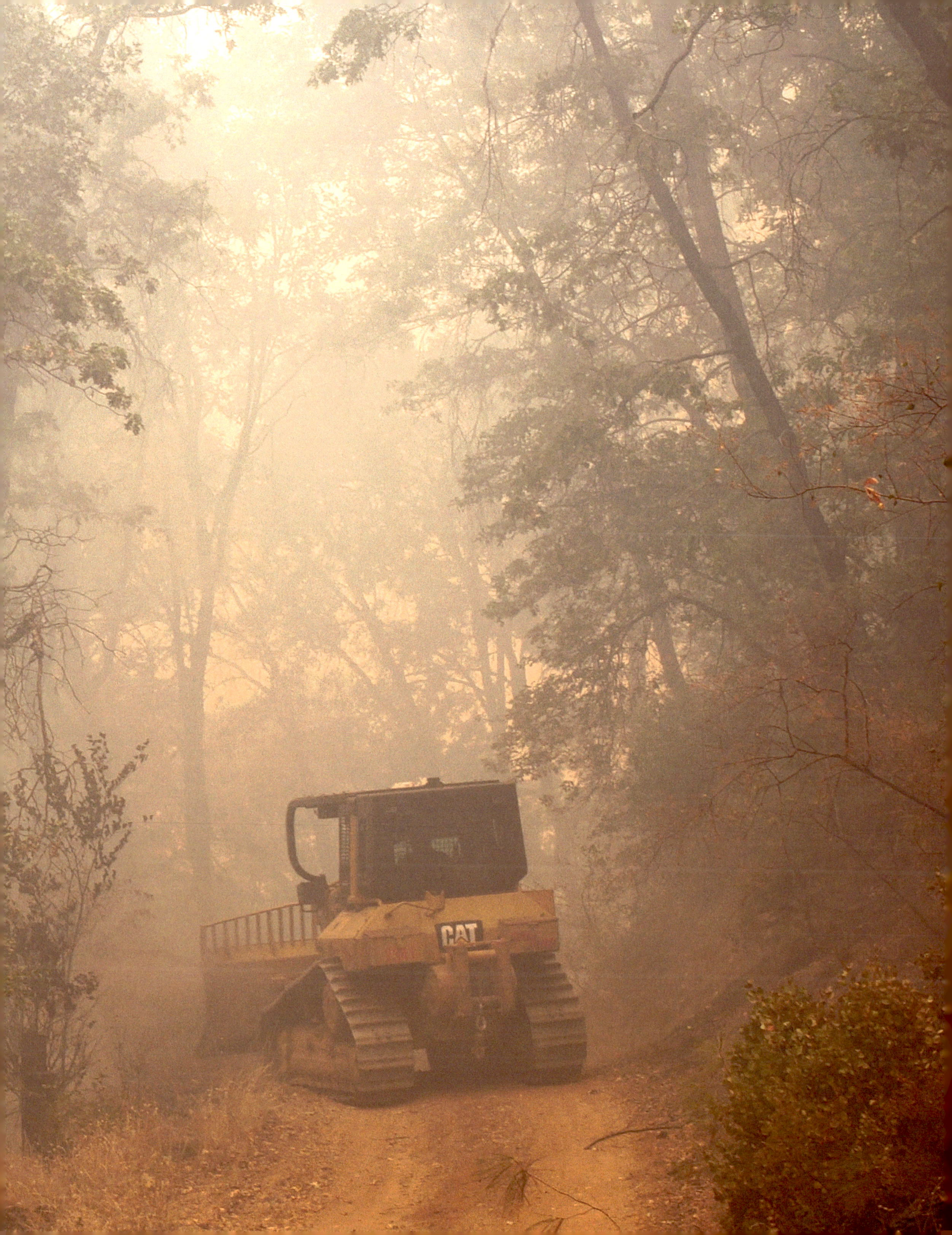
CAT

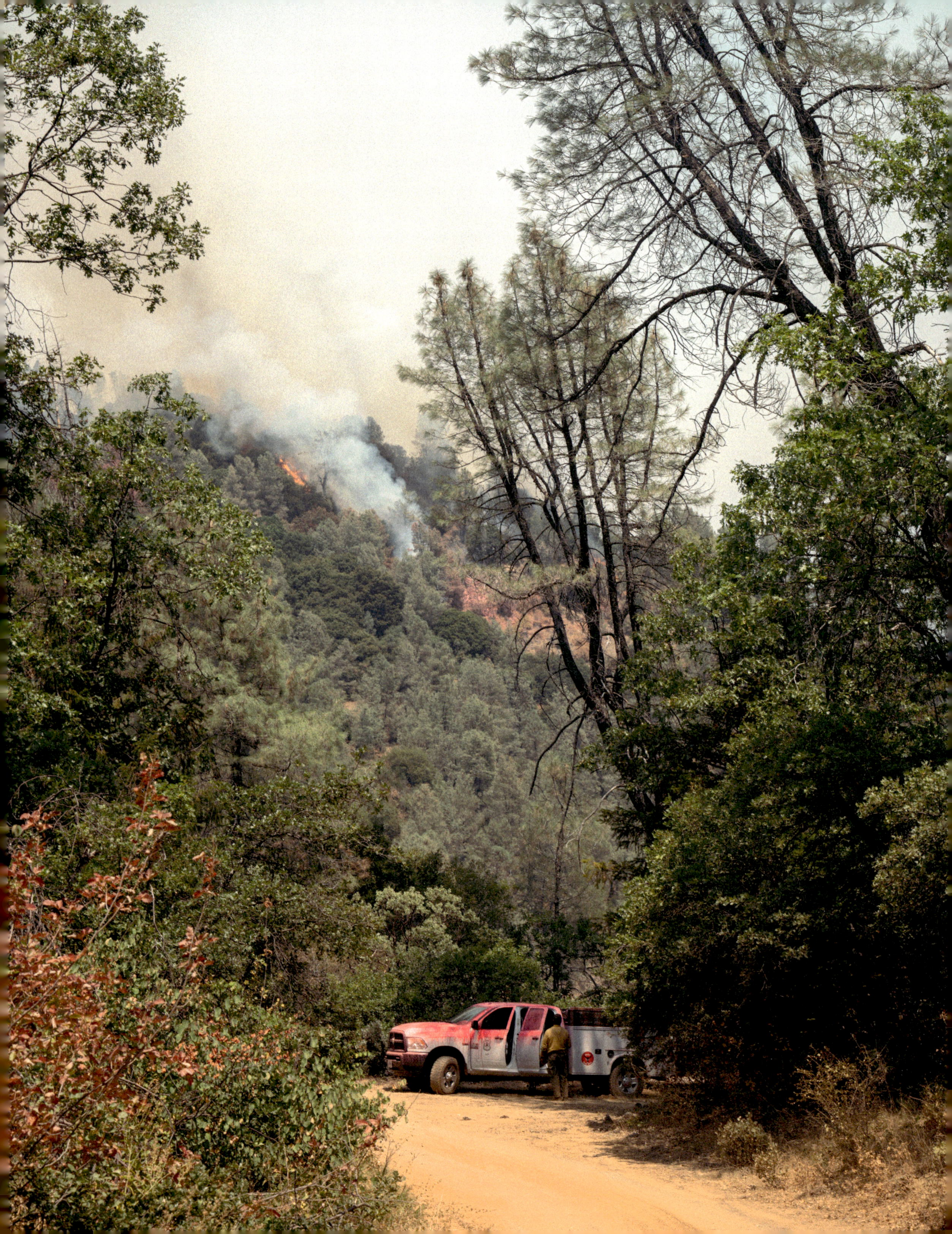

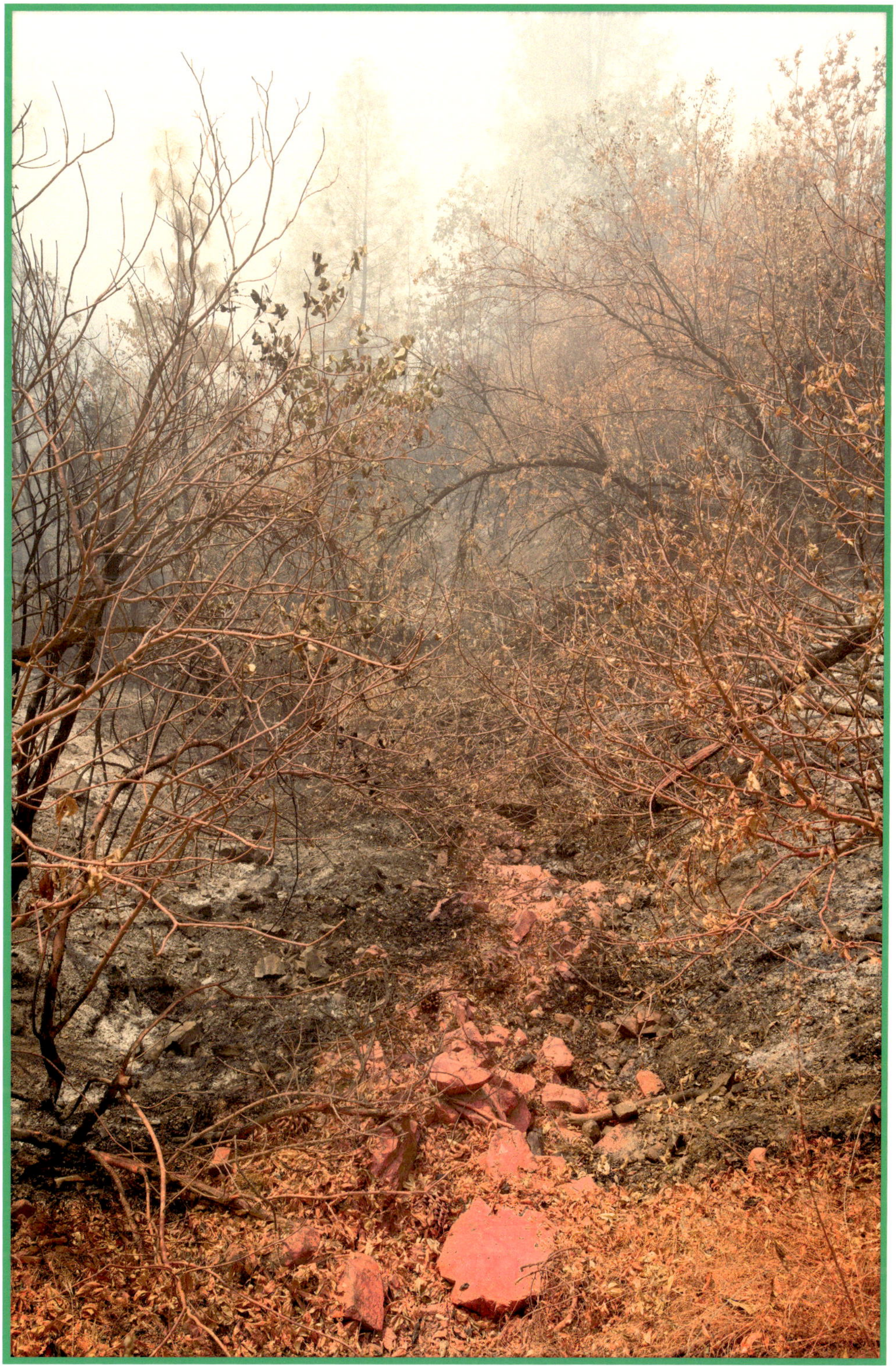

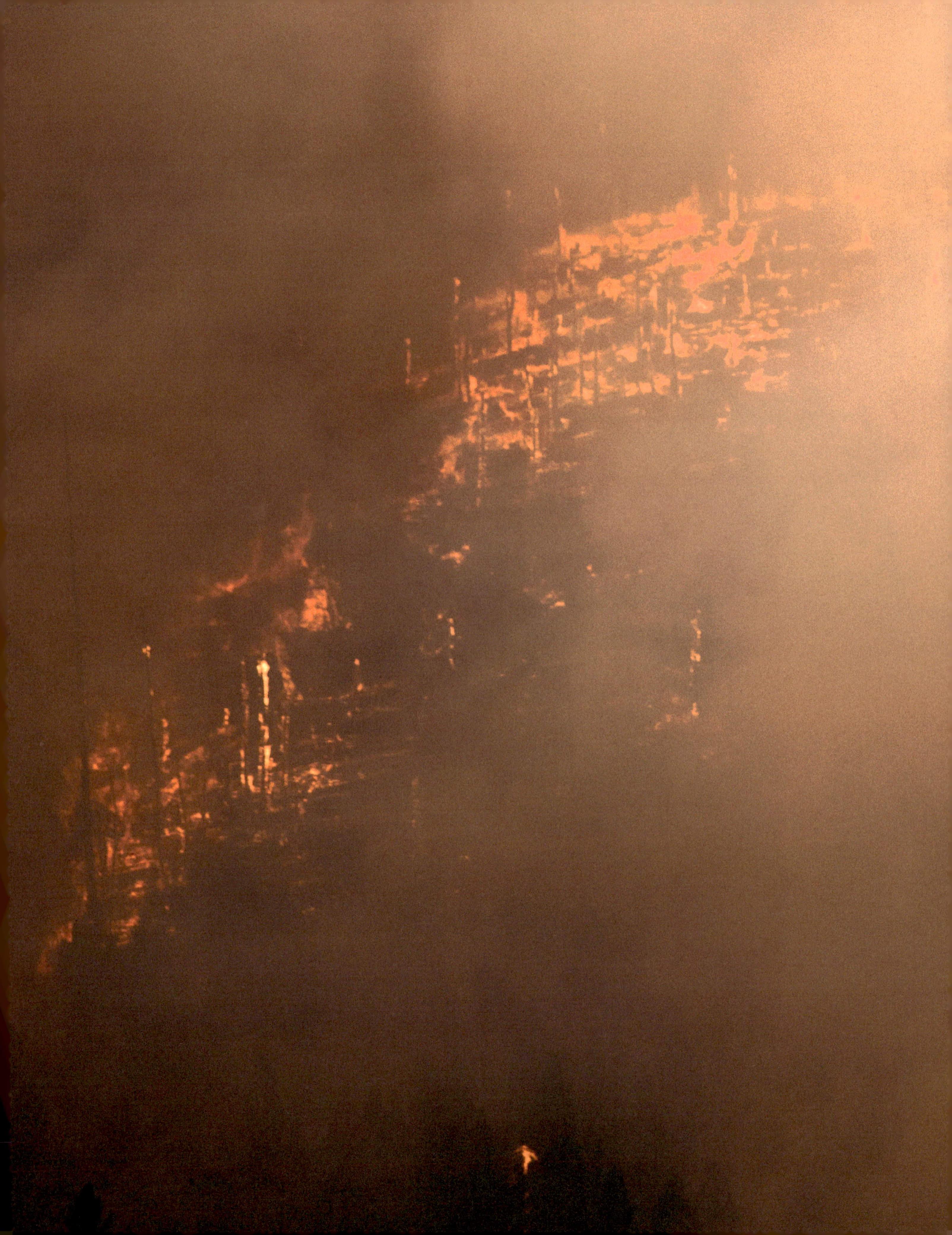

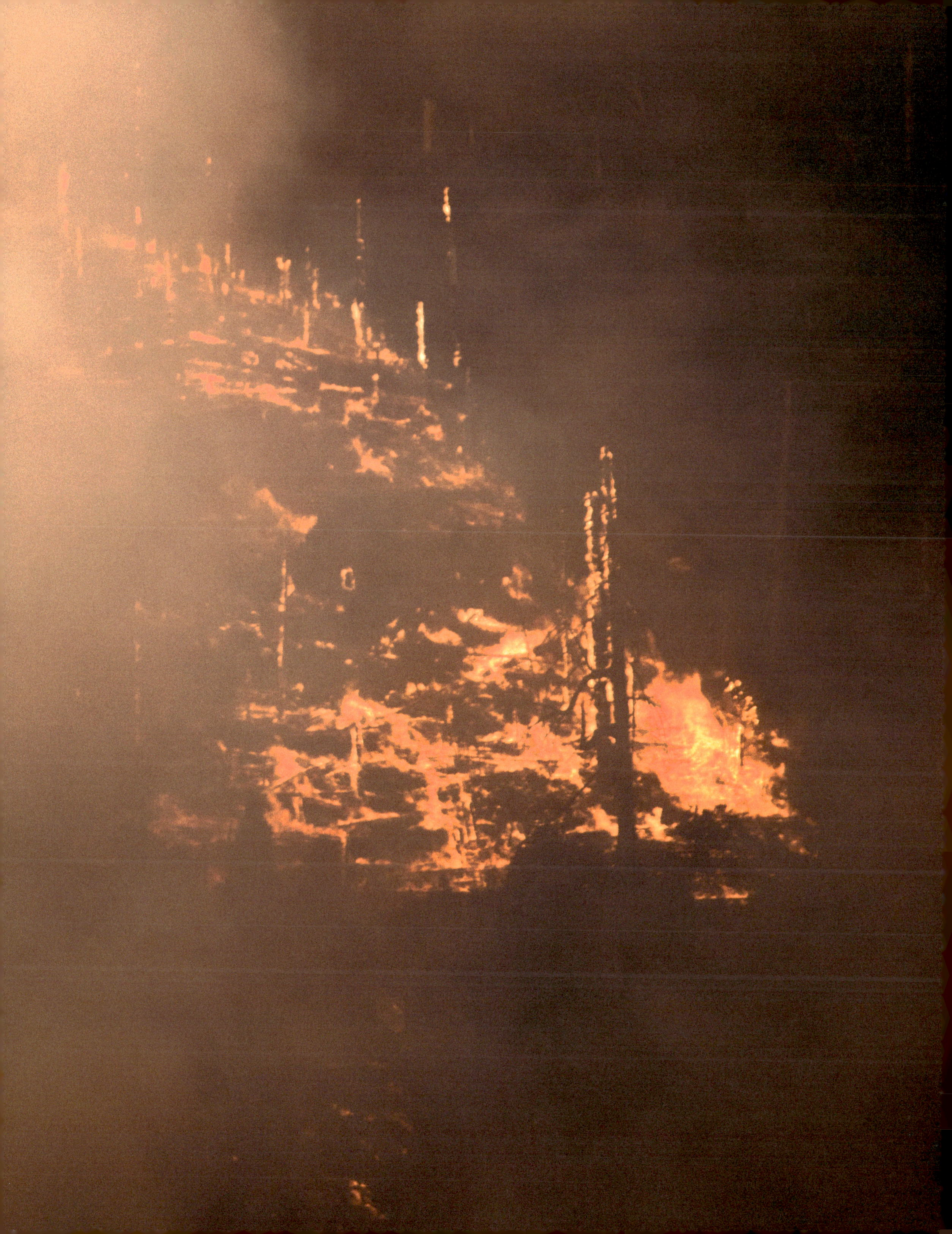

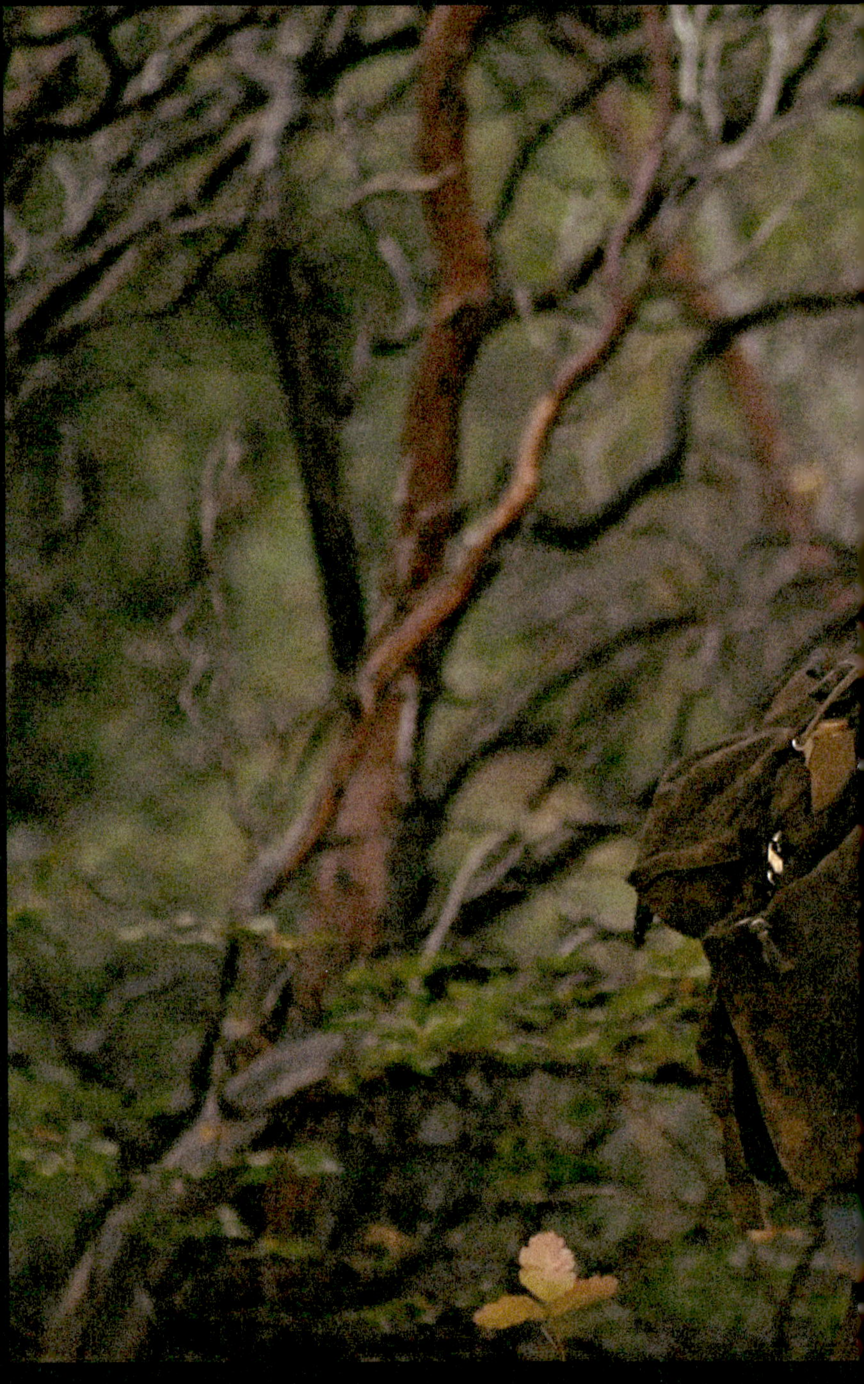

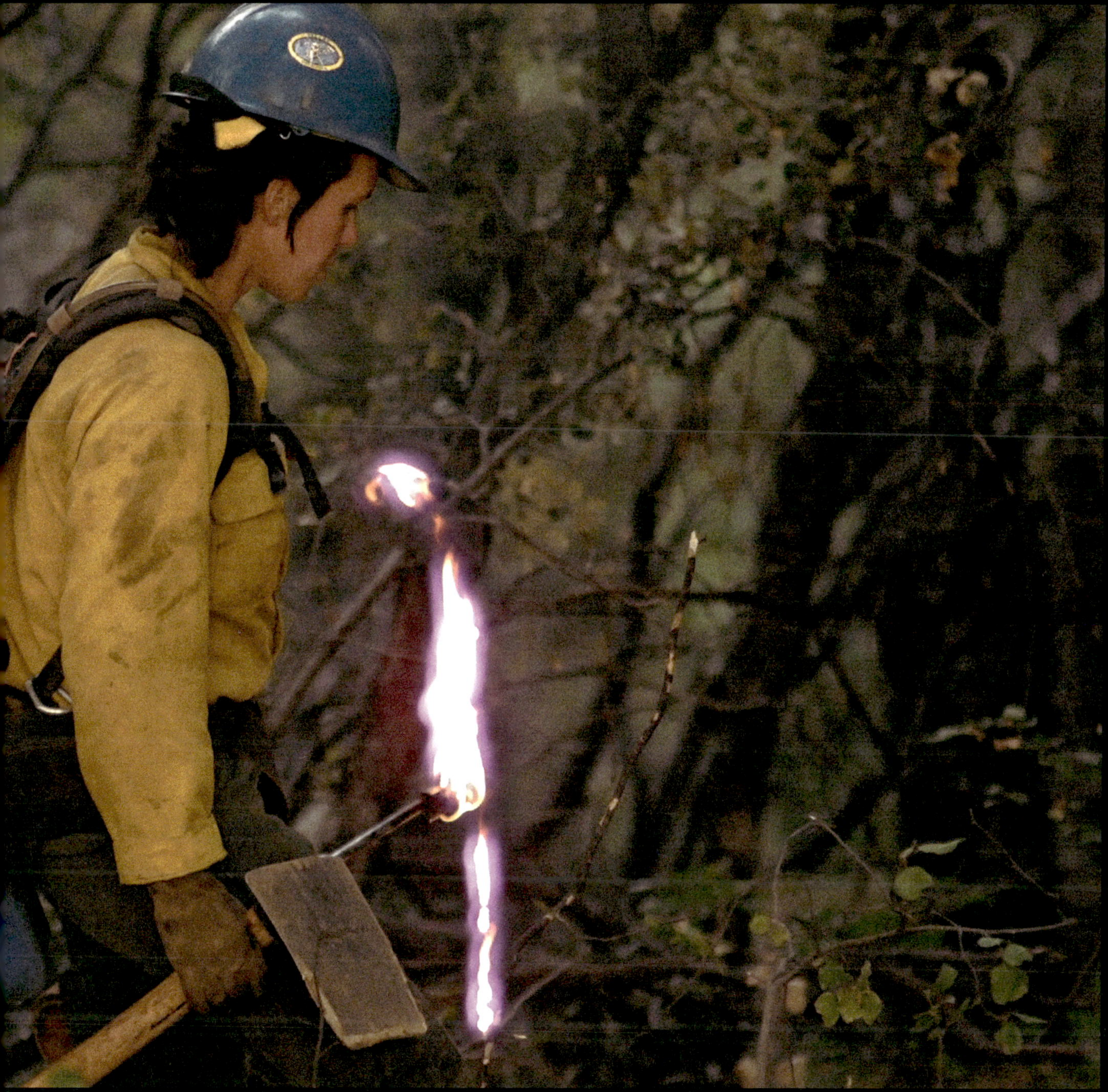

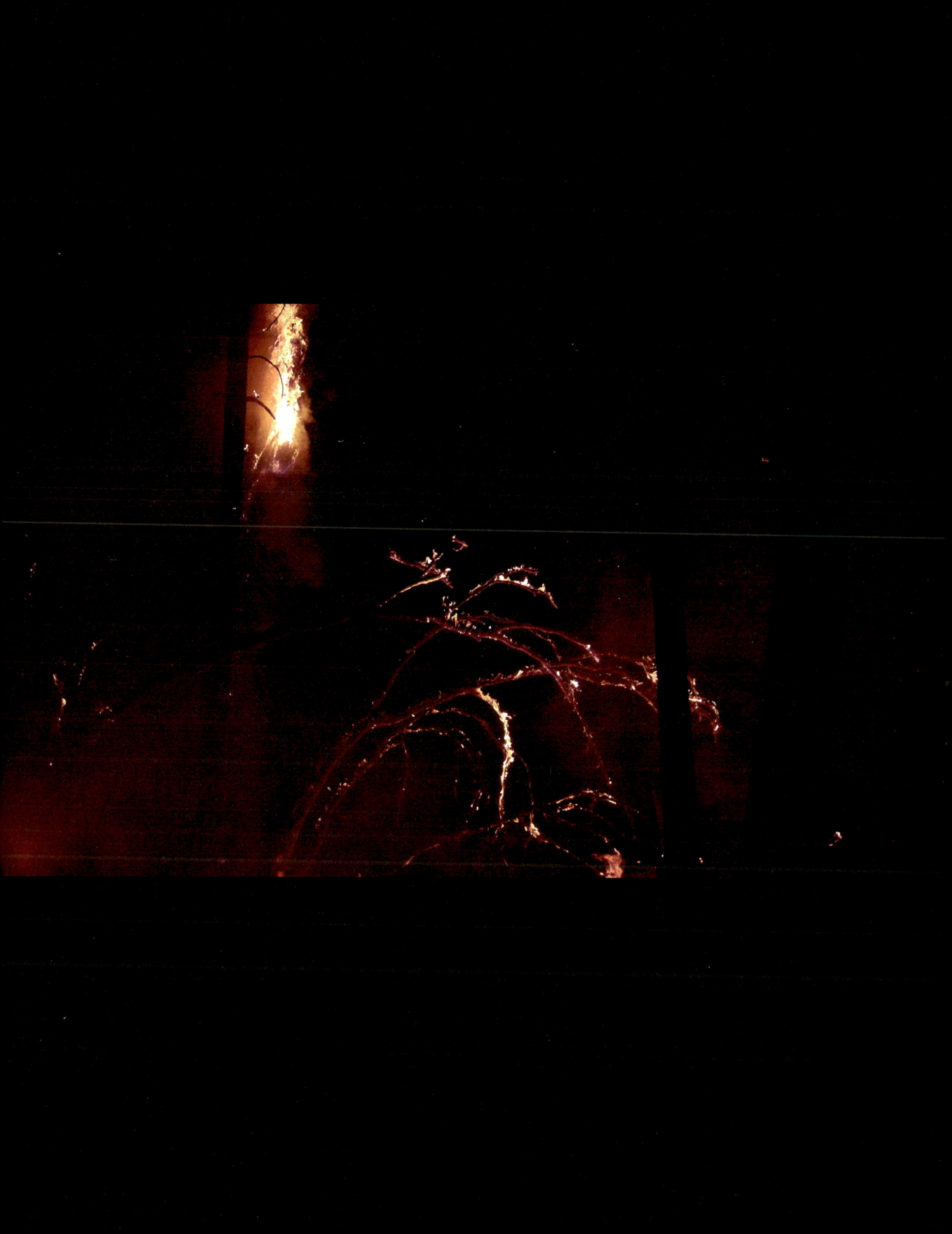

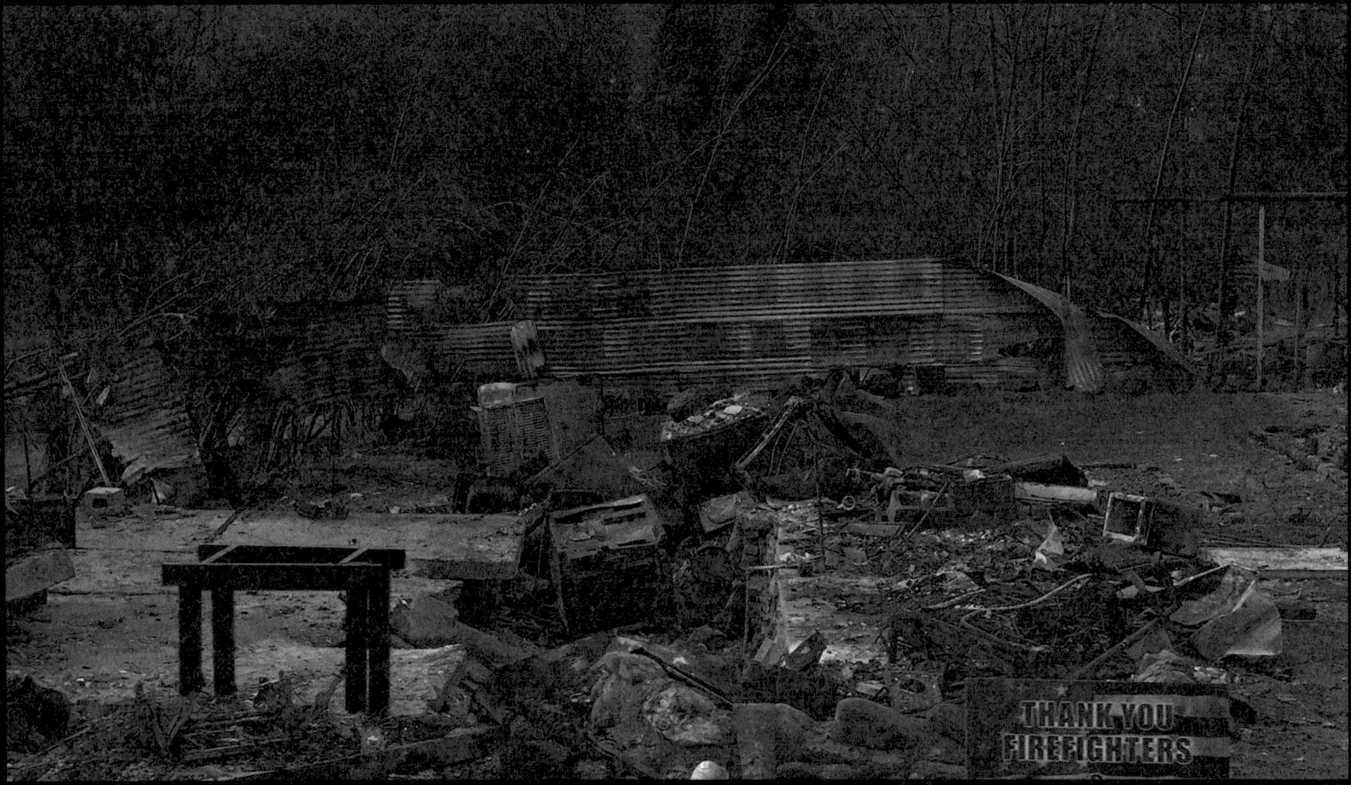
THANK YOU
FIREFIGHTERS

The Psychoanalysis of Fire

Gaston Bachelard

Psychoanalysis has already long been engaged in the study of legends and mythologies. It has prepared for studies of this kind a working stock of explanations that are sufficiently rich to throw light upon the legends surrounding the conquest of fire. But what psychoanalysis has not yet completely systematized—although the works of C. G. Jung have cast a bright light upon this point—is the study of scientific explanations, of objective explanation, which purport to account for the discoveries of prehistoric man. In this chapter we shall bring together and the complete the observations of C. G. Jung by calling attention to the weakness of rational explanations.

In the first place, we must criticize the modern scientific explanations which seem to us quite inappropriate for prehistoric discoveries. These scientific explanations originate in an arid and cursory rationalism which claims to be profiting by recurring factual evidence; but which is, however, quite unrelated to the *psychological* conditions of primitive discoveries. There is then a place, we feel, for an indirect and secondary psychoanalysis which would constantly seek the unconscious under the conscious, the subjective value under the objective evidence, the reverie beneath the experiment. One can study only what one has first dreamed about. Science is formed rather on a reverie than on an experiment, and it takes a good many experiments to dispel the mists of the dream. It should be noted particularly that the same action working on the same substance to give the same objective result does not have the same objective meaning in mentalities as different as those of the primitive man and the educated modern man. For primitive man thought is centralized reverie; for the educated modern man reverie is a loose form of thought. The dynamic meaning is completely opposite in the two cases.

For example, it is a leitmotiv of the rationalist explanation that the first men produced fire by the rubbing together of two pieces of dry wood. But the *objective* reasons that are invoked to explain how men are supposed to have been led to imagine this procedure are very weak. These writers often do not even venture to try and throw light on the psychology of this first discovery. Among the few authors who do concern themselves with an explanation, most recall that forest fires are produced by the "rubbing together" of branches in summer. They are applying just that recurrent rationalism that we wish to expose. They are judging by inference from a known science without seeking to recapture the condition of the primitive observation. Nowadays, when people cannot discover another cause of a forest fire, then end by thinking that the unknown cause may be the action of rubbing. But in fact we can say that *the phenomenon in its natural aspect has never been observed.* If one were to observe it, it would not be, properly speaking, a rubbing action that one would think of if one approached the phenomenon from an ingenuous standpoint. One would think rather of a *shock*; one would find nothing that might suggest a phenomenon which is so prepared, long-lasting and progressive as the rubbing which is to cause the igniting of wood. We arrive, then, at this critical conclusion: none of the practices based on rubbing that are used by primitive peoples to produce fire can be directly suggested by a phenomenon of nature.

These difficulties had not escaped Schlegel. Without putting forward any solution, he had seen quite clearly that the problem set forth in rational terms did not correspond to the psychological possibilities of primitive man: "The mere invention of fire, the cornerstone of the whole cultural edifice, as the fable of Prometheus so well expresses it, presents insurmountable difficulties in our conjectures about man in a crude state of civilization. For us nothing is more common than fire; but man could have wandered in the desert for millions of years without once having seen fire on earthly soil. Let us grant him an erupting volcano, a forest fire set by lightning: hardened in his nakedness against the rigors of the seasons, would he have run forward at once to warm himself? Would he not rather have taken flight? The sight of fire frightens most animals, except those which through a domesticated life have become accustomed to it . . . Even after having experienced the beneficent effect of a fire offered him by nature, how would he have been able to keep it going? Once extinguished, how would he have been able to rekindle it? Even if two pieces of dry wood had fallen for the first time into the hands of the savage, what previous experience would indicate to him that they could by ignited by a long-continued and rapid rubbing action?"[1]

On the other hand, if a rational and objective explanation is really quite unsatisfactory in accounting for a discovery made by a primitive mind, a psychoanalytical explanation, however overbold it may seem, must in the end be the true psychological explanation.

In the first place it must be recognized that rubbing is a highly sexualized experience. Merely by glancing through the psychological documents amassed by classical psychoanalysis on will surely have no difficulty in convincing oneself of this fact. Secondly, one need only make a systematic study of the items of information gained by a special psychoanalysis of the impressions pertaining to heat, to be convinced that the *objective* attempt to produce fire by rubbing is suggested by entirely intimate experiences. In any case, it is in this direction that the circuit between the phenomenon of fire and its reproduction is the shortest. The love act is the first scientific hypothesis about the objective reproduction of fire. Prometheus is a vigorous lover rather than an intelligent philosopher, and the vengeance of the gods is the vengeance of a jealous husband....

Our theory would appear less daring if the reader would only free himself from an intransigent utilitarianism and would cease to imagine prehistoric man as being automatically subject to misfortune and necessity. It is in vain that all travelers tell us about the carefree life of primitive man: we continue to shudder at our mental picture of life at the time of the cave man. Perhaps our ancestor was more receptive to pleasure, more conscious of his happiness in proportion as he was less sensitive to suffering. The warm sense of well-being arising from physical love must have been transferred into many primitive experiences. To set fire to the stick by sliding it up and down in the groove in the piece of dry wood takes time and patience. But this work must have been very agreeable to an individual whose reverie was wholly sexual. It was perhaps while engaged in the gentle task that man learned to sing. In any case it is an obviously rhythmic kind of task, a task which *answers* to the rhythm of the worker, which brings him lovely, multiple resonances: the arm that rubs, the pieces of wood that strike together, the voice that sings, all are united in the same harmony and the same rhythmic increase in energy; everything converges on to the one hope, on to an objective whose *value* is known. As soon as one engages in the action of rubbing, one experiences a pleasant objective warmth at the same time that has the warm impression of an agreeable form of exercise. The rhythms are mutually supporting. They are mutually induced and continue through self-induction....

In the field of psychoanalysis the naming of things is often sufficient to cause a *precipitate;* before the name, there was only an amorphous, troubled, disturbed solution; after the name, crystals are seen at the bottom of the liquid. The *Novalis complex* would synthesize, then, this impulse towards fire that is brought about by friction, the need for shared warmth. This impulse would reconstitute, in its exact primitivity, the prehistoric conquest of fire. The Novalis complex is characterized by a consciousness of inner heat which always takes precedence over a purely visual knowledge of light. It is based upon a satisfaction of the thermal sense and the deep-seated consciousness of calorific happiness. Heat is a property, a possession. It must be guarded jealously and only given as a gift to a chosen being who merits its communion in a reciprocal fusion. Light plays upon and laughs over the surface of things, but only heat *penetrates.*

Excerpts from "Psychoanalysis and Prehistory: The Novalis Complex," chapter three of Gaston Bachelard, *The Psychoanalysis of Fire*, trans. Alan C. M. Ross (London, 1964), pp. 21–24, 27–28, 40. Originally published in 1938 by Librairie Gallimard as *La psychanalyse du feu.*

---

1 Auguste-Guillaume de Schlegel, *Œuvres écrites en français*, vol. 1 (Leipzig, 1846), pp. 307–08.

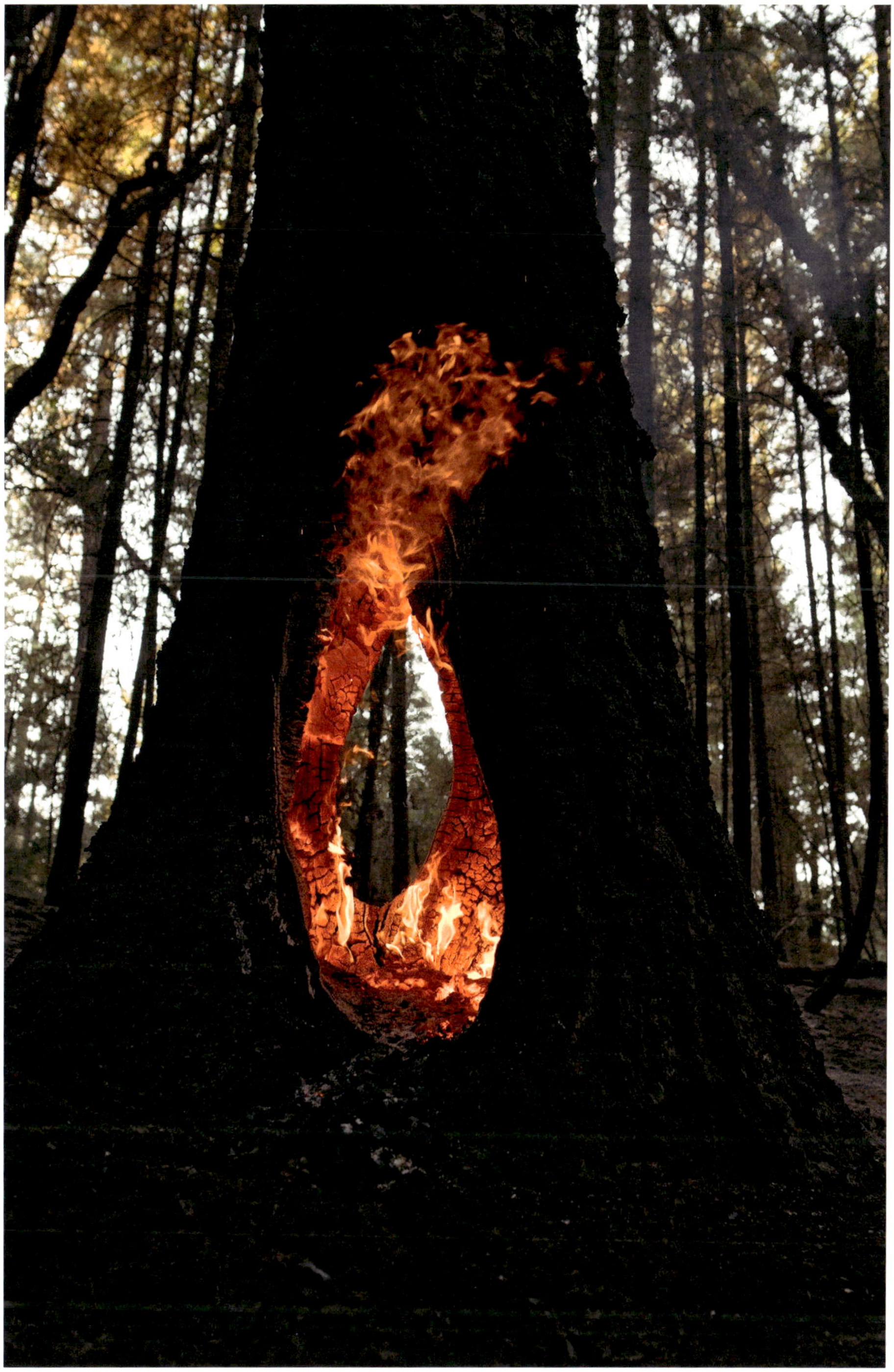

List of Illustrations

Cover, page 110
Alexei Denisov-Uralsky's painting *Lesnoi pozhar* (Forest Fire) being admired by James Symington, Joseph Duffy, and Anatoly Dobrynin (left to right) during its transfer to the Soviet Union in 1979

Page 6
Punishment #7
2011
Inkjet print
100 × 150 cm

Page 13
Page from Max Frisch, *Der Mensch erscheint im Holozän* (1979)

Pages 14–15
Untitled
2017
Antler tips, stainless steel struts
Variable dimensions
Installation view,
Sies + Höke, Düsseldorf

Pages 16–17
Herd of reindeer struck by lightning, Norway, 2017

Pages 22–23
Documentary footage, Berlin, 2016

Pages 24–35
Documentary footage, Venezuela, 2016

Page 37
Talking to Thunder (Palm Tree)
2017
Inkjet print
225 × 150 cm

Pages 38–41
Details of *Talking to Thunder (Lagoon)*
2017
Inkjet prints
Triptych, each panel 26.6 × 157.3 cm

Pages 42–43
Talking to Thunder (Lagoon) and *Talking to Thunder (Tree)*
Installation view,
Sies + Höke, Düsseldorf

Page 45
Talking to Thunder (Bright Tree)
2017
Inkjet print
225 × 150 cm

Pages 46–47
Video still from *Talking to Thunder*
2017
Video (1920 × 1080), stereo sound
21 min.

Page 49
Lightning Rockets
2017
Nine rockets, aluminum, Kevlar, copper, silver
Variable dimensions
Installation view,
Marlborough New York

Page 50
Third lightning expedition (Kiko, Celo, Julius von Bismarck, Natalie Körner, and Martin Schied), Ologa, Venezuela, 2016

Page 55
Unfall am Mittelpunkt Deutschlands #1
2013
Inkjet print
130 × 90.5 cm

Pages 57, 60–65, 72
Apocalypsoid
2017
Flint stone, granite, stainless steel, pigment ink, tables, apparatuses, prints
Variable dimension
Installation views,
Städtische Galerie Wolfsburg

Page 58
Apocalypsoid before explosion

Page 59
Sphericized 3-D simulation of the same *Apocalypsoid*

Pages 66–67
Apocalypsoid c
2018
Granite, stainless steel, pigment ink
26 × 22 × 22 cm

Pages 68–69
Apocalypsoid b
2018
Granite, stainless steel, pigment ink
26 × 25 × 26 cm

Pages 70–71
Flint stone *Apocalypsoid* before explosion

Page 80
General circulation model of the atmosphere, NSF Center for Multiscale Modeling of Atmospheric Processes

Pages 84–109
Video stills from
Irma to Come in Earnest
2017
Video (1920 × 1080), stereo sound
44 min.

Pages 117–21
Die Luft muss man sich wegdenken
(One Must Think Away the Air)
2017
Steel wire
800 × 1100 cm
Installation views,
Städtische Galerie Wolfsburg

Pages 122–23
Technical drawing, measurements, and bending radii

Pages 125–29
Installing the movement sensor system (accelerometers, barometer, GPS, computer, radio transmitters, antennas, batteries, and solar panels) for *Die Mimik der Tethys* (The Expressions of Tethys), Atlantic Ocean off the coast of France, 2019

Pages 130–34
Die Mimik der Tethys
(The Expressions of Tethys)
2019
Buoy suspended in parallel cable robot system
Variable dimensions
Installation views,
Palais de Tokyo, Paris

Page 135
Sebastian Muellauer, Julius von Bismarck, Arnaud Blangy, and Antoine Bertholon during installation of the movement sensor system off the coast of France, 2019

Page 137
Carr Fire, California, 2018

Pages 138–39
Wildfire, Sweden, 2018

Pages 140, 150–51, 167
Mendocino Complex Fire, California, 2018

Pages 141–45, 152–57
Hirz Fire, California, 2018

Pages 158–59
Slow-motion video still, Carr Fire, California, 2018

Pages 160–63
Slow-motion video still, Hirz Fire, California, 2018

Pages 164
Slow-motion video still, Keswick, California, 2018

Julius von Bismarck

1983
Born in Breisach am Rhein, Germany

2012–13
Universität der Künste Berlin, master class, professor Olafur Eliasson

2009
Universität der Künste Berlin, Institut für Raumexperimente, professor Olafur Eliasson

2007
Hunter College, New York, MFA program

2006
Universität der Künste Berlin, Visual Communication, Digital Class, professor Joachim Sauter

2005
Universität der Künste Berlin, Visual Communication

Lives and works in Berlin

Grants, Awards, Residencies

2018
Award of the Shifting Foundation, Beverly Hills, California

2017
Junge Stadt sieht Junge Kunst, Prize of the City of Wolfsburg, Germany

2013
IBB Photography Award, IBB Atrium, Berlin

2011
Prix Ars Electronica Collide@CERN, Linz, Austria, CERN, Switzerland

2010
Beep Electronic Art Award, Madrid

2009
Prix Ars Electronica with the Perpetual Storytelling Apparatus, Linz, Austria

Selection of the Jury—Japan Media Arts Festival 09, Tokyo

2008
Award Golden Nica with the Image Fulgurator at Prix Ars Electronica, Linz, Austria

Solo Exhibitions

2019
Die Mimik der Tethys, Palais de Tokyo, Paris

I'm Afraid, with Julian Charrière, Sies + Höke, Düsseldorf

Art Club, Villa Medici, Rome

2018
Immer noch der Lauf der Dinge, alexander levy, Berlin

I'm Afraid I Must Ask You to Leave, with Julian Charrière, Kunstpalais Erlangen, Germany

2017
Gewaltenteilung, Städtische Galerie Wolfsburg, Germany

Talking to Thunder, Sies + Höke, Düsseldorf

Good Weather, Marlborough, New York

2016
Approximately Three Dimensions, alexander levy, Berlin

Desert Now, with Julian Charrière and Felix Kiessling, Steve Turner, Los Angeles

Objects in Mirror Might Be Closer Than They Appear, with Julian Charrière, Villa Bernasconi, Grand-Lancy, Geneva

2015
Landscape Painting, Marlborough, New York

Tiere sind dumm und Pflanzen noch viel dümmer, Kunstverein Göttingen, Germany

2014
History Apparatus, Kunstverein Arnsberg, Germany

2013
Unfall am Mittelpunkt Deutschlands, alexander levy, Berlin

Les bêtes sont bêtes et les plantes le sont encore plus, Galerie Ilka Bree, Bordeaux

This Is So Romantic, IMO Gallery, Copenhagen

2012
Punishment I, alexander levy, Berlin

LE DICTATEUR: These Peanuts Are Bullets, Family Business, New York

2011
5 Minute Museum, Eindhoven, The Netherlands

2009
Kapelica Gallery, Ljubljana

Group Exhibitions

2019
MASKE Kunst der Verwandlung, Kunstmuseum Bonn, Germany

Nature in Art, MOCAK, Kraków

Elementarteile: Grundbausteine des Sprengel Museum Hannover und seiner Kunst, Sprengel Museum, Hanover

Ré-flexions: Autour des nouvelles acquisitions, Frac Alsace, Sélestat, France

Post-Water, Museo Nazionale della Montagna, CAI Torino, Turin, Italy

2018

Public Face, with Benjamin Maus and Richard Wilhelmer, Hamburg

Days without a Night, Goethe-Institut New Delhi

Entangle: Physics and the Artistic Imagination, Bildmuseet, Umeå, Sweden

Lichte Momente, Stadthaus Ulm, Germany

Without Nature, Nicoletti Contemporary, London

The Sensation of the Sea: In Honour of Bas Jan Ader, The Mesdag Collection, The Hague, The Netherlands

Züricher Theaterspektakel, Zurich

November, Haus am Lützowplatz, Berlin

Räumlichkeiten, Kunstwerk—Sammlung Klein, Eberdingen-Nussdorf, Germany

Impact, Kunst- und Gewerbeverein Regensburg e.V., Germany

Im Zweifel für den Zweifel, NRW Forum, Düsseldorf

Haus der Sinnsuche: Gutes Leben durch Kultur, Kunstsaele Berlin

Objects in Mirror Might Be Closer Than They Appear, with Julian Charrière, Swiss Institute, New York

Inside Ecologies, Weltkunstzimmer, Düsseldorf

Are You Satisfied? Aktuelle Kunst und Revolution, Stadtgalerie Kiel, Germany

Greffes, Galerie Rolando Anselmi, Berlin

Entfesselte Natur—Das Bild der Katastrophe seit 1600, Hamburger Kunsthalle, Hamburg

Between Realities, Färgfabriken, Stockholm

Power to the People, Schirn Kunsthalle, Frankfurt am Main

2017

Antarctic Biennale, Antarctic and Antarctic Pavilion, Venice

KULT! Legenden, Stars und Bildikonen, Zeppelin Museum, Friedrichshafen, Germany

Unboxing, LEVY Galerie, Hamburg

BEOBACHTUNG, Dittrich & Schlechtriem, Berlin

Small—An Exploration of Miniature, SEXAUER Gallery, Berlin

Unter Waffen: Fire & Forget 2, Museum Angewandte Kunst, Frankfurt am Main

Citynature: Vilnius and Beyond, National Gallery of Art, Vilnius

PRODUKTION: made in germany drei, Sprengel Museum, Hanover

Art Basel Unlimited, with Julian Charrière, Basel

Santiago Sierra: Mea Culpa, PAC—Padiglione d'Arte Contemporanea, Milan

NACH DER NATUR—Material, Form, Struktur, Museum Sinclair-Haus, Bad Homburg, Germany

Festival of Future Nows, Hamburger Bahnhof—Museum für Gegenwart, Berlin

The Raft: Art Is (Not) Lonely, Mu.Zee, Oostende, Belgium

2016

The End of the World, Centro Pecci, Prato, Italy

It's All Natural. . . /, Nassauischer Kunstverein, Wiesbaden, Germany

Über die Unmöglichkeit des Seins, Kunsthalle Exnergasse, Vienna

In Space No One Can Hear Your Laugh, Galleria Giovanni Bonelli, Milan

Kunstpreis der Böttcherstraße, Kunsthalle Bremen, Germany

From Science to Fiction, Florian Christopher, Zurich

+ultra: Gestaltung schafft wissen, Martin-Gropius-Bau, Berlin

Back to the Land, Studio La Città, Verona

5th Moscow International Biennale for Young Art, Trekhgornaya Manufaktura, Moscow

2015

OPENING ON THE FOAM, Schloss Sacrow, Potsdam

Art Basel Unlimited, Basel

In the Land of the Blind the One-Eyed Man Loses Sight, Dittrich & Schlechtriem, Berlin

Fusion, Knust x Kunz +, Munich

Welcome to the Jungle, KW Institute for Contemporary Art, Berlin

The Future of Memory, Kunsthalle Wien, Vienna

Invento: As Revoluções que nos Inventaram, OCA Parque Ibirapuera, São Paulo

Stranger Than Paradise, Sies + Höke, Düsseldorf

Beuys ohne Hut—Karin Székessy fotografiert Künstler, Horst-Janssen-Museum, Oldenburg, Germany

Fire and Forget: On Violence, KW Institute for Contemporary Art, Berlin

Group Show V, alexander levy, Berlin

8th Momentum Nordic Biennial of Contemporary Art, Moss, Norway

Höhenrausch: Das Geheimnis der Vögel—Mystery of Birds, OK Center for Contemporary Art, Linz, Austria

2014

Pencil / Line / Eraser, Carroll / Fletcher, London

Der schwarze Hund, Gesellschaft der Freunde junger Kunst, Baden-Baden, Germany

Lichtwark revisited: Künstler sehen Hamburg, Hamburger Kunsthalle, Hamburg

thingworld: International Triennial of New Media Art, National Art Museum of China (NAMOC), Beijing

Treasure of Lima: A Buried Exhibition, Thyssen-Bornemisza Art Contemporary Academy, Cocos Island, Costa Rica

ONE PLACE NEXT TO ANOTHER, Winzavod Center for Contemporary Art, Moscow

mira mira Neue Jahresgaben, Kunstverein Arnsberg, Germany

I CAN'T CONTROL MYSELF, Kunstverein Wolfsburg, Germany

CLOCKWORK, Oben, Vienna

Festival of Future Nows, Neue Nationalgalerie, Berlin

ONE TORINO: SHIT AND DIE, Palazzo Cavour, Turin, Italy

5th Annual Exhibition of Hybrid Art, VDNKh, Optika Pavilion, Moscow

Die Eigenheit der Dinge, Franz Josefs Kai 3, Vienna

Screening—Julius von Bismarck / Fabian Knecht / S. T. Paul, alexander levy, Berlin

2013

Festival of Landscape Objects ARCHSTOYANIE, Kaluga Region, Russia

BERLIN.STATUS [2], Künstlerhaus Bethanien, Berlin

TEA, National Taiwan Museum of Fine Arts Taichung, Taiwan

Let's Invent a Language to Narrate My Story, Dienstgebäude, Zurich

Ich bin dein Nachbar, Bromer Art Collection, Roggwill, Switzerland

Skulpturenprojekt Wallanlage, Stade, Germany

Berlin Masters, Arndt, Berlin

Public Abstraction Private Construction VI VII, Kunstverein Arnsberg, Germany

LE DICTATEUR: UN HOMME JUSTE EST QUAND MÊME UN HOMME MORT, Palais de Tokyo, Paris

Handlungsbereitschaft—Skizze einer Generation am Ende der Geschichte (3. Aufl.), Motorenhalle, Dresden

2012

Raumtrigger, taiga, St. Petersburg

13th International Architecture Exhibition—La Biennale di Venezia, a collaboration with Julian Charrière, supported by Vogt Landscape Architects Ltd., Venice

APO-CALYPSE, Montreux, Switzerland

Handlungsbereitschaft—Skizze einer Generation am Ende der Geschichte (2. Aufl.), Kunstsaele, Berlin

Grosses Feld, Institut für Raumexperimente, Janmeda, Addis Ababa, Ethiopia

Glasauge, Institut für Raumexperimente, Berlin

Addis Fotofest, Institut für Raumexperimente, Addis Ababa, Ethiopia

Syabi, Tokyo Metropolitan Museum of Photography

Raum #6, Zurich

Weltausstellung, Flughafen Tempelhof, Berlin

Life Clock, Den Frie Centre of Contemporary Art, Copenhagen

Cyberarts 12, OK Center for Contemporary Art, Linz, Austria

PHotoESPAÑA, Off Limits, with Santiago Sierra, Madrid

2011

URO, IMO Gallery, Copenhagen

Electron Festival, Geneva

Kackwald, Nation of Gondwana, Grünefeld, Germany

Pièce de Résistance, Mediamatic, Amsterdam

TGM, Munich

Impakt, Utrecht, The Netherlands

Solares Fondazione delle Arti, Parma, Italy

Almost Cinema, Vooruit, Ghent, Belgium

Seeing/Knowing, Gund Gallery, Gambier, Ohio

Index, Cabaret Voltaire, Zurich

Handlungsbereitschaft—Skizze einer Generation am Ende der Geschichte, Berlin

2010

Electrified 02, S.M.A.K., Ghent, Belgium

Transmediale 2010, Haus der Kulturen der Welt, Berlin

Reflective Interventions, Gallery Art Claims Impulse, Berlin

Provinz, Lindau, Germany

Shift Festival, Basel

Geist III, Berlin

Stadt am Rande, Today Art Museum, Beijing

Agents & Provocateurs, Hartware MedienKunstVerein Dortmund, Germany

Let's Start to Implement Little Errors, Institut für Raumexperimente, Berlin

StreetArtGalerie, Berlin

Persistence of Vision, Foundation for Art and Creative Technology (FACT), Liverpool

Persistence of Vision, Nikolaj Kunsthal, Copenhagen

2009

Illustrative 09, Berlin

Agents & Provocateurs, Institute of Contemporary Art, Dunaújváros, Hungary

My Map Is Not Your Map, Arteleku, San Sebastián, Spain

Cyberarts 09, OK Center for Contemporary Art, Linz, Austria

Geist, Berlin

Bilderschlachten, European Media Art Festival, Museum für Industriekultur Osnabrück, Germany

Pixelache 09, Kiasma—Museum of Contemporary Art, Helsinki

Artefact—BEHIND THE IMAGE | THE IMAGE BEHIND, Stuk Kunstencentrum Leuven, Belgium

The Infuancers, Centre de Cultura Contemporania de Barcelona

Japan Media Arts Festival 09, Tokyo

UM Festival, Lisbon

Are We Human?, New Media Scotland, Edinburgh

Beeldfestival, Rotterdam, The Netherlands

Fotofolgen, HFBK, Hamburg

2008

Humboldt-Universität zu Berlin, Institut für Physik, Quantenoptik, Berlin

Medienfassaden Festival 08, Berlin

Cyberarts 08, OK Center for Contemporary Art, Linz, Austria

Pixelache 08, Kiasma—Museum of Modern Art, Helsinki

Social Intervention, Gallery Sangsangmadang Seoul

Authors' Biographies

Dehlia Hannah

is a philosopher and curator who is currently Mads Øvlisen Postdoctoral Fellow at the Department of Chemistry and Biosciences at Aalborg University-Copenhagen and an affiliate of the School of Earth and Space Exploration at Arizona State University. She holds a PhD in philosophy from Columbia University, with specializations in aesthetics and the philosophy of science. Her most recent project, *A Year Without a Winter* (Columbia University Press, 2018), revisits the literary and environmental aftermaths of the 1815 eruption of Mount Tambora through a transdisciplinary thought experiment in order to reframe contemporary imaginaries of climate crisis. Her forthcoming monograph *Performative Experiments* examines contemporary artworks that take the form of scientific experiments.

Susanne Pfleger

is a curator and art historian. She studied at the universities of Heidelberg, Reims, and Florence. She has been director of the Städtische Galerie Wolfsburg since 1997. Previously she worked as a curator, both freelance and at the Wilhelm-Hack-Museum in Ludwigshafen. From 1991 to 1993 she was a Postdoctoral Fellow at the Kunsthistorisches Institut in Florenz—Max-Planck-Institut in Florence. Since 2002 she has been an adjunct professor at the Burg Giebichenstein University of Art and Design Halle. Susanne Pfleger's focus is art of the twentieth and twenty-first centuries. She has curated many exhibitions, including shows on Tony Cragg, Katharina Fritsch, Camille Graeser, Olaf Nicolai, and Thomas Schütte. She is an active member of various commissions and foundations.

Stephen Pyne

became a pyromantic by accident when, a few days after graduating from high school, he joined a forest fire crew at Grand Canyon National Park. He stayed for fifteen seasons and later wrote fire plans for Rocky Mountain and Yellowstone National Parks. He attended Stanford University and the University of Texas (Austin), training mostly in the humanities, and was a professor at Arizona State University until 2018. His publications on the history and management of fire include big-screen fire histories for the United States, Australia, Canada, Europe, and the Earth overall, and he has recently completed a ten-book survey of the American fire scene. He also examines questions of place and exploration, with books on Antarctica (*The Ice*), *How the Canyon Became Grand*, and the Voyager space mission.

Nadim Samman

is a curator and art historian. He studied philosophy at University College London before receiving his PhD from the Courtauld Institute of Art. He cofounded the 1st Antarctic Biennale (2017) and the Antarctic Pavilion (Venice, 2015–). In 2016 he curated the 5th Moscow International Biennale for Young Art and in 2012 the 4th Marrakech Biennale (with Carson Chan). Other major projects include *Treasure of Lima: A Buried Exhibition* (a unique site-specific exhibition on the remote Pacific island of Isla del Coco) and *Rare Earth* (at Thyssen-Bornemisza Art Contemporary, Vienna). In 2014 *Foreign Policy Magazine* named him among the "100 Leading Global Thinkers."

Jürgen Trittin

is a former Federal Minister for the Environment who has been a member of the Committee on Foreign Affairs in the German Parliament since 2014. He is also a deputy member on the Committee on the Affairs of the European Union and a member of the NATO Parliamentary Assembly. In 2015 and 2016 he co-chaired the Commission to Review the Financing for the Phase-Out of Nuclear Energy in Germany. In 2018 he was elected to the Board of Trustees of the Nuclear Waste Disposal Fund. Trittin has been a Member of the German Parliament since 1998. He was Chairman of the Parliamentary Group Alliance 90/The Greens in the German Parliament from 2009 to 2013 and Vice Chairman in charge of Foreign, Security, and European Policy from 2005 to 2009. He served as Federal Minister for the Environment, Nature Conservation, and Nuclear Safety from 1998 to 2005.

Colophon

This book is published in conjunction with the exhibition *Gewaltenteilung*, Städtische Galerie Wolfsburg November 11, 2017–July 29, 2018

Editors:
Dehlia Hannah
Susanne Pfleger

Project management:
Constanze Korb, Hatje Cantz
Laura Seidel, Studio Julius von Bismarck

Coordination:
Corinna Wolfien, Books Communication Art

Copyediting:
Tas Skorupa

Translations:
Amy Klement (Frisch, Pfleger, Trittin)

Graphic design and typesetting:
Karsten Heller, DiG Studio

Typeface:
Akzidenz, Hoefler

Production:
Heidrun Zimmermann, Hatje Cantz

Reproductions:
Josephine Tischer, Berlin

Photo Credits:
Havard Kjøntvedt, Environment Directorate/the Norwegian Nature Inspectorate (pp. 16–17); Achim Kukulies, Düsseldorf (pp. 14–15, 42–43); Sebastian Muellauer (pp. 126–27); Courtesy of Robert Williams (p. 110); NSF Center for Multiscale Modeling of Atmospheric Processes (p. 80); Uwe Walter, Berlin (pp. 57, 60–65, 72, 117–21)
All others: Julius von Bismarck

Printing and binding:
DZA Druckerei zu Altenburg GmbH, Altenburg

Paper:
Magno Volume 1.1., 170 g/m^2

Special thanks go to all the collectors and collections who have supported Julius's work over the years and whose artworks have been reproduced in this book.

In cooperation with:

alexander levy
Rudi-Dutschke-Str. 26
10969 Berlin
Germany
www.alexanderlevy.net

Marlborough
545 West 25th Street
New York, NY 10001
www.marlboroughgallery.com

Sies + Höke
Poststrasse 2+3
40213 Düsseldorf
Germany
www.sieshoeke.com

Published by
Hatje Cantz Verlag GmbH
Mommsenstrasse 27
10629 Berlin
Germany
www.hatjecantz.de
A Ganske Publishing Group Company

ISBN 978-3-7757-4561-1
Printed in Germany

MIX
Paper from responsible sources
FSC® C100411

Cover:
Alexei Denisov-Uralsky's painting *Lesnoi pozhar* (Forest Fire) being admired by James Symington, Joseph Duffy, and Anatoly Dobrynin (left to right) during its transfer to the Soviet Union in 1979